SOLO TRANSFORMATION ON STAGE

A Journey into the Organic Process of the Art of Transformation

RONALD RAND

Foreword by STEPHEN LANG

Includes interviews with Christopher Plummer, Olympia Dukakis, Ben Vereen, Billy Crudup, V (formerly Eve Ensler), Stephen Lang, Ronald Rand, Laurence Luckinbill, Tony Lo Bianco, Angelica Page, Hershey Felder, Marga Gomez, Adrienne Barbeau, Karen Eterovich, Susan Claassen, Elizabeth van Dyke, Anita Hollander, Sabera Shaik, Jean-Claude van Itallie, Libby Skala and Julie Harris

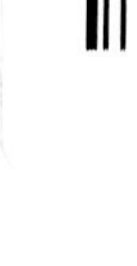

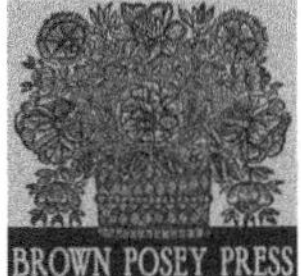

an imprint of Sunbury Press, Inc.
Mechanicsburg, PA USA

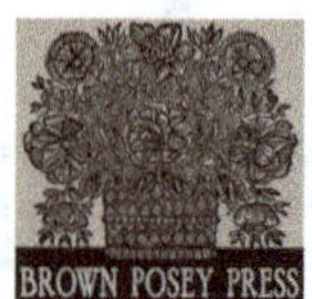

an imprint of Sunbury Press, Inc.
Mechanicsburg, PA USA

For information about special discounts for bulk purchases, please contact Sunbury Press Orders Dept. at (855) 338-8359 or orders@sunburypress.com.

To request one of our authors for speaking engagements or book signings, please contact Sunbury Press Publicity Dept. at publicity@sunburypress.com.

FIRST BROWN POSEY PRESS EDITION: November 2021

Set in Adobe Garamond Pro | Interior design by Crystal Devine | Cover design by Victoria Mitchell | Edited by Lawrence Knorr.

Publisher's Cataloging-in-Publication Data
Names: Rand, Ronald, author.
Title: Solo transformation on stage : a journey into the organic process of the art of transformation / Ronald Rand.
Description: First trade paperback edition. | Mechanicsburg, PA : Brown Posey Press, 2021.
Summary: *Solo Transformation on Stage* leads you through an organic process towards transformation using Stanislavsky's "Method of Physical Actions." Acclaimed solo performer in 25 countries, Ronald Rand takes you into his two-hour transformation as Harold Clurman. Included are twenty inspiring interviews including Christopher Plummer, Eve Ensler, Ben Vereen, Olympia Dukakis, Stephen Lang, and Billy Crudup.
Identifiers: ISBN : 978-1-62006-571-6 (softcover).
Subjects: PERFORMING ARTS / Storytelling | PERFORMING ARTS / Acting & Auditioning | PERFORMING ARTS / Theater / Playwriting.

Product of the United States of America
0 1 1 2 3 5 8 13 21 34 55

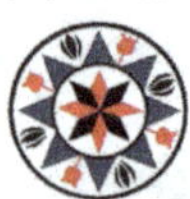

Continue the Enlightenment!

Books by RONALD RAND

Acting Teachers of America

CREATE! How Extraordinary People Live to Create and Create to Live

SOLO TRANSFORMATION ON STAGE:
A Journey into the Organic Process of the Art of Transformation

Dedicated to Harold Clurman,
whose inspiring words as the
conscience of the American Theater
continues to inspire me every day

"... The actor must be a leader. He must be true
to what is most eager, vital, and boldest within himself.
By being awake himself, the artist must awaken the audience.
This, ultimately, is what the audience also desires,
to be awakened."

—Harold Clurman

Contents

FOREWORD

STEPHEN LANG

Were Ronald Rand's fascinating and unique periodical, *The Soul of the American Actor*, his single contribution to the Dramatic Arts, he would have still earned his place as a highly regarded Man of the Theatre.

However, Rand's extensive Curriculum Vitae—playwright, painter, poet, essayist, publisher, editor, librettist, director, educator, cultural ambassador, and, not least, Actor—legitimately calls the sobriquet Renaissance Man to mind.

This cultured, knowledgeable, and singular individual is highly proficient in a wide range of semi-related fields, but I would not be in the least surprised to discover that he is a gourmet chef or a world-class badminton player—anything seems possible with Rand.

However, one calling is significantly missing from his resume: Critic. Now, it is possible, even likely, that Rand has done his share of dramatic criticism—I don't know—but I do know that manifest within both his person and his work is a spirit of such warmth, generosity, and old-world charm, that the crucial component of critical snarkiness (or downright nastiness), may simply not have found a home in his nature. It is difficult to imagine being panned by Rand.

This book, *Solo Transformation on Stage*, is framed around a single actor creating a solo performance. The form presents more than a few unique (sometimes lonely) challenges. If a scene between two actors written by Bernard Shaw or Aaron Sorkin can be likened to a volley of words or ideas being whacked back and forth like tennis balls, then the solo performance is more a feat of juggling, and a dropped ball or chain-saw can only be retrieved by the juggler. And then, of course, the cast parties are so boring.

This book is an astonishing outpouring of energy and experience, and it represents Rand at his warmest—quite hot actually—which is to say that his own belief in the importance of his subject glows from deep within. The chapters sweep along with evangelical fervor and surety, yet are gracefully tempered by a palpable sense of wonder and humility. These qualities do not merely stand in counterpoint but are organically coalesced into an even deeper quality of Faith.

Ronald Rand has unshakeable faith in the necessity of the art of Acting. He puts into words what every Actor feels in the heart; that what we do is in some elliptic way as crucial to life as bread, fire, or salt. Rand urges us to "seek out a greater realization of what life means to you. It will lead you on a path of allowing an even greater realization to flow through you."

In his solo play, *LET IT BE ART!*, Rand imbues those words with authenticity and utility by precisely describing his method of organic transformation into the person of the legendary Harold Clurman. Rand employs Clurman's own penetrating words as an inner path towards the symbiotic co-mingling of two souls, and so in a tangibly material way, the journey itself becomes the destination.

In referencing Clurman's "movement of molecules," Rand taps into the wondrous and mysterious shamanistic capabilities of an Actor in full performance mode.

In performing my own solo show, *BEYOND GLORY*, I have time and time again plunged into what is essentially a magical experience, emerging eighty minutes later in a state of exhausted exhilaration. There is an element of conjuring in the solo show; an intensely focused commitment, not to mention a certain sleight of hand. The solo Actor is not only a Player but a Prestidigitator as well.

With a trunk full of wardrobe, greasepaint, talismanic objects, and imagination, Rand begins his journey, and ours, by introducing the original touring actor, Thespis, the very founder of the craft. From his ancient perspective, we reflect on the ritualistic and animistic roots of the art and craft of acting, and we are reminded that these roots are still powerful and still run deep in the strange work that actors do. Rand's kinship with colossi of the past—Shakespeare, Ibsen, Stanislavski—is both mysterious and concretely reassuring.

Much has flowed through Ronald Rand—history, myth, technique—and much has been absorbed, refined, deeply personalized, and now transmitted through this noble and useful book.

PREFACE

Our humanity. Two simple words. Who would we be without our genuine humanness leading us forward—like the waves of the ocean, touching each other's shores of meaning, forever in movement. Every day we live in each other's atmosphere. Breathe the same world. Our sustenance is the rich soil of our minds. The deepening humanity in our hearts. The strengthening of our souls.

I wrote this book to explore the organic process of creating true life on stage through the 'Art of Transformation.' About what it takes to perform in your own solo performance, and how Transformation can help heal the world.

Creating is my way of life. I've been fortunate to do it in many different ways. What I love the most is sharing stories through the art of the theater. The fact is there's no right or wrong way to approach a role because there are many different techniques. Many ways to tell stories to reveal the essence of a person. Yet, at the same time, it's a craft that takes years to master to touch the hearts of those who come. I tell my students, if something I say makes sense, use it. If not, let it wash over you.

This book is an intimate journey that we'll go on together, almost like being in a performance. Our collaboration will be an exploration to find out how much we have in common about the nature of life and the nature of our art. It's my hope and faith that the work that you'll do will lead to greater harmony in the world.

For more than twenty years, I've traveled around the world to over twenty-five countries, across twenty states in America, bringing to life Harold Clurman in my solo play, *LET IT BE ART!*

Clurman had a profound impact on my life, as he did on so many others. Clurman is recognized as one the most influential individuals in the history of 20th century American Theatre. In 1931, he joined with Lee Strasberg and Cheryl Crawford founding the Group Theatre, which became America's first great acting ensemble company, dedicating themselves to make others aware through the plays they performed of the heroic human qualities of life. They led the American Theatre forward at a time during the Great Depression in the 1930s when it was needed more than ever. Clurman's dynamic passion woke everyone to appreciate the life-changing power of what theater can do in affirming the human spirit that sustains us on this planet.

During my play, audiences meet several inspiring individuals, including Stella Adler, Aaron Copland, Cheryl Crawford, Katherine Hepburn, Robert Edmond Jones, Clifford Odets, Jacqueline Kennedy Onassis, Constantin Stanislavski, Alfred Stieglitz, and Lee Strasberg. Each of them led lives that made a positive difference in this world. They inspired others through their work— challenging us to appreciate the wonder and beauty of art and life.

When I travel around the world in my play, before I depart to another country, I'm asked: "Will they know who Harold Clurman is?" I tell them: "That's why I'm going. After they meet him, they will." By the end of the performance—after experiencing his dynamic persona and passionate ideals—they're eager to learn even more about him and everything he accomplished. Recognized for 'talking the Group Theater into existence,' Clurman was an award-winning director of over forty of the most important plays of the 20th century, including the original productions of *A Member of the Wedding* with Julie Harris and Ethel Waters, *Bus Stop* with Kim Stanley, Clifford Odets' *Awake and Sing, Golden Boy, Paradise Lost,* and *Rocket to the Moon*, Jean Anouilh's *Waltz of the Toreadors* with Sir Ralph Richardson, Jean Giraudoux's *Tiger at the Gates* with Sir Michael Redgrave, Eugene O'Neill's *A Touch of the Poet* with Helen Hayes, Arthur Miller's *Incident at Vichy* with Joseph Wiseman and Roy Scheider, and directed Marlon Brando in his first adult role in *Truckline Café*. Clurman was invited to Japan to direct *Long Day's Journey into Nigh*t and *The Iceman Cometh* with the Kumo Theatre Company, and directed *Monserrat* at Israel's Habimah Theatre. He became America's foremost drama critic, renowned acting teacher, and author of several books, including *On Directing, The Fervent Years*, and *IBSEN.* Known as the 'Elder Statesman of the American Theatre,' his visionary ideals made him the theatrical conscience of America for over fifty years.

After each curtain call, I always give a speech of thanks in the language of the country I'm performing in—talking about how art shows us a way forward to live in peace and understanding, embracing our differences and our commonalities. Sitting on the stage, I have a 'Question and Answer' with the audience, usually with a translator. At times, well-known actors, personal friends, and former students of Clurman's have come to a performance including Clurman's step-daughter Ellen Adler, Group Theatre member Phoebe Brand,

Richard Clurman, Ruby Dee, Rita Fredricks, Sabra Jones, Rue McClanahan, Allan Rich, Lulla Rosenfeld, Joanna Rotté, Roy Scheider, Steven Scheuer, Lois Smith, Elaine Stritch, and the noted director, Jack Garfein—who presented my solo play in Paris a few steps from the Sorbonne, where Clurman had studied as a young man.

After answering questions, I step into the audience and shake hands with everyone who's come. Many times they're quite surprised and delighted to make contact this way. I believe it should be the norm. I'm always greeted with smiles—and we have another chance to talk together in a personal way. Later, when I remove my makeup and costume and the dust settles, I reflect on the beauty of each person I met. No matter what language we spoke, instantly, we became a 'family' through the great ritual and art of the theater.

In every country and state where I perform my solo play, I also teach my master acting Workshop, the 'Art of Transformation' for actors and students. Among those who have also participated have included lawyers, therapists, teachers, soldiers, taxicab drivers, teenagers, and children—all ages and many different backgrounds. We discover the common threads we share as I go through the tools on Constantin Stanislavski's 'Method of Physical Actions' chart. We open our hearts to explore the mysteries of how a creative art form is really the embodiment of our journey of being alive. We listen to one another, finding out how much we have in common.

Over time, actors and actresses including Ira Aldridge, Vinie Burrows, Ossie Davis, Ruby Dee, André De Shields, José Ferrer, Laurence Fishburne, Graham Greene, James Hong, Earle Hyman, Raul Julia, Eartha Kitt, Canada Lee, Rose McClendon, Claudia McNeill, Rita Moreno, Sidney Poitier, Chita Rivera, Paul Robeson, Will Rogers, Wes Studi, Cecily Tyson, and Ethel Waters, to name a very few, have despite overwhelming adversity—persevered with great integrity, tremendous courage, and fortitude—to say through their artistry: 'We need to respect each other. To care for and love one another.' Clearly showing how art brings us together with tolerance and empathy.

Through the theater—we become one. A thousand people laughing together in a singular moment can be life-changing—as is sharing a deeply painful moment.

One thing's for certain—the art of storytelling through solo performance continues to enlighten our lives—sharing our humanity—connecting us to one another in the most intimate way.

ACKNOWLEDGMENTS

This book was a lifetime in coming and could only have happened through the love and support of several special individuals. I'm eternally grateful to my teachers: Harold Clurman, Stella Adler, Jerzy Grotowski, and Joseph Chaikin, for their great insights in enlarging my soul as an actor, imbuing me with the responsibility of the theater artist.

Most certainly, I'm grateful to my publisher, Lawrence Knorr, Marianne Babcock, Crystal Devine, Victoria Mitchell, Joe Walters, and the entire staff of Sunbury Press for their invaluable assistance and support in making the realization of my dream come true.

A huge thanks with deep admiration to Stephen Lang for his inspiration as a true artist of the stage and film and his graciousness in writing the Foreword to this book.

With deepest thanks to each one of the extraordinary Performers who have shared their experiences as a solo performer in this book.

Heartfelt gratitude to Dennis D'Amico—and Nancy Cleary, Publisher of Wyatt Mackenzie Publishing.

My special thanks to every Theater Artistic Director, Festival Director, Professors, and Teachers at universities, colleges, academies, and schools around the world and across America, who made it possible for me to come and share my solo play as Harold Clurman for over twenty years.

I'm grateful for the love and generous advice of Martha Carpenter, whose life is a living example as a master painter of a committed artist in the pursuit of excellence.

My deep gratitude to my mother, Maribee, a master watercolor artist and teacher, for her unwavering love and belief as an artist, and my talented sister, Janice, for her bountiful love.

To the theater artists who have inspired me through their solo performances by their artistry and friendship: Olympia Dukakis, Julie Harris, Hal Holbrook, Stephen Lang, Larry Luckinbill, Christopher Plummer, and Phylicia Rashad.

What continues to give me my faith as an actor are those who continue to inspire my journey: Stella Adler, Joan Baez, Harold Clurman, Mahatma Gandhi, Thích Nhất Hanh, Louise Hay, Helen Keller, Martin Luther King, Jr., Jiddu Krishnamurti, the Dalai Lama, John Lennon, John Lewis, Abraham Lincoln, Nelson Mandela, Nancy Rhodes, Eleanor Roosevelt, Rita Fredricks, Albert Schweitzer, Constantin Stanislavski, Tim Stevenson, Rabindranath Tagore, Marilise Tronto, Elie Wiesel, and Oprah Winfrey—expanding the preciousness of life through their humanity.

Each day I draw from nature's inspiration for a greater mindfulness to flow through me. Making me more awake to the earth's vibrations. Allowing my soul's joy to be released in service in the art of acting.

Ronald Rand

INTRODUCTION

A Short History of Solo Performance

Over time, civilizations and cultures have appeared and disappeared as human evolution has ebbed and flowed. The need to 'make sense of the time in which we live' has always driven artists to examine the choices made in the name of progress by probing into society's deepest questions.

I tend to think solo performance may have begun among the earliest humans when a holy person—a shaman—stood up before others and 'acted out' through a ceremony—the embodiment of a spirit, a deity or an animal. They were allowed to 're-enact' because of their mysterious connection to the supernatural. Through a state of 'possession,' they could transcend time. Entering into a different dimension—an organic rhythm, in a sense—a realm of timeless eternity. The shaman would at times—through this 'trance-like' state—reach into 'a shadow world of spirits' through a heightened sensibility and receive a 'vision of truth.'

All of this occurred probably because, by that time, our brains had formed enough to hold a capacity to feel. What? Emotion. A desire to understand something larger than ourselves. Loss and grief. Desire and love. Beauty.

Eventually this oral tradition was carried forth from tribe to tribe. Over time, the human race accepted that others could have a similar capacity besides a shaman. The ability to get closer to the mystery of life and death, of spirit and the mysteries of existence. Through the art of story-telling, this eventually gave way to solo performance.

It's been said that during the 6th century, B.C. in Ancient Greece—Thespis of Icaria, which today is known as Dionysus, a city near Athens—was the first person to step out from the chorus to play a separate character in a play. Some say that Thespis actually introduced the first principal actor. Either way everything changed when Thespis sang separately the stories being told, and he actually was the first to go 'on the road,' carrying his costumes, his masks and other properties with him in a horse-drawn wagon, traveling from town to town. That's why we're called Thespians.

During Medieval England, there were entertainers known as strolling minstrels who would recite poetry, sing ballads and play instruments. In France, known as Troubadours, they traveled as poet-musicians. Both of them were story-tellers—an immediate link to how the solo performer developed and came into being over time.

The art of acting took a leap forward after centuries when actors of stature including Jacob Adler, Ira Aldridge, Sarah Bernhardt, Edwin Booth, Charlotte Cushman, Edwin Forrest, David Garrick, Sir Henry Irving, Edmund Kean, John Phillip Kemble, Charles Macready, Clara Morris, Rachel, Adelaide Ristori, Tomasso Salvini, Sarah Siddons, and Ellen Terry, among many others captured the audience's imagination through their powerful classic portrayals, bringing great depth into each of the roles they played. The modern actor was born at the dawn of the 20th Century. Eleanora Duse breathed life into the soul of a 'character' she was playing. For the first time, audiences forgot they were watching an actor and were swept up in the human drama. As a result, acting was no longer merely illustration—but illumination.

Over time, there have been many shapes, sizes and styles of solo performances including performers portraying several different people all at once, bringing to life an historical figure—or well-known comedians, musicians, performers, pianists, playwrights, poets, and singers telling their own stories through a solo show.

If we take a glance back and look at some of the most well-known originators of one-person performance by a monologist—among them include Samuel Foote, back in 1747, who entertained audiences in London in farcical entertainments, calling them, *The Diversion of the Morning*, which he continued performing for the next thirty years. Twenty years later, George Alexander Stevens presented a monologue performance entitled *Lecture Upon Heads*. Becoming enormously popular, as he lectured about important individuals of the time, historical and current events. So popular, in fact, that many other performers copied and adapted his shows into theirs. Between 1818 to 1834, a British satirist named Charles Matthews took to the stage performing in his 'one-man entertainment,' *At Homes*, to enormous response through his innate gift of mimicry and comic timing, portraying a wide range of eccentric men and women.

When the 19th century arrived, Charles Dickens became the premiere solo performer of his time. Stepping before huge audiences, he'd bring alive several characters by reading from his well-known novels. In fact, performing them as if he were the characters, across England, Ireland and America. Edgar Allan Poe and Mark Twain also regaled audiences reading from their most famous works. Those who attended were thrilled to not only listen to the writer reading in person from their own works, but were caught up in the sensational dramatic elements that accompanied each event. From her debut in 1920, Ruth Draper was recognized as the undisputed queen of one-woman theater in England for over thirty years, transforming herself into a vast array of characters. Emlyn Williams was widely received bringing Charles Dickens alive on stage for several years.

Over a period of time in New York City and across America, I was fortunate to see, and interview thousands of performers who have appeared within the pages of my newspaper, "The Soul of the American Actor." I've gotten to know many gifted solo performance artists, some who have become good friends.

When Julie Harris slipped into the essence of Emily Dickinson in *The Belle of Amherst*, and Hal Holbrook captured Mark Twain's great humor and wit in *Mark Twain Tonight!*—solo performance took on a life of its own as an art form in America. I became friends with Julie Harris after seeing her performances and interviewing her, and I met and talked with Holbrook twice, once onstage after his Broadway performance. Both of their inspiring artistry and personal words about their work planted a deep seed inside of me. Watching their innate gift as a storyteller in capturing the 'soul' of the person they were playing, and their dedication to the craft in creating a true theatrical experience, was the over-powering reason they were able to transport and inspired countless audiences. That spoke to me in a very deep place. Yes, a seed had truly been planted.

I personally have had the joy of experiencing many actors and actresses in their inspiring solo performances bringing to the stage a lifetime of dedication to the craft of acting, fusing itself into one moment of clarity and art.

Among those who have graced the stage in America and around the world through solo performances include: Richarda Abrams as Mary McLeod Bethune, Ed Asner as President Franklin D. Roosevelt, Eileen Atkins as Virginia Woolf, Michael Balogun in *Death of England: Delroy*, Adrienne Barbeau as Judy Garland, Bill Barker as Thomas Jefferson, Rob Becker in *Defending the Caveman*, Theodore Bikel as Sholom Aleichem, Jim Brochu as Zero Mostel, Vinie Burrows as Rose McClendon, Zoe Caldwell as Lillian Hellman, Simon Callow in *The Mystery of Charles Dickens*, Len Cariou as Ernest Hemingway and

Justice William O. Douglas, Pat Carroll as Gertrude Stein, Susan Claassen as Edith Head, Pauline Collins in *Shirley Valentine*, Tandy Cronyn in *The Tall Boy*, Billy Crudup in *Harry Clarke*, Gerant Wyn Davies as Dylan Thomas, Ruby Dee in *My One Good Nerve*, Karen De Mauro as Rachel Carson, André De Shields as Frederick Douglass, Roy Dotrice as Abraham Lincoln, Olympia Dukakis as *Rose*, Charles S. Dutton as Ira Aldridge, Karen Eterovich as Jane Austen and Aphra Behn, Hershey Felder as George Gershwin, Irving Berlin, Frédéric Chopin, Ludwig van Beethoven, Claude Debussy and Pyotr Ilyich Tchaikovsky, Tovah Feldshuh as Golda Meir, Frank Ferrante as Groucho Marx, Ralph Fiennes in *Beat the Devil*, Laurence Fishburne as Justice Thurgood Marshall, Henry Fonda as Clarence Darrow, Sherry Glaser in F*amily Secrets*, Marga Gomez in *Latin Standards*, Frank Gorshin as George Burns, Julie Harris as Emily Dickinson and Isak Dinesen, Andrew Harrison as Charles Darwin, Valerie Harper as Tallulah Bankhead, Noni Hazleworth in *Mother*, Krister Henriksson as Doktor Glass, Judith Ivey as Ann Landers and in *The Women of Lockerbie*, James Earl Jones as Paul Robeson, Sarah Jones in *Bridge and Tunnel*, Anna Khaja as Benezir Bhutto, Bob Kingdom as Dylan Thomas, Sir Ben Kingsley as Edmund Kean, Stephen Lang in *Beyond Glory*, John Leguiziamo in *Latin History for Morons*, *Freaks*, and *Spic-O-Rama*, Laura Linney in *My Name is Lucy Barton*, Tony Lo Bianco as Fiorella LaGuardia, Priscilla Lopez in *Class Mothers of '68*, Laurence Luckinbill as President Lyndon B. Johnson, President Theodore Roosevelt, Clarence Darrow and Ernest Hemingway, Marco Michel in *A Kiss—Antonio Ligabue*, Jefferson Mays in *I Am My Own Wife*, Ed Metzger as Albert Einstein, Audra McDonald as Billie Holiday, Robert Morse as Truman Capote, Romy Nordlinger as Alla Nazimova, Deidre O'Connell in *Dana H.*, Angelica Page as Sylvia Plath and Geraldine Page, David Payne as C.S. Lewis, Pete Postlethwaite as Scaramouche Jones, Christopher Plummer as John Barrymore and in *A Word or Two*, Andrea Reese as Jacqueline Kennedy Onassis, Ronald Rand as Harold Clurman, John Rothman as H.L. Mencken, Ruben Santiago-Hudson as August Wilson and in *Lackawanna Blues*, Andrew Scott in *Three Kings*, Sabera Shaik in *Puteri Saadong*, Herbert Sigueza as Pablo Picasso, Libby Skala in *LILIA!* as Lilia Skala, Jean Stapleton as Eleanor Roosevelt, David Strathairn as Jan Karski, Holland Taylor as Governor Ann Richards, Lily Tomlin in *The Search for Signs of Intelligent Life in the Universe*, V (formerly Eve Ensler) in *The Vagina Monologues* and *The Body of the World*, Elizabeth Van Dyke as Lorraine Hansberry, Billie Whitelaw in *Rockabye*, and James Whitmore as Harry S. Truman, Will Rogers and President Teddy Roosevelt.

Master comedians, musicians, pianists, poets, and singers have also presented unforgettable solo shows including Riz Ahmed, Laurie Anderson, Michael Ball,

Sandra Bernhard, Victor Borge, Billy Crystal, Dame Edna, Judy Garland, Whoopi Goldberg, Jackie Mason, Mandy Patinkin, Bernadette Peters, Edith Piaf, Bruce Springsteen, Ben Vereen and Robin Williams.

Playwright/performer Anna Deavere Smith created her own unique style of solo performance in her solo plays including *Fires in the Mirror*; *Twilight, Los Angeles*; and *Notes from the Field*, based on a series of extensively-researched interviews from real-life encounters and has brought these unforgettable 'portraits of people' on stage to pierce complacency and challenge the status-quo.

Dael Orlandersmith through her solo performances, including *Beauty's Daughter*, *Yellowman*, and *Until the Flood*, allows composites of people to speak through her as a storyteller surrounding traumatic events at the heart of her explosive solo plays.

V, (formerly Eve Ensler), created two one-woman solo plays: *In the Body of the World* based on her memoirs, and *The Vagina Monologues* based on her interviews of two hundred women, which went on to become a world-wide cultural phenomenon performed in over 140 countries.

Classic texts have come alive through the art of an extraordinary solo performer. Among them include Simon Callow in *Being Shakespeare*, Len Cariou in *Broadway and the Bard*, Sir John Gielgud in *Ages of Man*, Bill Irwin in his nearly one man show *On Beckett*, Charles Laughton reading "Aseop's Fables," Mariam Margolyes in *Dickens' Women*, Alec McCowen in *St. Mark's Gospel*, Sir Ian McKellan in *Acting Shakespeare*, Michael Pennington in *Sweet William*, Christopher Plummer in *A Word or Two*, Fiona Shaw in *The Waste Land*, and Sir Patrick Stewart in *A Christmas Carol.* Each carried onto the stage an undeniable challenge, not only for themselves to carry forth the majesty of the poet's 'leaps of faith' in capturing our humanity in words, but they melded themselves into the text in an unforgettable performance on stage.

Another unique type of a one-person performance that has captured audiences' imagination have been by actors and playwrights who have revealed their own personal life experiences or have illuminated the stage performing in a playwright's powerful 'confession of a soul's story.' Among them have included Mike Albo, Luis Alfaro, Brenda Wong Aoki, Mitchell Anderson, Beatrice Arthur, Leslie Ayvazian, Bobby Baker, Eric Begosian, Mel Brooks, Charles Busch, David Cale, Nigel Charnock, John Cleese, Quentin Crisp, David Drake, David Edgar, Tom Etchells, Karen Finley, Carrie Fisher, John Fleck, Elena Marcia Garcia, Marga Gomez, Guillermo Gómez-Peña, Luba Goy, Spalding Gray, David Greenspan, Valerie Hager, Darrell Hammond, Evan Handler, David Hare, Aleashea Harris, Danny Hoch, Wendy Houstoun, Holly Hughes, Grace Jones, Josh Kornbluth, Lisa Kron, Oni Faida Lampley,

James Lecesne, Ann Magnuson, Aasif Mandvi, Deb Margolin, Robbie McCauley, Tim Miller, Carey Mulligan, John O'Keefe, Monica Palacios, Petronia Paley, Michael Palin, Chazz Palminteri, Mike Pearson, Colin Quinn, Phylicia Rashad, Lynn Redgrave, Rachel Rosenthal, Dawn Akemi Saito, Madeline Sayet, Benjamin Scheuer, Heidi Schrek, Claudia Shear, Roger Guenveur Smith, Ryan J-W Smith, Elaine Stritch, Bob Stromberg, Nilaja Sun, Jean-Claude van Itallie, Phoebe Waller-Bridge, Lucy Wang, Alison Wearing, Marc Wolf, Charlayne Woodard, and Heather Woodbury. Plus Elaine Bromka, Lemon, Heather Raffo, and Anthony Sher.

These are just a few examples of the almost countless performers who have chosen solo performance as a way of reaching into the inner climes of an audiences' consciousness with searing and unrelenting truths that strengthen our lives and mend our hearts.

While some solo performers have appeared in only a limited number of performances, others have reprised their incarnation at periodic times or over several years. Among many of those who have chosen to continue in one role over an extended continuous period of several years, include Hal Holbrook who brought Mark Twain to life in *Mark Twain Tonight!* for sixty-three years in nearly twenty-six thousand performances in fifty states and twenty countries, Tovah Feldshuh in *Golda's Balcony* set a record as the longest one-woman show running in Broadway history of nearly five hundred performances, Rob Becker in *Defending the Caveman* was the longest running solo show on Broadway for over two years, Roy Dotrice as the 17th century writer John Aubrey in *Brief Lives* performing in over eighteen hundred consecutive performances, Sherry Glaser in *Family Secrets* became the longest-running female show in Off-Broadway history, Frank Ferrante has darted across the stage for over thirty years in *An Evening with Groucho*, Stephen Lang has told the story of eight Medal of Honor recipients for over a decade in *Beyond Glory*, and Ronald Rand has taken Harold Clurman to twenty states and twenty-five countries over twenty years in *LET IT BE ART!*

I was also given the unique opportunity to present five memorable performers in solo plays in New York City: Vinie Burrows as Rose McClendon, Karen Eterovich as Jane Austen, Andrea Reese as Jacqueline Kennedy Onassis, John Rothman as H.L. Mencken, and Libby Skala in *LILIA!* It gave me great pleasure that I could help them realize their dreams in bringing to audiences their life-giving solo performances.

Today, solo performers around the world have unique opportunities of performing their plays before audiences including at theaters, international theater festivals, monodrama and solo play festivals, universities and colleges, academies and schools, and in a variety of performance spaces.

Theater is not separate from who we are. It's our birthright. In a world filled with untold mysteries and myriads of unbelievable stories—the art of solo performance carries on a tradition stretching back millenniums—and will continue to enlighten, ennoble and shape our destiny on this planet.

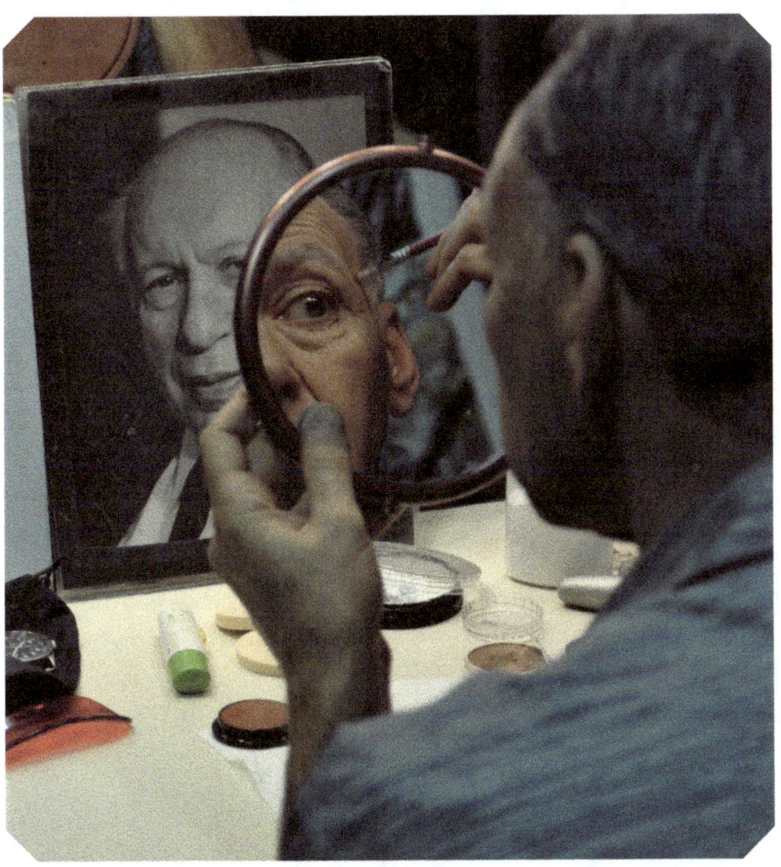

Ronald Rand, during his 'Transformation' process, becoming Harold Clurman in *LET IT BE ART!* (Courtesy Martha Carpenter.)

ONE

From Your Passion Comes Your Courage

Everything you've done up to now. Everything you've tasted, touched, breathed into, every time you stood your ground has led you to this moment. You've searched, you've studied, you've slept, you've shaken the dust off your shoulders from all the steps you've taken. Nobody said it would be easy, but neither should it be. You want to hold on to your doubts, your fears, past mistakes. They want to hold on to you. But you're going to have to let them go because the molecules are already talking to you. They've begun their magic dance. In this moment, in this instant, you know more than you think you know.

Something's rooted deep inside of you. You know it when you feel it. Your passion. One of the greatest forces on earth. Passion comes from deep in the core of your being. All the work you've done up to now—that's been the most meaningful to you—has come because of your passion. When it's aligned with your soul's desire, it moves you to do what you must do. To live the life you desire. To achieve the things you want to happen. Yes, your passion may shift. It may change over time. But when it's coupled with your over-arching dreams, all your energies will tap into the deepest part of your consciousness. You'll become transformed with greater freedom. A greater clarity. Your courage will overcome all fears and limitations.

You may be drawn off your path by the unexpected. Your faith may waver in a moment when you least expect it. That's when you'll need to draw even more from your passion. So you can share your truth with others. That's why the theater becomes a transcendent communication of the human spirit. Trust that everything that's been placed in your path is there for a higher purpose. Why? To allow you to grow, to expand. Your willingness to accept this with a glad heart, an open mind, will bring you the strength necessary for your 'path as an artist.' Even when things don't turn out the way you expect them to. That's part of your journey. Your inner voice will lead you to challenge all your preconceptions, your bad habits, your prejudices. Let them go. LET THEM ALL GO! This is how you'll develop your 'moral compass,' and move into a higher and stronger state of vibrancy.

August Wilson, through his plays, asks us to look at ourselves. He wants you to think about all of those in your family who have come before you so you can be who you are. He's asking you: 'What's your identity? What do you identify with the most? How has that molded you?'

Take a look. Look closely. It's not going anywhere. It's there waiting for you. Because it's made you who you are. It's given you your strength. It's what you're going to need. It's your 'rock.' It's where you come from.

So now that you know that you've got it—what are you going to do with it? Because it shaped you. This 'rock' has existed for a long time. You can count on it. Don't ever let it go. The question becomes: What *are* you going to do with it?

How strong is your faith as an actor?

Because one thing you can rely on in this process—is that you're never alone. We're on this journey together—you and I. So are all those who've come before you. They're right there next to you. They've seen it. They've done it. They reached for the stars. So can you. And you can feel them. We're talking about mindfulness. Intuition. Discernment. Now is the time you're going to have to open yourself up to the miracle of creation. To surrender and listen to that 'still small voice' inside you. Because you've got a journey ahead. We're talking about releasing 'truth.' What truth? Who's truth? What is true? Well, that's what you're going to have to find out. Because on the stage, you're a 'truth-teller.'

When you're going to become a person, other than who you are, and I'm not talking about acting like a 'character'—I'm talking about becoming a real breathing human being with as much passion that's inside of you—this is what it's going to take. This is where all your craft, your technique comes into play. You've already got a lot of talent. You've got loads of talent. I know you do. You've got tons of emotions. You've got sensitivities. You're filled with imagination. You've got spirit. You've got *spirit*! WOW!

So it really comes down to *this* moment. Because nothing's in your way—except you! How do you get out of your way? Well, we all like going into our heads. It's the quickest place to go when everything's coming in every direction. Our mind is one busy place. Never satisfied. Never gets enough. Always wanting to keep dragging everything from the past in front of you. Judgments. What other people think about you.

But that's not going to help you now. This is a different kind of path. This is a path that leads to 'Transformation.' You've got to be here—right now—in this moment. We're talking about 'a step off the cliff.' Nothing there but air. It's scary, but that's where you're going. Because you've chosen this path. That's where the path leads. You've got it in you, or else you wouldn't be reading these words. It's a 'leap of faith.' There's no two ways about it.

So now that you know what it's going to take—what are you going to do? And this is not going to happen overnight. This isn't going to happen by taking classes for a couple of weeks, or a couple of months, or even a couple of years. This path—once you're willing to go down it—is going to take all of you. Everything you've got. Where you're going—by the time you get there—you won't even recognize yourself. That's what happens. You become a new self. The minute you step out 'there.' Because there's risk out there. There's freedom. Yes, and 'Transformation.' But to get there, you're going to have 'burn some bridges.'

What's the first step? Well, it's pretty clear, isn't it. Calling upon all of your courage. Your passion. CLAIM IT! It's yours! Because once you do—all these invisible molecules that are ready will join with you. Yes—and they will come! And they'll keep coming when you least expect them. They're going to come and keep you up in the middle of the night. They're going to keep knocking at your door until you decide to 'swim with them.' They're not going to let you go. Why should they! You've chosen this path! So grab them! Look at them! Shake them! You're on fire! This is what it takes!

You're like a tree. It doesn't need to know how to grow. It rises with an innate knowledge inside! Have you ever thought what the inside of your heart looks like? Take a look. It's everything you've loved. Everything you've suffered. Everything you feel deeply about. It's who you are. It's what's going to keep making you a greater 'who you are.'

This world's been around a long time. It's seen a lot. But what it hasn't seen is what you're going to bring to it. This world needs a lot of help. And if you don't help it, who will. There's a lot of people out there hurting. Many out there on the march. A lot is hanging by a thread. You're the thread we're counting on. You've the march. You're the heart of art!

Do you think most people know what they want? Do most people get what they want? Are most people happy? Are most people satisfied? Are most people up in the air? What do you think? That's why there's art. That's why there's you! They want to find peace. Courage. They want a chance to look at themselves. In their heart. In their soul. They want to know there'll still be a world tomorrow.

Who's going to give them that courage? Where are they going to find it? That strength? That 'rock' that they can hold on to. A way forward. This is where you come in. But we can't even begin to shake the 'coconuts from the trees' until we look at what's in front of us. What's in front of you. EMBRACE THE MOMENT!

If you want to give something to others, they'll welcome it only when you reach out and say: "Look what I've discovered!" That's what you're going to give them. But there's no 'half in or half out.' Choose the 'light' and GIVE IT AWAY!

Every day actors are bombarded by the realities of the 'business.' Either 'you've made it,' or you haven't. What's your 'worth' in the marketplace? A lot of the time, you're considered a commodity. Is that how you want to define yourself? Is that the way you want to be defined? To have your life and your art in the hands of someone who doesn't know anything about you? You want them to decide your worth? And even if you show them, they may still look at you like you're from another planet. But your future is not about them. It's about what you have to say! What this world needs. That's why you're alive.

I'm not saying anything that you don't already know. What do I know? I've lived a couple of years on a planet that's billions of years old, and now all of a sudden, we have a couple of answers. Do we know where we come from? Where we're going next? See—it's all one big mystery. But what we do know is that we've got to do a better job of living together. We've got to look around and make others more aware of how we can help one another. That's why you're here. But you're going to have to be willing to be strong.

Because take a look. Artists have been persecuted, vilified, forgotten, tortured, even killed for being an artist. Yes, they have been championed, remembered, celebrated, and lauded. They can shake their art at a government—jar their fellow human beings to re-think their entire lives—and at the same time—entertain and inspire. So, you have a path ahead of you. It's up to you to take that step into the unknown to show us a way forward.

Anton Chekhov wrote: "He who desires nothing, hopes for nothing and is afraid of nothing, cannot be an artist."

TWO

With Faith, Everything's Possible

To create something that's never existed before. How does that happen? For some, it comes more easily. Probably because of their habits, because of a great deal of practice and hard work. Sometimes it doesn't come at all, and you have to start all over and work your way through each step. Thomas Edison, who invented the light bulb, made thousands of unsuccessful attempts before achieving what he was after. It's certainly unlike a magician who taps on a black hat. Says a few 'hocus-pocus' words and makes a rabbit appear out of 'thin air. But even good magicians have to practice for a long time to make it look easy. Everything worth doing takes a great deal of practice—and this has nothing to do with 'tricks.'

Something can come through you in an instant. You can leave reality and step into another. The choice is entirely up to you. I'm talking about the organic process of the 'Art of Transformation.' For it to occur, you have to believe it. To believe it, you have to do it. To know you have that power. But it's not magic—although it's mysterious—and it is a ritual. Rituals have been around a long time. They're as simple as shaking hands or as complex as a Presidential inauguration, a coronation, a sacred ceremony inside a house of worship—or the two-hour Transformation I go through to bring Harold Clurman alive in my solo play.

All rituals require a process. Before a performance, I have to initiate a sequence, followed by activities and actions during my preparation for creation to take place. Special gestures. Reciting of dialogue. An order and use of make-up and special objects that I have placed out in front of me. Dressing into Clurman's clothing, which some refer to as a costume. Finally, surrendering to allow Transformation to occur. All of this is just the beginning.

The first words Clurman utters in my play before an audience sees him: "If this be magic, let it be art!" immediately sets molecules flying between the audience and myself. But for all of this to occur—many things have to come into play. That's why we have to begin at the beginning. To examine what's leading up to that moment.

Tiny vibrations of molecules are tricky things. Floating around inside of you. Around you. These words are molecules. Your thoughts. Everything you know. Everything you see. Everything you don't see. Literally everything. And when these tiny little molecules line up to light your way. Ah, that's when it becomes interesting. But you can't touch them. Taste them. See them. Still, that doesn't mean they don't exist. They're as real as you and I. As real as the universe. If they weren't, all the most inspiring art that's ever been attempted or exists wouldn't exist. It's a crazy thought. But life had to start somewhere. I'm talking about what's inside you that makes you tick.

Most of the time, we take a lot of it for granted. But when you need to make sense of something, to find a way through—at that moment—time can stop, stand still—and a thought can come through you in an instant. But you have to be willing to be open to receive these 'vibrations of molecules.' Whispering to you. Bringing their own life force of energy. Showing you your destiny.

You're a part of a 'tribe' of all those who've come down this path. What matters now is it's up to you to see it for what it is. To recognize the impossible is possible. To leave no stone unturned. Letting nothing stand in your way. Sure, it brings up a lot of questions. But most of them, you already know the answer. You knew the answer when you asked the question because the way forward chose you. That's how it works.

Scratch the surface of anyone—what are you going to find? Yourself. We're all alike. Of course, we look at the world differently. We've had different experiences, different parents. We grew up differently, in a different place. Still, that doesn't mean that we're not the same. We may eat different foods. Like different clothes. Still, it doesn't mean we're not the same. Do you think what you believe is different than what others believe? Of course, there's always going to be differences. Still doesn't mean we're not the same. That's what makes us human beings. A lot of folks have tried over centuries to explain that. Books after books line bookshelves the world overwritten by poets, philosophers, psychologists, scientists, artists—all trying to make sense of who we are. But guess what? Everything comes back to how *you* see the world.

That doesn't mean you're the center of the universe. It means we're all in the same universe. With the same problems, same issues, and we're trying to make sense of it all. How do you take a step forward? Faith. That's what's behind everything you do. And what is it based on? Love. The most powerful force in the universe. That's why we're still around. It's what keeps the world turning. "It's up to you how you shape your daily life," Clurman says in my solo play.

One morning, when I was in my teens, I decided to climb a tree. I thought if I could get high enough, I'd have a clue about where I was. I grabbed one branch after another, climbing higher and higher. The bark cut into my hands. But I wasn't going to stop until I reached the top. Still, there was too much in the way. I tried pushing the branches, the leaves out of my face so that I could see. When I stopped, I looked down. I realized I was going to have to figure somehow how to get back to the ground. What was I doing in a tree? What are you doing in your life?

Finding a way forward every day is about recognizing what you can offer others. When you wake up in the morning, you decide what you're going to do with the time you're given. See what's in front of you. Feel the rhythm of life. When you listen with all of your heart, nothing can get in the way of what's leading you forward. It's taking you where you need to go, creating something that's never existed before. All your own. Larger forces than even you and I are aware of are guiding our every step. When you get out on stage in a solo performance, you're never alone because you have the audience with you all the time and all of those who have shown you the way forward. They're coming through you so you can say what needs to be said.

Catching the dawn.

Now that's a simple phrase. But what does it mean? How often do you get up early enough to watch the sun appear in the sky? We're on a turning planet, and every day, the sun greets us—and with it—comes light, bringing a new day. A new dawn offering unlimited possibilities. It's like a new person coming into your life, approaching you for the first time. It's as if you've never seen life quite like this before. This is what you can bring so others can see. As if it's the first time they've really 'seen the dawn.'

It's why the audience is coming to join with you when you do your solo performance. They've come to have their world 'lit up'—and in turn, they're illuminating your life. When you burst upon them with everything you've uncovered—everything you've discovered through the 'Art of Transformation'—the world we live in and what we think about it—everything changes. As if you've opened an entirely new world for them.

Just like every truthful living performance has never happened before, each new audience experiencing your 'light' becomes a miracle showing a way forward. Because with faith, everything's possible.

THREE

Claiming Your Path

There are certain questions you always have to ask yourself when you begin working on a role. After all, you're creating a human being. That has to think. That has to breathe. That has to live, just like you. Certainly, you have to answer: Who am I? Where do I come from? Where am I going? Why am I here? What do I want? Who am I talking to? What's the purpose of all of this?

Of course, it's more than that. And you know it, or else you wouldn't have picked up this book. There's a need inside of you. A curiosity. That's great. That's what you've got to have. That 'need' is what's going to make all the difference. Because without it, there's no point in going ahead. You might as well 'close up shop' right now. I listed a lot of extraordinary individuals in the introduction. Not only did they come here to say what they needed to say, but they said it through someone else who had to say what they had to say, or else the world wouldn't go around. Of course, the world will keep going around for a long time. But not in the same way. Not in a better way. It would be missing something. That 'something' is what people need to understand about themselves. And they need to hear it from you. Or else we'll forget who we are.

Can someone be even stronger than 'the truth'? After all, we know truths change. What's true today may not be true tomorrow. Still, some things always remain true. Some things are eternal, and they flow through you. They flow through everyone. I'm talking about the human spirit. That's something everyone feels. It's what saves us. And it's going to keep saving you. It's the one thing you've got going for you, more than practically anything else. And when you tap into that . . . Ah, you know it when you feel it. So does the audience. That's when the molecules take off. But to get there? Well, there it is. That's the big question.

What is it going to take for you to find it? To live it? To claim it and then—give it away! Because after all, it's never yours. The only way it works is when you give it away. Remember—'it' finds you. That's the long and short of it. It finds you because it's all about being 'open to receive.'

So what's guiding you? A flow. That's right. A flow into a state of wonder. Can something be even greater than your imagination? I know, you can imagine a lot of things. But this—this is something different.

How to explain it? Something triggers something. That's the key. We all love being inspired. Stuff always happens then. But you can't always depend on it. So it's even more than that. Something triggers something, and everything becomes clear. That's when you know you're 'inside.' Something's arrived that will take you where you've got to go. Now you can't *make* that happen. It's not about making something happen. It's about—'giving yourself permission.' That's right. But to what? To whom? To *you*. To allow it to happen. Something has to arrive to join with you.

This is what happens when I step into the dressing room. Or what I refer to as the 'Creation Room.' It's where creation takes place. A place of 'letting go.' Of slipping into another realm, allowing another energy to arrive. Letting molecules have 'free rein' making everything possible. This is what happens every time I prepare. It's what's necessary for the 'Art of Transformation' to occur.

It's said we stand on the 'shoulders of those who have come before us.' As a young actor, I often wondered: 'How does that work? What's that about? How can it be a part of what I do on stage?'

We live in a translucent age today. It's become a glorified art to achieve one's 'fifteen seconds of fame.' Well, if that's what you're after, I'm afraid you're reading the wrong book. This process is about the moment when you decide: I have to do something that holds great meaning. Others have realized this. They've realized their responsibility. They've recognized in themselves where they come from. You come from the same place. This 'mantle' being passed to you is inside of you. That no matter what you're faced with. No matter how tough it gets. When you see yourself going backward, well, then you've lost touch with it. But it's there—in your heart. In your soul. A sustaining power that will never let you down. It'll stir the deepest waters in every part of your being. When you see yourself going forward—that's what's inside of you.

Now, you've got to grab hold of it. Once you do, it'll lift you higher than you ever thought possible. That's the power inside of you. Feel its force. You can see clearer because of it. Take a look around. You can see the past, the present, and the future. You're going to need it more today than ever before. You might ask yourself: "Is this art that I'm immersing myself in going to make a difference in today's world?" You'll only find out when you decide to add to the larger vision of the human experience.

Bertolt Brecht, the German director, and playwright, once said: "It's most difficult to discover a truth which is socially useful. It's precisely this truth we need." How are you going to challenge yourself to penetrate to the audience with a truth that's socially useful?

To start with—it requires being open. Honest. To discover your 'truthful impulses.' Sometimes at a rehearsal, or a read-through, or during a performance, you may become inspired. But we know that inspiration is not something we can always rely upon. A craftsman building a table or a bridge, or an actor discovering all the subtleties inside another human being, builds through a learned discipline because that's what it takes.

Wolfgang von Goethe, one of the great poets and writers of all time, stated: "I wish the stage were as narrow as the wire of a tightrope dancer so that no incompetent would dare step upon it."

To act on the stage is to put your life at risk. I know that sounds pretty heady. Your desire to inhabit another person's skin—to tell their stories—to reveal their soul through the actions you portray—calls into play not only all of humanity but everything that hangs in the balance from one moment to the next. Your performance contains our essence as human beings.

Recently I read the screenplay of *My Dinner with Andre* by Wallace Shawn and André Gregory. After watching the film again, I was drawn to Gregory's words when he said: ". . . We're talking about trying to find the truthful impulse, to not do what you should do or ought to do or what is expected of you, but trying to find what it is that you really want to do or need to do or have to do."

Every thought you bring to the stage has within it the potential to shine 'a light' for others to see. I believe, as Harold Clurman reminded us: "We retain our human stature and possibly enhance it when we learn to walk in the outside world, and at the same time find a quiet place within ourselves, where consciousness and conscience dwell and develop." Think hard and long about those few words within his sentence: 'To find a quiet place within ourselves.' See, that's where the journey begins.

There. By going there. Finding that quiet place within yourself. Once you're there, you'll start to become much more aware of a larger world inside an even larger universe. This is when the molecules start flowing in ways you never thought possible. It's similar to when you're inside a dream that's extremely clear, and it's showing you a way forward. At the same time, you become grounded in ways you never imagined were possible.

Time is not reality. It may seem real when you're passing through it, but it doesn't exist except in your mind's logic. You can slow down time—and make it appear as if an instant is an eternity.

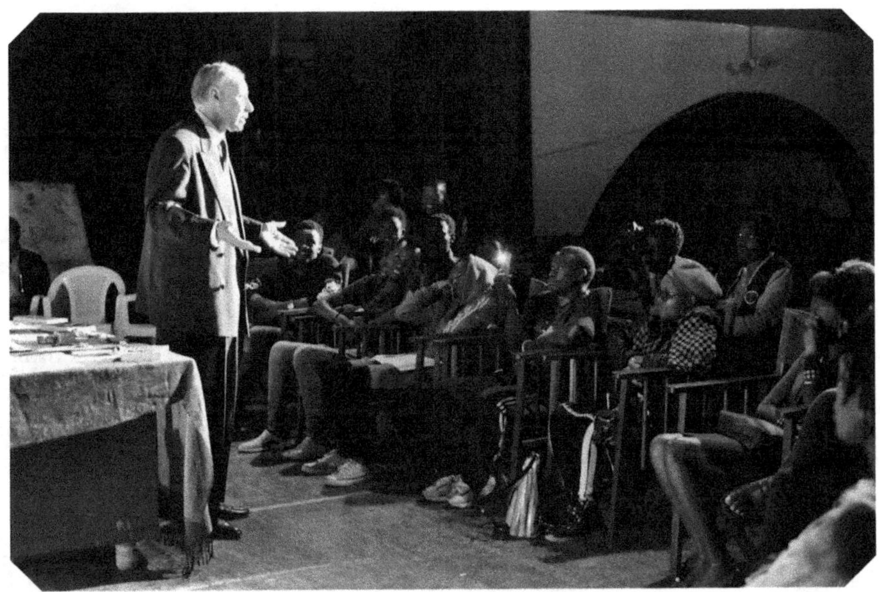

Ronald Rand as Harold Clurman in his solo play, *LET IT BE ART!* performance at Nakuru Players Theatre in the Kenya International Theatre Festival. (Courtesy Ronald Rand.)

FOUR

Your Task as a Truth-Teller

You've chosen to tell stories on the stage. With that comes a responsibility as a 'truth-teller.' What's a 'truth-teller'? Once you tap into the unalterable 'truths of life' that hold us all together, you'll begin to fathom a greater sense of what's inside that world. But how's it possible to know for sure what truth really looks like? What it consists of?

Perhaps that search for an answer started a long time ago. When a primal urge was born in someone like you who wanted to make sense of something. Maybe they saw a mirage in the desert. The water appeared to be right there in front of them. They could almost reach out and touch it. But when they got there. It totally disappeared. That water may have meant life and death. But where did it go? How could it not be real? At that moment, it may have made the person question—what is reality? How can my eyes show me something that appears to be true—and for it to turn out not to be true? So, what is true and what isn't? And over time, our mind has had to grasp somehow that that's also a part of our reality—and even in that, a mystery exists.

Today we're faced with an even greater dilemma, and the stakes have gotten higher. We want to try somehow to 'stay in the loop,' but as Olympia Dukakis reminded me: "There is no more loop."

The ground has shifted. But still—truth is truth. Yet, it changes over time. So how do we know what 'truth' really is? How do we know when we've seen it or heard it? Something deep inside tells you when something *is* true. It's amazing because we always know it. Deep down. Whether or not we want to recognize it or not, it's still going to be the truth. You are a 'barometer of your own truth.'

Does that mean every thought you think is true? No. That's why we have to find out what 'truth' is made of? How did *your* truth get shaped? This is what great poets, writers, and playwrights, artists of all dimensions have given their lives to uncover. To grapple with. To tap into. The simple difference between right and wrong.

When Henrik Ibsen, the great Norwegian playwright, in his plays uses words like Truth. Love. Justice. Honor. You have to discover what they mean to the person using them at that time and what they mean for us today, what they represent. What they mean for *you* today in the way you live your life.

That's why it's necessary to look deep inside yourself. To shine your search-light on everything you believe in. Because you're going to have to come to grips with the 'truths' you've been given—and find out that some of them are true—and that some of them aren't.

It also requires telling yourself 'the truth' about your work, with no hedging. Are you doing what you want to do with your life every single day? Remember, you can't let anything get in your way. And if you're doing it, are you doing everything you can to make it an even greater reality? This is where daring comes in. Courage. It's the same when you're telling the truth on stage. There's no 'in-between.' It must be revealed with the complete authenticity of your soul. With total sincerity. All of your compassion. Because some truths are even larger than you and I. The stakes are that high. That's why it's up to you to uncover them—and reveal them to others.

Picasso said once: "I do not seek. I find."

So must you! Find that unshakable truth. That faith inside yourself. To allow the deepest currents of nature to come through you. The ripples of time and all those who have fought for what they believed in so you can live the life you live. Because you're reading this book, I have faith you will. It tells me that you want to know more. You're not willing to settle.

In his book, *The Actor's Eye*, renowned actor Morris Carnovsky wrote, ". . . no truth can be expressed except your own truth. Artistic control means the intelligent management of what you're driving at—the imaginative perception . . ."

The theater remains one of the few places on earth where we can come to hear the truth. We also know that on stage that there's something referred to as an 'artistic truth.' Nothing is real on the stage—and yet, at the same time, it is. What is real is your 'truth-telling'—the reality and truth created through your imagination 'in the moment.' A belief that's so strong, built on a resounding, resonating truth being born in the moment, capturing the imagination of all those who have come. Through your craft. Your intelligence. Your understanding. Your humor. Your imagination and humanity.

In that moment, the world may go on outside, but a new reality has been born within the sacred space. Every audience is different. Everything you do as a performer will never happen in the same way ever again. In this singular moment, the infinite possibility of a purer way of seeing has come into being. Hearing. Listening. Revealing our humanity.

Seek out the most relevant discovery that you can make at this moment—artistically, emotionally, and spiritually.

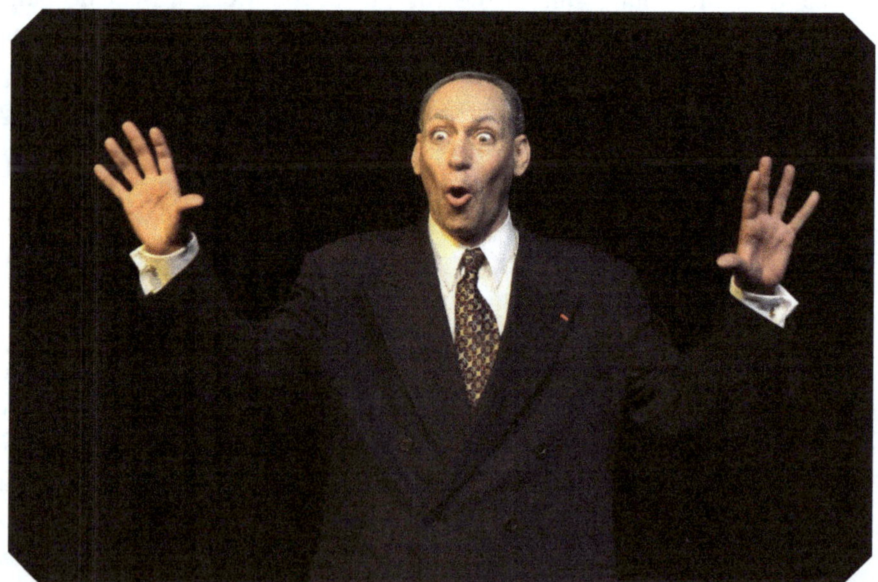

Ronald Rand as Harold Clurman in his solo play, *LET IT BE ART!* (Courtesy Ronald Rand.)

FIVE

Preparing the Way for Creation

Just as important as building confidence in your abilities and your skills is allowing space for 'not knowing.' I know that may sound strange. But we certainly don't have all the answers, do we? We live our lives inside a complete mystery. Yet, as we go along, part of the riddle is revealed to us. Keeping that in mind will allow you to experience a state of amazement every day of your life. Innocence. Wonder. Each time you approach an opportunity to create on the stage—allow the molecules to surround you to keep you discovering what exists inside every moment.

I've learned that this will also bring you innumerable opportunities of coming in contact with other like-minded individuals in your personal and artistic life. Through your decisions of who you study with. The kind of projects and plays you choose to work on. Especially the solo performance you wish to create. The story that you have to tell. Who you want to collaborate with. Who your director will be and why. Who your audience will be and where. Ultimately—what they'll be left with after they've experienced what you brought them.

I take my solo play around the world. So, for the most part, audiences that meet Clurman for the first time have probably never heard of him. That's okay. That's the same way it is with every new play we've never seen before. That's why it's such an amazing experience when their eyes and ears, and hearts discover what kind of a person Clurman is. Because at that moment, he's coming to life in front of them. They're learning about the world that he comes from. The way he thinks and speaks and expresses himself. His great passion. That's what they connect with.

It's about making audiences aware of an entirely different way of looking at life. Making them think: What more can I bring into my own life. That's one of the greatest gifts you can bring through your solo play. Clurman draws each person into his world and what's at stake. And even though my solo play takes place in 1980, everything Clurman says is just as relevant today, especially when he takes audiences back to the 1930s. Audiences know we're still faced with the same problems. He makes them laugh. He makes them cry. Everything he says affects their attitude about their own life.

In that singular moment, that's what you have to offer. An opportunity to expand their vision. Keep in mind that continuing to expand your own vision will have a definite and direct bearing on how you grow as a creative artist—as a person—as a solo performer. Your audiences are just like you. They want to discover more about themselves.

Always take time between performances to stop and reflect and ask yourself: 'What did I accomplish today that brought me closer to my dreams?' 'Step inside' and connect with your subconscious. Allow time to restore and re-energize your creative cells. Let your molecules connect with all your energies. Let go of any doubts. They won't do you any good. Let your body express any fears you might be holding inside by physically releasing them through exercises. Get them out of your way so you'll be completely open to bringing audiences the fullness of your entire being. To allow the person or persons in your solo play to exist in their complete fullness.

Every moment in life, and on stage—has its own rhythm. Every moment has its fullest expression, its deepest meaning. Through your preparation, the creation that's coming into being will take you into these 'worlds of meaning' that you wouldn't have normally found by simply 'thinking' about them or rehearsing without tapping into this kind of 'flow.'

This is how you'll be able to create your solo play and allow what needs to come through you to manifest itself. As a conduit for greater meaning, astonishing thoughts will appear. Everything you need is embedded inside your soul, urging you on to greater freedom. Though sometimes, some things can get in the way, color what you do. Your ego may feel the need to impress someone. Moliere called it: "Le grand art est de plaire." The need 'to succeed in the art of pleasing.' The work we're doing is not about that. If that's what you need to do, do it and get it out of your system. Then we can move on and allow creation to occur.

Have you ever thought about what it means to be 'ego-less'? I took the time to read Eckhart Tolle's book, *A New Earth: Awakening to Your Life's Purpose.* Well, I must have read it a couple of times to try and wrap my mind around the concept of what it means to be 'ego-less.' There's a great deal to be learned from Tolle's ideas, the stories he shares. You need to understand how much of a role your ego plays in how you create, in how you live each day. The effect it has on your work, how you judge yourself and others. I believe it's impossible to do away with your ego entirely in our field because it serves several purposes. But the moment your ego makes you 'second-guess' your true nature, it's getting in your way. The ego has been known to dredge up past mistakes, doubts, disappointments because it thrives on conflict. You have to be aware of when your ego is doing that, how to deal with it, and to let those feelings go. That's why books like Tolle's can be extremely useful in giving you greater insight. He shows you how strongly you can come to believe in your own identity. But is it really who you are? It's essential to think about this, especially when you're creating another person in your solo play.

When an actress told Ibsen how much she loved his characters, he replied, "I do not write characters. I write human beings." He made it clear every person he created as a playwright—or eventually that will be created by you in your solo play, is a human being that has to come and live fully through you. That's where your technique and talent come in.

There was a time in my life when I was studying at New York University that I decided I needed to 'educate' myself in a deeper way. I was going to read beyond just the plays and theater books that I had been assigned. I needed to understand how things came into being, why we think the way we do. Why I believe in what I believe in. Of course, we're all, in a sense, brainwashed from the moment our brain can hold thoughts, whether we're aware of it or not. I'm not saying that's a good thing or a bad thing; it's just the way it is. It's a matter of survival—of being human. But we have to be aware of how we've been influenced, in many ways unconsciously. And try and recognize how it continues to influence the way you think now. Who taught you? Who taught your parents, your teachers?

I was intent on trying to unravel why we believe the things we do, especially if I'm going to become someone else. I'd have to know why *they* think the way they do. What they learned growing up, the books they read. The life-changing consequential life experiences they had. This all plays a significant role in how Clurman comes to life through me. I set myself the task—and it must have taken me over five years—of reading every masterwork that the great master authors had written. I became a voracious reader—reading every play written by the master playwrights. Many of the master texts of the world's great religions. Books written by the greatest philosophers, scientists, thinkers, humanitarians, psychologists, and more! This is something you can do yourself. Believe me, it will expand your vision and understanding of life and nature—bringing you a greater perspective of existence—a greater appreciation of history, art, civilization—and everything in between.

Seek out a greater realization of what life means to you. It will lead you on your path of allowing true creation to flow through you.

SIX

When the Stage Disappears

You're backstage, and you hear 'places.' What happens? Well, we all react in different ways. What do you do? Perhaps your body tightens a little. Your pulse quickens. You might take an extra swallow of water. A deep breath. Because you're getting ready to 'travel.' Or you might be full of energy and completely relaxed to arrive in the 'wings' next to the stage—to prepare to enter into a new reality. But who's actually leaving the 'Creation Room'? Are you still in the 'state of transformation'? Is it you or the person you're bringing to life who's 'traveled'?

Let me tell you what happens during my process when it comes to this moment. At least a half-hour before 'places,' Clurman has already 'arrived.' He already exists in 'his world of 1980.' Of course, I'm *inside* aware that he has to go to where the stage is. But he's not going to a stage. He's returning to his apartment. So I have to usher him—and if there are heavy doors to be opened or an elevator or stairs—when I had arrived at the theater earlier—I made sure that he doesn't have to deal with figuring that out now. After all, he's a gentleman approaching eighty, and I have to do everything beforehand to ensure he has a smooth and easy path.

Clurman is on his way to return to his apartment to go on with his life. It has nothing to do with a theater, an audience, or a stage. On this spring afternoon, he's traveling back after attending a play at the Brooklyn Academy of Music. He's coming home by taxi. He has to get out of the taxi, make his way into his apartment building across from Carnegie Hall in New York City, arrive at the second floor via an elevator, walk down the hallway and enter his apartment. All of which is happening, and I'm experiencing through my imagination. I'm aware that he needs to enter 'on cue.' But he doesn't care about that or that there's a specific time for him to enter. Because *he's* not in a play. He's simply entering his apartment—and all of a sudden 'discovers' that his assistant is still there, along with two other students—and he goes on with his life.

Let's say you've gotten to the 'wings,' and there are a few moments when you have to wait to hear your 'cue' before you enter. What's going through your mind? Who's doing the listening? Whose eyes are you looking out of? Whose heart is beating? Of course, it's all yours. And someone else who has arrived. You're now holding another life that must be expressed in their reality. You know that as the actor inside. Yes, a new reality has taken place to allow organic life to occur at that moment.

This is the mystery of 'the moment before' and how it works. But actually, it's not this one moment 'in the wings.' It's the entire flow of molecules that began when you invited another person to come alive—to live through you. And it begins even before you enter the 'creation' room. Making this process work requires accepting that the 'Creation Room' is a necessary step in this person's life. They're coming from a reality where they were—and now they're moving into another part of their day. It's all one continuous stream of consciousness. There's no separation. Molecules moving you forward, almost in an unconscious way. By being totally aware of everything that's occurring allows this 'other' person to come into being. Because they're a real person just like you. Who has come to do what they have to do.

The moment Clurman arrives, and the audience meets him, they make a whole slew of judgments. We all do, the moment we meet someone new. Who is this person? Why are they dressed this way? Do I want to get to know them? Do I want to listen to what they have to say? In the theater, we have our work cut out for us—so that the audience willingly suspends their disbelief—and is swept up into an entirely different reality.

We've all heard the phrase—'breaking character.' For me, there is no 'character.' There is only this person who's living through me. The only time 'I' return is when Clurman leaves his apartment at the end of the play, and I come out on the stage for the curtain call. This is part of the mystery of theater.

Today we have to keep finding new ways of engaging and involving the audience, connecting with people from all different parts of the world to understand one another. The audience is always an essential part of this process, part of the journey. They become part of the Transformation that takes place.

With my solo play, that's very much the case. Through the invitation extended by Clurman crossing the 'fourth wall'—his passion leaps 'across the footlights,' so the audience becomes entirely engaged. Especially when Clurman talks directly to them, giving his first 'Talk,' as if they're the group of actors who have to consider joining the Group Theatre in 1930. His words fly out, encouraging them, exhorting them, lifting their spirits in the middle of the Great Depression. To join in the beginning of a new theater that will change the very meaning of what theater can be.

Over more than a hundred years ago—Edwin Booth, Ira Aldridge, Sarah Bernhardt, Edwin Forrest, Joseph Jefferson, James O'Neill, who was the father of Eugene O'Neill, and several other actors—would travel across this country and around the world, performing in plays and comedies, exciting melodramas and Shakespeare, bringing the power of live drama right to the people. Audiences in small towns or in large theaters, under tents, or at mining camps were transported by these 'larger-than-life' actors through their grandeur and size, their language, and gesture. But it was even more than that. Their storytelling transported the listener to believe in the story being acted out in front of them, and their entire lives were changed in an instant.

America may have begun with shutting down theaters because of our forefathers' puritanical background. However, once theater took root, nothing could stop it. Everywhere performers traveled, it was as if the audience wanted to reach out and feel the electricity of the performer. They didn't care if what was occurring wasn't real. At that moment, it was. A life force in front of them. Vibrations—molecules—rippling through each person in the audience. The power of the actor's voices, their tremendous willpower, and Transformation sending life-giving energies directly into the audience's psyche—into their souls. Each person became the embodiment of the imaginative story coming to life. To each of them, the impossible became real.

Pretty much everyone has seen the masterful performance by Tom Hanks as Chuck Noland in the film, *Castaway*. Hanks continues to be one of our finest storytellers as an actor in film, including in another 'storytelling' film, *News of the World*. When I had the pleasure of working with him on a John Patrick Shanley film, we spent at least a half-hour talking together about the process and our love of acting.

In the film, *Castaway*, there's a moment when Noland is unable to make a fire and has cut himself. He angrily picks up a volleyball and throws it. However, he leaves an imprint from his cut hand on the ball in the shape of what appears to be a face. Noland stops and stares at the imprint. A transmission is occurring between Noland and this object. He discovers a new 'friend' in the face and decides to call him 'Wilson.'

At that moment, once this Transformation has occurred—not only does it change the person Hanks is playing, as well as the life of the object—it changes us. A life-giving transference has taken place. A shift in consciousness has come into being through the power of the imagination. That's how molecules shift. The need is so great at that moment to find a way to go on—and we, the audience, completely accept it, believing that somehow magically—this ball has become imbued with 'life.' Because the actor has made it real for us.

Later, when 'Wilson' becomes lost and is stranded among rocks, he's rescued by Noland. We see his love towards this inanimate object. But it's now no longer just a ball—it's become his dearest and closest friend. 'Wilson,' first, a bloody smear, has now been further painted, taking on an even stronger life-force of hope and safety. When Noland is finally able to break free from the island, 'Wilson' joins him on the raft because they're both breaking free together. However, it soon leads to their parting. In a weakened state, Noland hadn't made sure 'Wilson' was tied down properly, and on the open sea, 'Wilson' floats away. This time, Noland cannot rescue his friend. We feel the loss just as much as he does because we believe entirely in the bond that has taken place. Something indeed sacred. Although it's not a 'live' performance, it's 'alive' in the moment in our hearts. It's 'alive' because we feel it through Hank's performance in our souls. In our need to feel. It's what keeps us human.

Everything you see and use on the stage must be imbued with this kind of 'life force'—and it begins in the 'Creation Room.' Actually, for me, it begins weeks before a performance. Molecules are floating around me as I prepare in several different ways. Reading, rehearsing, readying myself.

On the day before I arrive at the theater, I usually go through the entire play, letting the dialogue stream out of me as I re-discover where I am, what I'm saying, what's occurring moment-to-moment. When I prepare in the 'Creation Room,' I become a 'willing vessel' giving myself over to allow the organic process to occur. The immersion that takes place through Transformation is always a part of the mystery of the actor's art. When it comes time for the performance, I invite a stream of molecules to join with me in a flow of creation.

The mind's a miraculous thing. It's accepting. Challenging. Demanding. Willing to believe the unbelievable. Its strength depends entirely upon you to defy gravity. To immerse yourself into another world that doesn't even exist. But at that moment—your breath, your body—accepts it and believes it. Essential ingredients for the organic process to take place, leading to Transformation.

After a performance, deep resonating energy continues to reside in the audience. It's how the theater renews and heals everyone who comes. It's how we feel more human. In a world where hope's greatly needed, we desperately need to keep reaching out to one another.

Another way to study Transformation is to examine and 'feel' the inner life inside great paintings. You may already appreciate certain artists who touch you deeply. I've been painting since I was a child, and when I spend an hour or two in front of a painting by Vincent van Gogh, I'm taken over by the colors he chose, the different shapes and forms. His emotional strokes teaching me how to see all over again. Van Gogh literally taught himself how to draw, to paint. But his paintings don't merely depict what was in front of him. They became an extension of his soul. His longing to connect with the deepest recesses of the eternal. The flow of molecules that moved through his focus, his concentration, the depth of his soul poured into the paint—passing through his brush and onto the canvas—became the 'life-force' of existence. The more he released his passion with each stroke, he allowed nature to flow through him—and bring him 'a peace that passeth all understanding.'

Take the time to let the colors wash over you. Feel the collision of space and time. Van Gogh's starry sky reveals reflections of the glittering light of passion, traveling further and deeper into the depths of the unknown. Who are we, it asks. How did we come here? Where are we going? How do I touch the unknowable? Take the time as you go down your path to keep searching—reaching out to go even further. Embrace everything you come in contact with because you've been put here to say what your soul has to say.

The role that art and nature play in your life is a sustaining force bringing you closer and closer to realizing and releasing all the gifts you hold inside yourself as a storyteller.

SEVEN

The Organic Process of the Art of Transformation

Imagine it's late at night. You're sleeping. Myriads of thoughts are passing before your eyes. Your mind's in motion. You're dreaming. In a state of wonder. Where are you? How did you get there? Where did you go? Why does your mind do that? You see, we're faced with mysteries at every turn of our life. It's been said that your dreams reveal more about you than even your conscious thoughts. Do you keep a dream journal? If you don't, start one. Always make sure it's right there next to you. So when you dream and you hear thoughts when you're sleeping—try in your conscious/unconscious state to stay with what you're seeing or hearing—and in the darkness, grab your pen and paper, and write down what's coming. Keep your eyes closed. Don't stop writing it down until 'it' stops. In the morning, type it out. See what came through you. Dreams are powerful revelations. Not all of them. But some may uncover riddles about who you are. How you think about your present, your past, and future. There are so many pathways to release all the wonder inside of you.

Over a period of three months from out of my dreams, I heard a series of words in the darkness. I wrote them down. I never knew when they would come. A few weeks later, more words came in my dreams. What was so unusual was that they came in verse, not prose. After a few more weeks, I began to see that these 'words' held something of a deeper meaning, especially since it was Henrik Ibsen talking to his Muse. A few weeks, Ibsen was talking to Nora, a person he had created in *A Doll's House*. I still wasn't sure what these words represented. More people showed up in my following dreams, including Ibsen's wife and Hedda Gabler. What was going on?! Did I say: "Ignore it. It'll go away." No, I recognized that there was something definitely occurring. So I continued typing out everything I had written down. After three months, the dreams stopped. I thought: What is this? An epic poem? A play? Why did Ibsen come through me?

Eventually, I showed them to my good friend, Jill Navarre, the Artistic Director of the Auroville Theatre Group near Pondicherry in India. She had invited me to come and perform in my solo play and teach Workshops for the Auroville community. If you don't know about Auroville, look it up. It's a life-changing community built on harmony, goodwill, and consciousness. Well, I told her what had happened, and she asked to read the words that had come to me in my dreams. After she did, she said, "These words are an opera." "An opera!?" "Yes! And I know a German composer, Hartmut von Lieres, who lives here in Auroville during part of the year, and together, you and he will turn it into a new opera."

Did I have any idea that this would be a part of my destiny? Of course not. So I had to learn how to create a libretto and spent several months learning to do just that. Why opera? I can only think it must be amazing synchronicity. As a teen growing up, I would watch 'Live from the Met' operas every weekend, reading the translations at the bottom of the television screen carefully, swept away by the power and impact of the extraordinary performances.

After several years of collaborating, we've created the first opera written about Henrik Ibsen and his life. I have to believe Ibsen 'came through me' to say what he has to say to us at this time. I became a conduit—very much in the same way it can happen to you when you allow molecules to come through you to create your solo performance. This is the wonder and miracle of the universe. You never know what you will receive. I couldn't have written these words for my new opera, *IBSEN*, consciously. It's the same way my solo play, *LET IT BE ART!*, also came through me.

By continually leaving yourself open—as a pathway—giving yourself permission to go even further than you thought was possible—molecules will come and dance with you. This is what the organic process of creation is all about.

What is an 'organic process?' It can be defined as 'a sustained phenomenon,' according to the dictionary, 'that manifests itself through a series of gradual changes.' Now this definition contains the word: phenomenon. 'Six degrees of separation' is also considered a phenomenon. But in our case, it simply means a way in which to work to create life. To invite freedom to take place. To focus all your energies with a willingness to set aside all doubts. To take a leap of faith into the unknown. To be 'in sync' with all that you are. Not in your head but in your gut. To allow 'another' person to come and speak through you.

Playwrights, directors, teachers, of course, refer to this person as a 'character.' They had to call it something. Now you can 'play a character' if you want to. But I'm talking about something different. Allowing the opportunity to 'invite' a human being to exist within a play through the organic process of the 'Art of Transformation.'

Ibsen was very clear about this, remember? Because he knew by calling a person 'a character'—they're not thought of as a 'real' person—and that will certainly affect how you think of them and bring them to life. Like you—they have their own thoughts—their own life that has to come alive, without a moment of hesitation during your solo performance.

Every rehearsal. Every day when you're not rehearsing. Every moment is always a search for finding out more about who they are. This is what it takes to create your own solo performance. It's a constant 'breaking through the ice.' Fusing yourself with this 'other person.' Finding out how different they are from you—and how similar. Once you say: 'Let's go on this journey together,' you're 'breathing them into existence.' For this to happen, you're going to have to accept there's no longer a separation. At this moment, you allow their 'trains of thought' to become yours. There are no longer periods at the end of sentences, no longer commas separating thoughts. Each thought becomes part of a flow—expressions of meaning—that have to be set loose to express what must be shared.

How do you begin to allow this to happen? You first have to find what the impact of these ideas means to you. The simplest way to get inside is to allow your body to express each word or the idea—and see what it makes you do physically. The body will reveal what even words can't. So now, when you come back to the idea—it's pulsing inside of you. Vibrating. The need to express it is so strong.

Why did Hamlet say: "My words fly up, my thoughts remain below. Words without thoughts, never to heaven go." Words are all we have, but they only become yours through how you bring each word alive using all of your instrument.

That's why you have to constantly work on your breath control—your voice—developing the flexibility to release all the ideas that words hold within them. Of course, it's never about 'acting out' a word. It's about allowing these ideas to 'flow through you.' How do *they* want to be released? Through your eyes? Your fingers, your chest, your legs, your heart, your soul? With every breath you take—the ideas become life moving through you, shaping your storytelling—empowering you to go even further! Feel their meaning deep inside your being—then give them away! This is how you'll discover where ideas will take you. Don't take a single word for granted.

When you reach the day of your performance, you'll enter what's called the dressing room. But that's not what I call it. As I said before, I refer to it as the 'Creation Room.' It's not simply a place to spend some time preparing. Going over lines. Putting on make-up. Jumping into a costume. This is actually where 'creation' takes place. Where it begins. Where it's born. Where everything is set into motion. Where a whole new world of possibilities arrives. So, it's always necessary for a type of 'cleansing' to take place—to allow 'creation' to come into being. The 'Creation Room' has to become an environment for the organic process of the 'Art of Transformation' to take place.

My good friend, Joanna Rotté, has talked about the time she and other acting students were studying with Stella Adler, and they had decided to create their own acting company. Talk about initiative! Then they took a chance and asked Adler if she would direct them in a production of Thornton Wilder's one-act play, *The Happy Journey to Trenton and Camden*. Amazingly, she said yes!

Well, when the day arrived for their first performance, all the actors were preparing in a small dressing area right behind the stage, and Adler arrived. She took one look at the condition of the dressing room—how the actors had haphazardly thrown their belongings down—items and trash scattered across the floor. She stepped away, returning with a bucket of water and a hand towel. Getting down on her knees, she began to scrub the floor. Immediately, the actors rushed, offering to take her place. She refused, continuing to clean the floor until it was spotless. It was a clear lesson of how you can't act in a state of chaos. Stella Adler followed it by saying: "The actor is the sanity of the theater. It's up to you to keep the theater healthy."

Very much, your process, in a way, is a similar kind of ritual. It can be thought of, in the same way, as doctors and nurses when they prepare their instruments and clothing for a birth. They have to go through an entire cleansing process. Do you know how clean the floor needs to be in an operating room? How clean everything they touch—every instrument—has to be for an operation? Just think of all the preparation that's required because nothing can be left to chance. There's so much at stake. A new life will only come into the world if all of this is done properly. Nothing can be overlooked.

When you begin your preparation—everything must be laid out. Your make-up. The things you'll need. Not only for you—but also for the arrival of the other person or persons you're bringing to life. The clothing they'll wear.

Everything that is a part of their existence. What others refer to as 'props.' However, I never refer to a person's personal object as a 'prop.' Others can. But I don't. They're an extension of this person who's coming to life through you because it's what they wear, what they use in their life. They're just like the personal objects in your life. Your wristwatch or a ring. A necklace or a hat. They're certainly not 'props.' Without them, this person would not be who they are, neither would you. Each 'object' holds 'life' within them. They tell their own stories, a world of meaning. They must be imbued with their own unique 'life force.' They're 'life-giving' for you and the audience.

Why do I compare creating on the stage and the preparation necessary for such an enormous moment of new life being born and coming into the world? Because your creative work can be just as profound. With the same kind of enormous life-changing possibilities. The creation you're bringing into life is essential for the progress and the well-being of our society. With the potential to change life as we know it. One human being can change the world. The human being you're bringing into life through your solo performance can have the same impact in ways that you can't begin to imagine.

That's why your approach to creating organic life through the process of the 'Art of Transformation' requires an enormous focus—clarity—concentration—bringing you into a creative frame of mind—allowing you to 'swim' with the molecules. Acting is living and breathing *in the moment.* It's not about 'acting.' It's 'living' with the audience, so they will find a way to go on living.

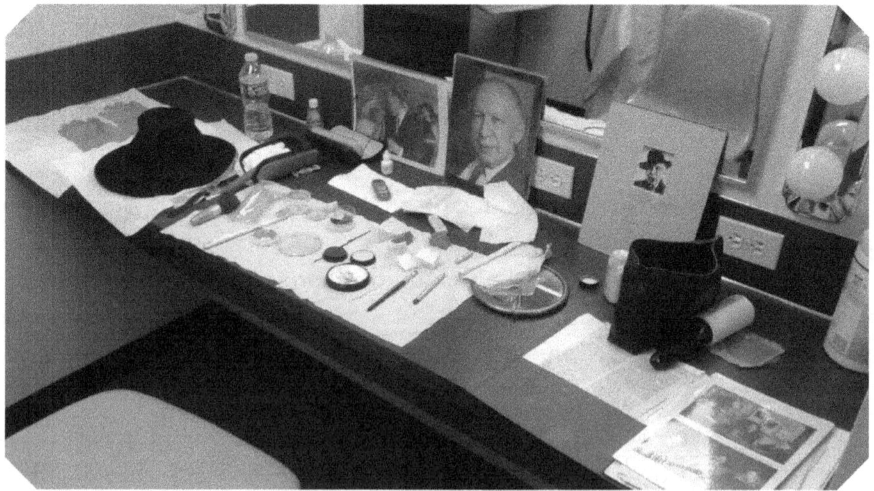

Ronald Rand's 'Creation Room' for his 'Transformation' into Harold Clurman. (Courtesy Ronald Rand.)

What happens when you have to prepare in an unusual dressing area that's not set up for 'creation' to occur? Or it's extremely noisy and almost impossible to concentrate?

Over the years, I have prepared in countless 'creation' rooms, all different shapes and sizes. From a 15th century Moroccan apartment inside the Dar al-Makhzen palace in Tangier's Casbah—to a cave in Tbilisi. Even in the middle of the Colombian jungle. Nevertheless, every time I prepare, I have to make sure that I allow the molecules to come to dance in the space. To change into different shapes. To breathe through me, around me. Ushering me into a different reality so Clurman can live when he arrives. Because it's not about me—I'm a vessel for Transformation to take place.

Every 'Creation Room' you'll prepare in will be different. It'll have its own energies when you arrive. But you'll still need to turn it into a space where 'creation' can take place. For that to happen, it's necessary to give yourself the time that you need. Always make that a requirement. I can't do performances at certain festivals or theaters when they say that I'll only have a small amount of time to prepare or share the 'creation' room with other groups, or I have to put the set up myself right before I perform. It won't work for my preparation.

You decide what you need for creation to take place. No one can tell you what way works best, except you. I always give myself at least two and a half hours for my preparation—for the 'Art of Transformation' to take place. Although, there have been times when I've had to adjust to circumstances beyond my control and prepare in a much shorter frame of time. But by that point, I had been doing my solo performance for over fifteen years, so I understood what was necessary.

On one particular tour, I had flown into Moscow, and when I arrived, I was immediately whisked off on a drive for two hours to Vologda, a large city between Moscow and St. Petersburg. As we approached the city's suburbs—in the distance on the horizon—the sky had darkened, as if the heavens had unleashed whirling dervishes swirling through the clouds in a blackened cauldron. Traffic slowed down considerably. When we finally arrived and entered Vologda, we had to skirt large tree limbs. Wide pools of water, to the right and left of us, covered the streets. With only a little over an hour to go, the lobby filled by an eager audience, I entered the theater. Somehow, I had to set up the stage quickly—go over the lights and sound—and cleanse and prepare my 'creation' room for 'creation' to take place. Then I could go through my 'Art of Transformation' process for Clurman 'to arrive.'

Over the past two decades, I have served as Artistic Director, stage manager, and performing artist during my tours. On the day before a performance, I always try and hold a technical rehearsal. In this instance, it wasn't possible. Owing to the technical limitations of touring to the different countries I've traveled to, I always keep everything as simple as possible. I arrange a general 'wash' of lights to cover the stage unless there's more time available for special lighting. And during the performance, I only have three sound cues—music by George Frederic McKay, Aaron Copland, and George Gershwin. Some theaters have constructed a set for my show—like they did in the Mary Welch Theatre at Lycoming College.

While on other occasions, I've performed on the set of an entirely different show. At one performance, Clurman's apartment was on the set of Eugene O'Neill's *Long Day's Journey into Night* at North Coast Repertory Theatre. Another time at Syracuse University, the set was from the musical, *The Wild Party*—which meant Clurman entered through a shiny brilliant red vinyl door at the center of the set, and to my far left, a partially visible toilet could be seen onstage!

Sometimes, the audience will be right in front of me or surround Clurman in ways that will transform the performance into an entirely different experience than I could have ever imagined.

When I performed in Zimbabwe, my performance took place in a large tribal hut built by the Shona People on the grounds of Harare's Gardens, with an audience of over two hundred surrounding me on tiers of bleachers circling up to the roof. Another time the audience was two feet in front of me when I performed in the ornate inner courtyard of the majestic Dar al-Makhzen palace. I have faced audiences sitting in pews inside a church or on all three sides in the famous Chamber Theater 55 in Sarajevo. No matter the configuration, every space becomes Clurman's apartment as soon as he arrives.

Before I arrived in Vologda, I had sent a photo of what the set looks like along with a list of what I needed: three chairs, three tables, a carpet, and a few plants. In this instance, everything was laid out on the stage as I had requested. When I began my preparation in the 'creation' room, this time, I entered into a deep state of relaxation, breathing into an endless flow of timelessness. Allowing energies to shift and molecules to arrive. It was as if Plato had spoken directly to me: "Necessity *is* the mother of invention."

When I set my stage for each performance, I always specifically place on top of 'Clurman's desk'—papers that I bring with me for every performance, including those with a personal connection for Clurman. There are copies of pages from his dairy and notes he took when he met with Stanislavski on his

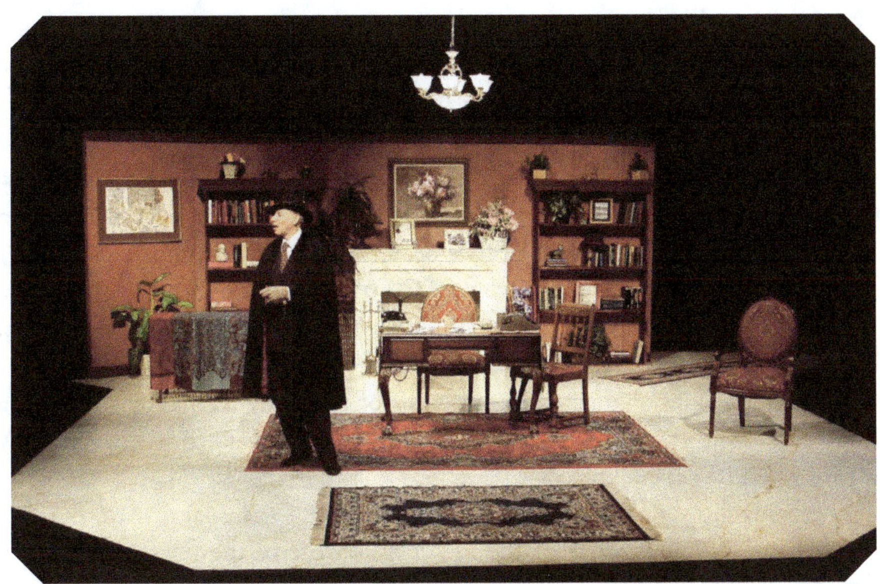

Ronald Rand as Harold Clurman in his solo play, *LET IT BE ART!* at Mary Welch Theatre, Lycoming College. (Courtesy Ronald Rand.)

visits to Moscow, a handwritten copy and a typed-out version of the new essay Clurman is working on, a Japanese doll which he had been given when he directed in Japan, an ashtray for his cigar which he arrives holding but has gone out, two of his books: *The Fervent Years* and *On Directing*, plus other odds and ends which he has accumulated over the years.

When I performed at the Century Center for Performing Arts in New York City, J.C. Compton, Clurman's second wife, gave me Clurman's original 'taxi wand' that he would wave and light up in the dark to get a taxi on the streets of New York City.

It's 'Clurman's' desk—where he works and writes and thinks. So everything must be made available for him to 'live' when he arrives at his apartment. All holding personal deep meaning for him—allowing the space to become transformed into Clurman's apartment on West 57th Street.

What surrounds Clurman on the walls is just as important. Sometimes, there may only be black curtains. So, everything has to come to life in Clurman's mind. But if I have the time, I have placed original paintings on the walls of his apartment, including some by America's leading artists, including Martha Carpenter and Tim Stevenson. At several performances, I have also hung my paintings, which on occasion, I present to those who have made my performance possible.

The clothing you wear is exceptionally important. It needs to be imbued with personal energy because it will become a container holding all of the person's passion and lifeforce you're bringing to life. I step into Clurman's suit, his shirt, cape, and fedora. The cape I wear is an exact duplicate of Clurman's cape that he wore when he went to the theater. It was given to me as a gift by a dear friend, Steven H. Scheuer, who would attend the theater with Clurman in this same cape. When these clothes become transformed, molecules are set flying, flowing into them, as they're now Clurman's clothing.

By allowing organic life to occur in the 'creation' room—Clurman can 'arrive.' I can only describe it as a 'giving over' when Clurman enters my body. I feel the molecules change inside the cells of my body as they go through a Transformation. This may occur as I'm doing my make-up. But I never know exactly when it will take place.

Learning how to prepare your instrument is like the launch of a rocket ship. All the different parts of the vessel must receive the necessary fuels to blast off into outer space as it prepares for liftoff. The procedure that astronauts and those that assist them leave nothing to chance. It's a matter of life and death. One little detail overlooked is a recipe for disaster. It's what Constantin Stanislavski, the great Russian master acting teacher/director and co-founder of the Moscow Art Theatre, kept reminding his actors: "It's all in the details."

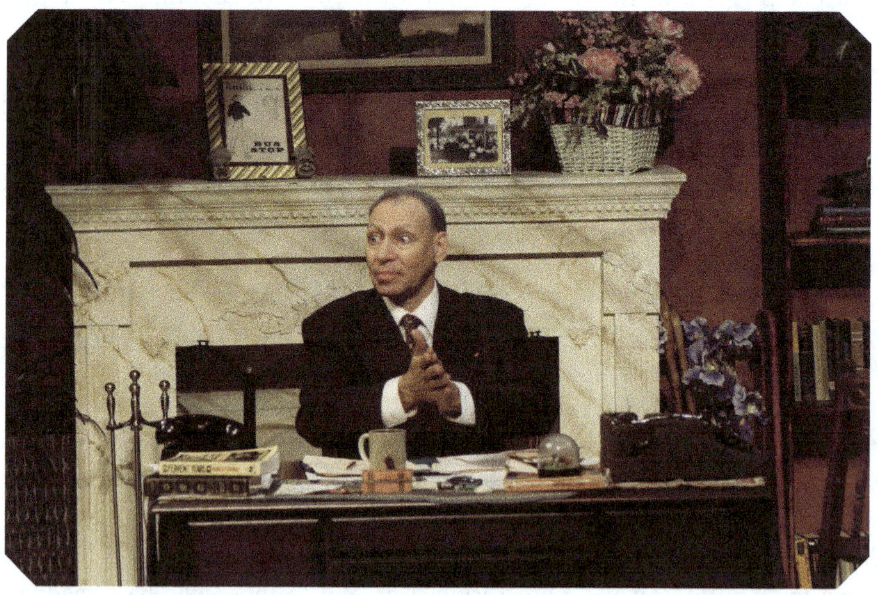

Ronald Rand as Harold Clurman in his solo play, *LET IT BE ART!* at Mary Welch Theatre, Lycoming College. (Courtesy Ronald Rand.)

There have been times when I have had to 'hold'—waiting longer in the 'Creation Room,' even though the scheduled time for the performance was seven or eight P.M. Another performance before mine may have taken longer, and I've had to wait an extra half hour, or even an hour or longer.

But Clurman is not 'waiting' for anything. He's in the midst of his day. Having gone to the theater, he's returning to his apartment to go on with his life. He has to finish working on his essay. He's going to the theater in the evening and planning to have dinner at The Russian Tea Room with Stella Adler. He has a busy afternoon ahead. But just in case—I place several pages of his writings on the table in front of him, and other things for him to look over—photographs he may recognize from his life—all of which are part of the organic process of the 'Art of Transformation.'

Acting is how I have lived and breathed since I was a child. I've certainly accumulated a lifetime of experience on stage. And yes, certain aspects have become what is referred to as 'second nature.' However, I work hard never to leave anything regarding the tech side of the show to chance. Clurman was once asked: 'What do you do, after you're gone through all your rehearsals with fine actors, and still the production doesn't come together as you expected?' His reply was simply: "I forgive myself." That's all you can do when you've given your absolute best.

There may be instances when you're on the road with your solo play, when things may go wrong, certainly not as planned or expected. Things can happen beyond your control. Since I have performed in many countries where several different languages are spoken, things may have been misunderstood by the lighting/sound person, or the set will be changed or moved for some reason other than what had been worked on during the tech rehearsal. They may think 'their way' will be work better. I've actually come out on stage, and my set has been moved quite a distance from the position that I had set it during rehearsal. Of course, *I* notice it and mentally have to deal with it. Clurman is simply entering his apartment. He's going on with what he has to do, and he goes to his desk wherever it is.

When I first began working on my play in 2001, I rehearsed with a director for the original production, Gregory Abels, although I had a general idea of what I wanted to do. I thought it would be a good idea to have a 'third eye.' This is something you're going to have to decide. What works best for you. To have a director—or direct your solo play yourself.

We both agreed to have a simple beginning when Clurman arrives as he enters his apartment—and the music that has been playing is supposed to stop.

His 'assistant' who's in the apartment turns it off, and Clurman discovers he's not alone. Well, you can imagine, that has not always been the case, especially in as many countries I have performed in and the different languages.

On more than one occasion, the music doesn't go off when it's supposed to, even though it's all been rehearsed during the tech rehearsal. In fact, sometimes, it can take a while for the music to stop. Of course, Clurman barrels on saying what he has to. There was even one instance when the music never stopped during the *entire* performance! Which was quite challenging to me inside of Clurman since I had to make sure he was heard in his 'quiet' moments. Yet, I could also see there were times when he thoroughly enjoyed listening to the rhythms of Copland.

There exists a 'real' time within the 'given circumstances' of the reality where this person is living. Their time. They've come to do what they need to do. It's why they're alive. And once they've done that, they go on with the rest of their life. They're not going 'off stage'—because they're not in a play. That's why it's essential that where they're coming from—what they were doing before—and where life is taking them next—is all one continuous stream. This sustains the truth and believability of everything they're doing, of everything that's occurring. If at any moment, your mind takes you out of the reality of the life of the person you're bringing to life—what will bring you back—is their life—where they are and what they've come to do.

You might ask: What if I'm in a play like *No Exit* or the playwright has written, 'The play takes place nowhere.' Well, there is no such place as 'nowhere.' Or they might write: "It's on a planet someplace or in heaven." Well, you still have to ask: Where exactly am I? What's around me? Where did I come from? Where am I going next? Every place affects who you are and shapes what you're doing. That's why it's absolutely necessary for the audience to know exactly where you are—without a doubt. Your actions completely tell them everything.

Right out of high school, I was fortunate to study with several master acting teachers: Stella Adler, Harold Clurman, and Jerzy Grotowski. Later, with Joseph Chaikin, John Strasberg, and Robert Lewis. I learned the craft of acting and unlearned many bad habits from one of the greatest acting teachers of all time—Stella Adler—over a period of more than five years. She was the only American acting teacher to study for over four weeks with Stanislavski personally. Stella Adler changed the course of acting training in America, teaching many successful actors and actresses, including Warren Beatty, Marlon Brando,

Robert De Niro, Benecio del Toro, Melanie Griffith, Mark Ruffalo, Elaine Stritch, Leslie Uggams, and Henry Winkler.

Of course, she was the first to say, "I didn't teach Brando anything he didn't already know." However, her extraordinary insights awakened his genius and everyone else she taught.

As inspiring as it was to be in her presence and listen to her inspiring ideas—way beyond her theatrical glamour and beauty—her fiery strength would hold you and force you to come to terms with why you wanted to act—to transform yourself into a cultured human being. To be an actor who wanted to devote one's entire self entirely to the craft of acting and to be in service to the playwright's vision.

Adler never stopped pounding into us: "An actor represents two thousand years of civilization the moment you walk on the stage." "That it's up to you to study and understand all of the great arts," reiterating: "Keats died at twenty-five, and he knew everything!"

Every day in class, her gaze would pierce into me. Nothing would slip by that was less than necessary. "Feed your spirit!" she would say. "Feed your heart! Feed your mind every day with the nobility of art! Feed your soul with the great

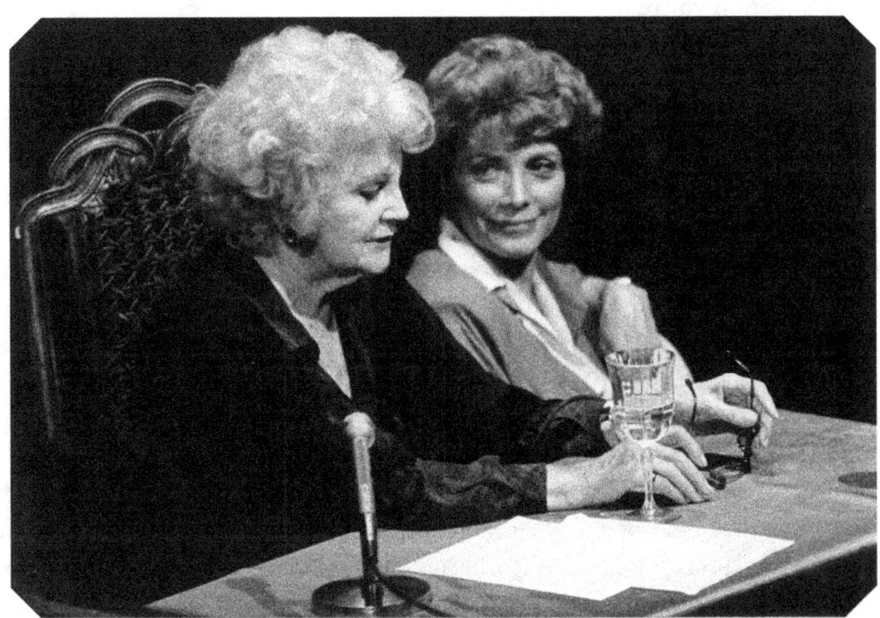

Stella Adler with Irene Gilbert.

playwrights, the universal humanity of all time! You carry within you all the seeds of knowledge! The life inside you reflects the life outside of you!"

Utterly demanding, Adler never ceased to squeeze every ounce out of me to get me to understand the power of an 'idea.' Loving to a fault—because she loved actors—she knew we, as students, were young. But still, that was no excuse. The stage demanded that the actor rise to understand the legacy that we've been handed. She never let anything get in her way to impart that to us.

Time and time again, I'd feel her deep insights sweep over me. Into me. Through me. Molecules swimming in the air. About the depth one must go to rise to the heights of the great actors before you. To dive deep into the playwrights and their vision. You can find her passionate insights in her engrossing books on acting and script interpretation.

Adler came from a rich theater tradition. Her father, Jacob Adler, was the 'King of the Yiddish Theatre.' She understood the power of the actor's art, having acted the entire part of her early life in her father's acting company. She made it clear that once you have a craft, you can take something that's on the page of a script or inside an empty space—and transform it through your imagination into life to make it true. "Never start with words," she'd tell us. "Start with moving. The doing makes you talk . . . The truth of art is the truth of the situation you're in, not your own situation."

By letting the depth of a great playwright come through you, you'll be able to make their words come alive. You not only have to interpret—but allow a new-found 'truth' to sweep into your entire consciousness and being—in order to become a creative artist.

Day in and day out, we'd delve into the life-giving works by Henrik Ibsen and August Strindberg, Anton Chekhov and Arthur Miller, Tennessee Williams and August Wilson, Clifford Odets and Edward Albee, Lorraine Hansberry and William Inge, and many, many others. Each class was a life-changing journey uncovering the 'buried gems' inside a playwright's work. There were no shortcuts to analyze what the playwright wanted the audience to experience. A mantle was passed to us in the name of truth. It was our responsibility to bring that into everything we did.

During one particular class, Bill Paxton and I got up to present a scene from Edward Albee's one-act, *The Zoo Story*, that we had been working on for months. You probably have seen Bill in epic films such as *Twister* with Helen Hunt, and *Titanic*. Sometimes Bill and I would sit on frozen park benches along Central Park's many byways in the middle of the winter, exploring, unraveling the dense reality of Peter and Jerry's relationship in the play. The ground was frozen. Our hands were frozen. But we didn't stop. We pushed through. The snow would be coming down on us, around us. I couldn't see Bill. I'd think he was there—probably about ten feet away shouting at the sky—while I fiddled to try and light my pipe in the frigid whistling wind. We had to feel the reality. To get it inside us. To understand the play. To taste it. Letting Albee's words swim through us, along with all the molecules they held. What was real was where we were. Nothing was going to stop us from finding out what was occurring moment-to-moment in the play's action.

When the day finally arrived, and we decided to present the scene in class—quickly, after a few moments—Adler stood up from her throne-like chair. Sweeping past Bill, she immediately stepped into the scene, taking over the part of Jerry. I continued lighting my pipe and reading my book. She started striding around the stage, pointing at what she 'saw in the park.' Asking me all sorts of questions. Demanding to know where we were. "Is that 86th Street?" "And what's that street over there!" "Have you been to the zoo! I said, have you been to the zoo!" She kept throwing more and more of the play's dialogue at me, literally thrusting her face into mine, trying to throw me out of my reality. Grilling me over and over again. Examining my efforts as I fought to light my pipe as Peter. Inside I was shaking like a leaf. Outside I went on with who I was and what I had to do. All to no avail, she finally drew herself up and proudly announced: "There! An actor who knows where he is!" And Bill and I went on to finish the scene.

The drive to 'uncover the truth' is what will set you apart. How important that is to you will allow you to go even further as you create your solo performance. Once you say: "I will do this, and nothing will stand in my way!" You push through, just as we did in Central Park.

Acting on stage is never knowing what's going to happen 'moment to moment.' It was the same when I performed in the inaugural Harold Clurman Festival of the Arts at the Stella Adler Studio of Acting, in the Irene Gilbert Theatre at the Stella Adler Academy of Acting in Los Angeles, and in the shadow of Mt. Everest in Kathmandu. Because it's not about acting. It's about 'giving over' to the human being you're bringing to life. I never know what Clurman will say or do, where he'll go. I'm assuming he'll say the words that represent the play. But *he's not in a play*. He's living his life. He's come to say the things he has to say—because it's who he is. It should be the same for you every time you go on the stage. Breathing life into meaning through your imagination in the instant, as this other person.

In class, Adler would talk about her time with Stanislavski. How he had worked with her on a scene from John Howard Lawson's *The Gentlewoman*, one of the plays that she had been cast in as a member of the Group Theatre.

In 1934, the Group Theatre had a huge success with a play by Sidney Kingsley called *Men in White*. It was the first successful 'doctor drama' on Broadway and influenced all similar kinds of movies and TV shows you see about doctors that have become so popular. Because of that, Clurman and Adler were able to travel to Russia to see productions by the Moscow Art Theatre, plays directed by Vsevolod Meyerhold, and hopefully, to meet Stanislavski. But he wasn't there. On their way back to America, they stopped off in Paris. By chance, Jacques Copeau, the famous French theater director, told them, "Stanislavski is in Paris." He was there recuperating from a heart ailment and seeing his family. The meeting between Adler and Stanislavski I actually bring to life in my solo play.

Adler related to us in class that when she first met Stanislavski, she was despondent. She had lost her joy as an actress. She told him: "You've ruined the theater for me. Before I studied your System, I loved the theater. Now I hate it!" Well, you can imagine! What could Stanislavski say? His reply, in other words, was simply: "If it's not helping you, forget it." And he invited her to come and work with him during his time in Paris.

Stanislavski had been a successful actor for many years on the stage. This was back in the 1890s. But he was never completely satisfied in finding a way to 'live' as the person he was portraying. After some of his performances, he would feel like he had captured what he was after, but other times, nothing seemed to go right. When he felt he had given one of his best performances, he was asked why it didn't go so well at the end of the performance. He became obsessed with finding out exactly what it was that great actors do that allows them to become inspired—and live on the stage as someone else. When he watched Salvini, the great Italian actor playing Othello, he saw the entire palette of the actor's craft in action. It was everything he dreamed could be possible. But why couldn't he do it himself?

He went on a search. At the same time, he revolutionized the Russian Theater filled with a prevalent declamatory, exaggerated mediocre acting style. He watched performances by great actors around the world, which thrilled him.

It's what you should be doing. But don't just 'watch' other actors perform. Examine what they're doing. How they achieve what appears to be a seamless Transformation, living 'moment to moment.' An actor spends his life being a 'sponge'—examining, dissecting, exploring.

Stanislavski went ahead and joined forces with another talented individual—a playwright and a director. His name was Vladimir Nemirovich-Danchenko. Together, they set out to create an ensemble company of actors calling themselves the Moscow Art Theatre. They presented a play by Tolstoy—*Tsar Fyodor Ivanovitch*—a historical melodrama set in the sixteenth century during their first season. How did Stanislavski create the atmosphere that appeared to be so real that the audiences believed they were in the sixteenth century? He introduced the 'music of nature' from offstage, smells coming from the cooked food on stage, and through the naturalistic behavior of the actors. Everything made it appear as if the story was taking place in feudal Russia at that time, allowing the given circumstances to tell the story even before a word was spoken.

Now he needed another play. He had seen a production of Anton Chekhov's new play, *The Seagull,* described as a failure by the critics. However, Stanislavski felt whoever directed it didn't understand what was going on inside the play. He felt he knew how he could bring it to life. But he first had to convince Chekhov to let him direct *The Seagull.* Chekhov wasn't that enthusiastic about having his play done again. Do you think that stopped Stanislavski? He convinced Chekhov that he understood who these human beings were, that he could make the play come alive. Again, he took the time to create the atmosphere, the reality of what was occurring in each moment.

Even with all of this, Stanislavski still had to find a way to convince the actors in his company to 'not act.' He wanted something entirely different from them—to see themselves trapped in pain, the joys, the loss, the struggle, the life of each person in *The Seagull.* Take the time to read how he worked with his actors, laying the ground for what would become The Stanislavski System.

Opening night came. As the audience watched the production—they could feel 'actual life' happening in front of their eyes. The ground shifted. It was as if 'a stream of nature' was coursing through their cells—the actors were living on stage in harmony. Molecules had been set loose, flying like never before.

This is why once you create an atmosphere, an environment for your solo performance—the space will speak. It will have its own life. You have to allow that to come into being. The environment you create on the stage is completely connected to what you create in the 'Creation Room'—as you move from one environment into the next.

Well, even after a successful tour with these two plays, Stanislavski still wasn't satisfied. Something gnawed away at him. Everything still seemed to be haphazard in how the actors prepared. How could they possibly become

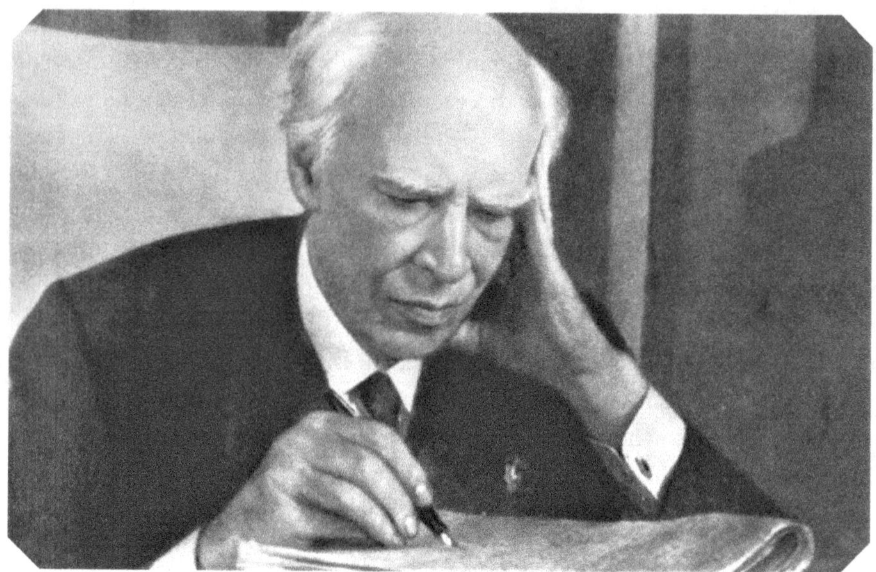

Constantin Stanislavski, 1938.

inspired for every performance when they were relying on bad habits? With a desire to please the public? He began to explore what was missing. Could there possibly be an elusive ingredient for an actor to slip into a creative state of mind? To not only rely upon becoming inspired in the moment—but actually 'live' on the stage. Again and again, he kept at it. During rehearsals. During classes. He kept searching.

Was it actually possible to 'live on stage' as the person in the play again and again over a long period? To become relaxed enough to capture the inner realm of the person's thoughts created by the playwright—and allow the 'life of the human spirit' to appear.

He traveled to Finland during a break from his rehearsals. This was in 1906. While he was there, it just so happened; he was watching children play together. When was the last time you did that? Watching that kind of abandoned freedom. They don't have to think about becoming a horse or a pirate; they do it without a moment's hesitation.

Molecules were set loose in his mind. At that moment, he had a break-through. What 'if' the soul and the imagination of the actor could join forces? How could that happen? Stanislavski was now on an evitable collision with history. No one had ever undertaken a search like this—to uncover the actor's creative process. To come up with a 'roadmap' for the actor to use to create on stage. He still had to convince the actors in his company of this new approach, which, by the way, some were initially resistant. Nonetheless, he was going to find a way to make this possible for all actors.

Luckily, Stanislavski had working for him an unusual 'jack-of-all-trades.' His nickname was 'Suler,' and he took care of everything at the theater. Actually, his real name was Leopold Sulerzhitsky, and he had the most unusual background. Along the way, he had been trained in yoga. And as time would pass, he and Stanislavski began to work closely together. He observed Suler guiding his actors to become more relaxed in their work by using yoga. Stanislavski wanted to know as much as he could about it. He began to realize, perhaps this was a way 'in.' Once the actors were relaxed enough, they could possibly invite a connection to their subconscious—even to their superconscious.

How's it possible to enter a superconscious state? Well, as you know, we live in a 'conscious' state, where all five of your senses are available while you're awake. The subconscious resides in your lower brain and spine, remembering everything you do—and when you enter into a state of relaxation or through yoga, you're able to access your subconscious—by allowing yourself to enter into this 'other' state of mind. Once Stanislavski put this together, he called it 'a temple of spiritual atmosphere.' Where we allow creation to take place.

He coupled it with a set of rhythmic breathing exercises. He was now getting closer to unraveling the mystery of prana—the 'breath of life.'

Have you ever thought about how it's possible you're able to manifest certain things in your life? It's almost beyond logic that they occur. You might be thinking about someone, the phone rings—you pick it up, and you hear their voice! I was walking down the street—and the person I was thinking about—materialized right in front of me!

Stanislavski now realized there was a connection between this life force and how yogis can make the impossible appear possible. Through the mastery of one's breath, coupled with a state of relaxation, it's possible to tap into one of the great mysteries of life—your subconscious—leading to your superconscious. And in turn, open up a whole new way of accessing your imagination.

We've all heard about quantum physics. Simply put, it's telling us that's nothing solid in the universe. Yes, there are all these molecules flying between everything and everywhere. Well, what if it was possible to tap into that universe? It's often been referred to as the 'ether.' So, if we're talking about the 'essence of the universe,' we're also talking about where the greatest inspirations and ideas come from. Now, if we go even further and allow molecules to take off—we'd be able to tap into our superconscious. When does that happen? Well, you had probably felt it when you were in a state of complete bliss or inspiration—in love—or a deep state of meditation. It does require a great 'letting go'—an immersion into a higher state of awareness. In our art—it allows the wonder of creativity to flourish.

Among the many exciting ideas that Albert Einstein shared, one stands out: "The finest emotion of which we are capable is the mystic emotion. Herein lies the germ of all art and all true science . . . To know that what is impenetrable for us really exists and manifests itself as the highest wisdom and the most radiant beauty."

What if you could tap into this energy and allow your awareness, your intuition, to flow from the entire universe? Wouldn't that be amazing! When that happens, all the molecules of the universe will join forces with you. Stanislavski knew the actor had to be the master of his own inspiration.

He began to explore what could evoke 'memory.' Could that be another way 'in' to achieve a creative state—and ultimately, to act in an inspired way? Stanislavski focused on the discoveries of the well-known French psychologist Théodule-Armand Ribot and his work called 'The Psychology of Emotions.' What if there was a way to tap into the deep-seated memories that we hold onto and never let go of? To control them by bringing them into our creative process. Making them accessible through a sense memory. Stanislavski called it a 'self-feeling.' Eventually, it became known as 'affective memory' or an 'emotional memory.' It's a tool that allows the actor to draw from their memories and subconscious behavior. To use them to feed the emotions of the 'person' you're bringing to life in a play.

But 'affective memory' is not simply about dredging up bad experiences from your past and using them when you need to feel great emotion on stage. It's a tool that you have to learn how to use over years and years of practice. To study and learn how to master it. Because you're dealing with your personal memories. If you bring them up, they've got to be dealt with, and sometimes that can have a great traumatic effect on your personal life. Stanislavski came to realize this as he kept experimenting on the 'art of experiencing.' He kept searching.

In the latter part of his life, he shifted his emphasis. He came to believe that through a person's actions—by their living in the 'given circumstances' that they find themselves in—through your imagination—you'll find the 'emotion' that the person is feeling in the play. He made it clear that 'affective memory' can be a useful tool, but to use it when you need it.

When Stanislavski worked with Adler, she said he introduced her to a tool in his System called 'Justification.' Immediately, she began 'justifying' everything she saw around her as the person she was bringing to life, as she spoke her thoughts out loud. Why she was there. What she wanted the most. What her strongest action was. What she was feeling. What was in her way. This tool can be extremely useful during rehearsals to ground you where you are in the given circumstances.

Towards the end of their five weeks of working together, Stanislavski showed Adler a chart he had created called 'The Method of Physical Actions.' He described it as the culmination of his entire life's work. Adler copied the chart down and made a promise to bring it back to America.

When she returned to the Group Theatre, she showed the chart to all the actors—and gave a Talk about what she had learned from Stanislavski during their time together. The actors felt they were released from having to dip into their own lives and dredge up their past memories. However, this was a direct challenge to the way that Lee Strasberg has been working with the actors, how he had taught and directed them in the Group Theatre productions. This caused a great rift to occur.

By that point, Strasberg had developed his own way of teaching and directing and believed Stanislavski's earlier work, especially the use of 'affective memory' and relaxation, was essential in bringing an actor to their greatest freedom in expressing their emotion. Like every master teacher, he created his way of teaching acting to fit his personality and what he believed.

Across America, and around the world, for more than a hundred years, there have been many influential acting teachers, actors, and directors who have shaped their approach to teaching acting through their personality, their insights and their vision, including Susan Batson, Eugenio Barba, Herbert Berghof, Augusto Boal, Phoebe Brand, Joseph Chaikin, Michael Chekhov, Harold Clurman, Vladimir Etush, Christopher Fettes, Giles Foreman, Jack Garfein, Uta Hagan, Wynn Handman, Bill Hickey, Anupam Kher, Alvina Kraus, Oleg Kudryashov, Martin Landau, Harold Lang, Robert Lewis, Yat Malmgren, Paul Mann, Sanford Meisner, Sonia Moore, Austin Pendleton, Warren Robertson, Carol Rosenfeld, Sinead Rushe, Richard Schechner, Boris Shchkin, Viola Spolin, Oleg Tabakov, Yegevny Vakhtangov, Boris Zakhava, Igor Zolotovitsky, as well as the many teachers, actors, and directors found within the pages of my book *Acting Teachers of America.*

Adler's and Lee Strasberg's disagreement led to a split in American acting training about which aspects of the Stanislavski System best suits an individual's quest in using themselves in service to the play. This is something you'll have to decide for yourself. Which way of working best suits you. Your nature and your instrument. As you grow and change, you may consider exploring one technique and then another. Finding more and more ways of using your body and your voice. How to use the space to create a profound and moving experience to tell your stories. There's a myriad of amazing ways to usher in gesture and language.

Many actors have found astonishing directions to go in. Among some highly useful avenues to explore the craft of acting include Michael Chekhov's technique and his Psychological Gesture, Viewpoints created by Mary Overlie and Tadashi Suzuki's training exercises used by Anne Bogart's SITI Theatre Company, Augusto Boal's techniques, the Laban Movement, the Jacques Lecoq method, Atlantic Practical Aesthetics, explorations by Grotowski, physical theater including yoga, tai chi, and Butoh, commedia dell'arte and clowning, the Feldenkrais Method, The Williamson Technique, Brechtian techniques that originated from Bertolt Brecht, and many and more ways which clearly show how vast the possibilities exist for you to explore the art of creating on the stage.

Whomever you study with and whatever technique you're introduced to, as you move through it, within it—learn and use its principles as your foundation. Remember: it's a means to keep expanding. By continually reading all kinds of plays, literature, poetry, biographies of actors, poets, dancers, musicians, directors—movers and shakers from every walk of life—you'll gain a clearer understanding of life and see how human beings have struggled with the impossible, their fear of failure, nerves and stage fright, and how they have coped with it. All of this will keep bringing you further insights into the organic process.

Always remember—learning one's craft is not like putting on a suit of clothes—one size fits all. The craft of acting takes a lifetime of study and working at it. Learning and un-learning and re-learning. Discovery after discovery after discovery. Until eventually, you may, if you're diligent, gain a mastery of the craft of acting. The mystery of our art will only continue expanding for you through your willingness to challenge everything you come in contact with—to keep growing your vision.

Adler would often tell us in class: "Stanislavski told me that the actor has the power to create life on stage. That it's always a matter of finding the truth first in life." But what does that mean exactly? Of course, you can find 'truth in life.' But you can't just put what you see in life and stick it on the stage. Because on stage, it has to become 'heightened' truth. That's what you're ultimately responsible to create. And it's not only *in the words*. The play's only a skeleton—like an iceberg buried ninety percent under the water.

Almost every day, Adler would say: "Your talent lies in the strongest possible choice that you make every moment, in everything you do on the stage." The choices you make must be bold and clear, expressing what must happen. Anything less, and there's no reason to do it.

Adler again would remind us: "When I worked with Stanislavski, he told me: "Everything is created and comes to life through where you are. See it through your inner imagination. You have within you the seed of every human feeling, every sensation. The truth in art is in the given circumstances, not in your own feelings."

It really 'struck home' to me in one particular exercise that Adler had us do in class. All of us including Paxton, and Kate Valk (who is a leading actress at The Wooster Group), another of my classmates, did an exercise of becoming chickens—living in the reality of their environment. Adler had also done the same exercise when she taught Marlon Brando. All of us began immediately running around, screeching, living as chickens. Suddenly, Adler announced: "A bomb is falling!" Instantly we became frightened and started running around in every possible direction. As the story goes, when Brando heard it, he sat down 'on his nest and laid an egg.' All the other actors 'as chickens' in his class ran at him, tugging at him, trying to get him to hide. He simply replied, "A chicken doesn't know what a bomb is."

To 'live truthfully in the given circumstances of a play' has often been described as what acting is. But both you and I know that it's more than that. Because your name is not in the list of the playwright's 'characters.' If it were, the play would be about you. But it's not. You're bringing to life a completely different person than who you are. That's why you need to find out—as much as you can—who this other human being is. We're collaborators and interpreters of a playwright's creation, and at the same time, we go even further to find out the essence of what makes this other person who they are. What drives them forward. Who they are 'inside.' Their reason for being alive, why they exist in the world of the play.

It's really like breathing. For the most part, people don't think when they breathe. They just do it. And a lot of the time, most people are holding their breath without even realizing it. How you breathe every day has a direct bearing on your health, on how you think. But there's an enormous difference when it comes to breathing on the stage. There—how you breathe with your diaphragm sustains the strength of what you're communicating.

When you're in front of others, it may cause an element of tension. You might get uptight from fear or judgment—and your breathing can 'go out the window.' That's why it's necessary for your instrument must be there for you to perform in the most natural, stress-free way. Completely open and available for you. Several of my good friends, including the late Kristin Linklater, and two gifted teachers, Carol Fox Prescott and Dru Pilmer, have devoted their lives inspiring others about the importance of breathing correctly through their teaching. Teachers such as Cecily Berry, Florence Birdwell, and Patsy Rodenberg taught how to use your voice in the most natural way possible—powerfully releasing our need to communicate. Study their books. Work hard to release all the passion you hold inside.

Every single one of these ingredients is necessary for creation to take place on the stage. Surprisingly, I think maybe, there have been maybe three or four times, during my many years of performances as Clurman, when there have been microphones at the foot of the stage, or I've worn a microphone. Mainly because many theaters weren't set up that way, and I would be performing in an unusual setting—in a tribal hut or under the stars—in a large garden theater—and it wasn't possible. I had to have a 'voice' that would support and sustain Clurman's dynamic passion, filling the entire space.

A lot of great explorers have gone down this path. When Stanislavski's different books were published—including *My Life in Art*, *An Actor Prepares*, *Building a Character*, and *Creating a Role*—they gave us a window into his System. But it was only a beginning. It's one thing to read his books. It's another to comprehend and use these ideas and put them into practice. That remains your challenge—to bring your unique voice as a storyteller to all those who need to hear what you have to say.

At one point here in America, three theater leaders got together. They said to each other: there needs to be a place where actors can come and practice their craft. It's not an easy thing to do, especially away from all the glare and commotion of the outside world. Nevertheless, they said it's necessary for the growth and nourishment of the actor in this country. Elia Kazan, Cheryl Crawford, and Robert Lewis said: 'We've got to do this.' When these three former members formed what would become known as The Actors Studio—in a sense, it became an 'out-growth' from what the Group Theatre had stood for. This happened back in 1947 in New York City. They invited actors and actresses to become a part of The Actors Studio and work on their craft. To peer into the inner workings of what it takes to create organic life on the stage. It was like the way Stanislavski worked with his actors in Russia.

They invited guest directors and teachers to talk about and teach the craft of acting, including Harold Clurman, Jack Garfein, Daniel Mann, and Sanford Meisner. They also said playwrights should have a chance to work on their plays, so they created a Playwrights Unit. Playwrights came, including

James Baldwin, Lorraine Hansberry, Tennessee Williams, and Norman Mailer, having a chance to explore their new work working with The Actors Studio members. Directors eventually joined, including Arthur Penn, Mark Rydell, and Sydney Pollack. When they invited Lee Strasberg to come and teach in 1951, he ultimately became the Studio's Artistic Director.

Many amazing actors and actresses were invited to join because they don't always get the chance to explore their craft and work on roles they wouldn't usually get cast. Among them: Alec Baldwin, Marlon Brando, Ellen Burstyn, Roscoe Lee Browne, James Dean, Robert De Niro, Jane Fonda, Ben Gazzara, Lee Grant, Julie Harris, Dustin Hoffman, Harvey Keitel, Stephen Lang, Marilyn Monroe, Paul Newman, Al Pacino, Geraldine Page, Estelle Parsons, Sidney Poitier, Kim Stanley, Maureen Stapleton, Rip Torn, Eli Wallach, Shelley Winters, and Joanne Woodward, just to mention a few. They joined because they wanted to keep searching—exploring all of the dramatic possibilities of human truth—to release everything inside them in service to the role. To this human being that has to live in a play created by a playwright.

I mentioned Robert Lewis, one of the founders of The Actor Studio. He went on to become an influential Broadway director and teacher. At one point, he wanted to try and clarify Stanislavski's chart. I studied with Lewis for over a year and was mentored by him on a scene from Odets' *Waiting for Lefty*. The same play that he had appeared in when the original production was first performed in 1935.

Now, as I had mentioned, Lewis had been an actor in the Group Theatre. When Adler returned from Paris, she brought back Stanislavski's chart—and gave a Talk explaining to the Group Theatre actors what Stanislavski told her—referring to the chart she drew on a large blackboard. Of course, Stanislavski had first written his chart down in Russian. When Adler studied with him, he wrote it on a board for her in French. She copied it down and then wrote it out on a blackboard in English before the Group Theatre actors. Lewis copied it down, and that's the chart that you and I will be looking at.

As it turned out, in 1957, Lewis stood on the stage of a Broadway theater in front of a packed excited audience over a couple of days, and he told them: "I'm going to try and solve the mystery and mystique of the Stanislavski System through a series of Talks." That's just what he tried to do after he showed them his original copy of the chart that he had copied down.

Now I'm sure Stanislavski had his specific aims regarding each tool on his chart when he created it. But here we are at the beginning of the 21st century—and it's up to you and me to examine these tools—to see how they can help fuel the creation of your solo performance on stage.

For more than twenty-five years, I've traveled the world teaching Stanislavski's 'Method of Physical Actions' chart at many state acting academies, acting schools, universities, and colleges, through my master acting Workshop called 'The Art of Transformation.' In Russia, they call the chart: the 'Method of Analysis through Physical Action.' I believe it's a most accessible way to work to achieve organic life on the stage. The deep-seated need that has driven actors over thousands of years on their search for laying bare truths rooted in the human heart is ultimately connected to our human nature and the need to explain the meaning of life.

These tools have worked for me—so I want to go over a few of the elements on the chart with you—and when you're in my Workshop, we'll undoubtedly cover a great deal more. So, let's dive in and see where it takes us.

What do you see before you on the chart? Why would Stanislavski devote his life to create a chart like this? Why should it matter to your work or to actors who'll be creating on stage today or a hundred years from now? Perhaps even longer? Techniques come and go. Yet, some remain because of what they continue to offer us. In my approach to the craft and the art of acting, coupled with my life experiences—I've discovered the steps on this chart allow a way to 'slip the light fantastic'—so when Clurman comes to 'live' on the stage—it's occurring through a completely organic process.

What's the first thing you see when you look at the chart? Does it look like a stairway? Steps? Or 'keys' on a piano? I look at it as a foundation, as if we're leaping from one pillar to the next. Mounting a stairway taking us upwards, step by step—until we reach the top—E—the Part—which, of course, everything is leading to.

As you can see at the top left corner, it says '1934.' Directly across from it at the top right corner. Do you see it there? It's a quote written in 1830 by the poet Alexander Pushkin. He's considered the father of modern Russian literature. What does he say?

"The truth of passion, the verisimilitude of feeling,' placed in the given circumstances, that is what our reason demands of a writer or a dramatic poet."

Take a moment. Reread it. What do you think it means? Well, there we are—back at 'truth.' But this time, it's connected to passion. 'The truth of passion.' What truth do you think Pushkin's talking about that lies 'inside of passion'? Something sparks your creativity. Your passion. What do you think the essence of your passion is? This is what we're talking about.

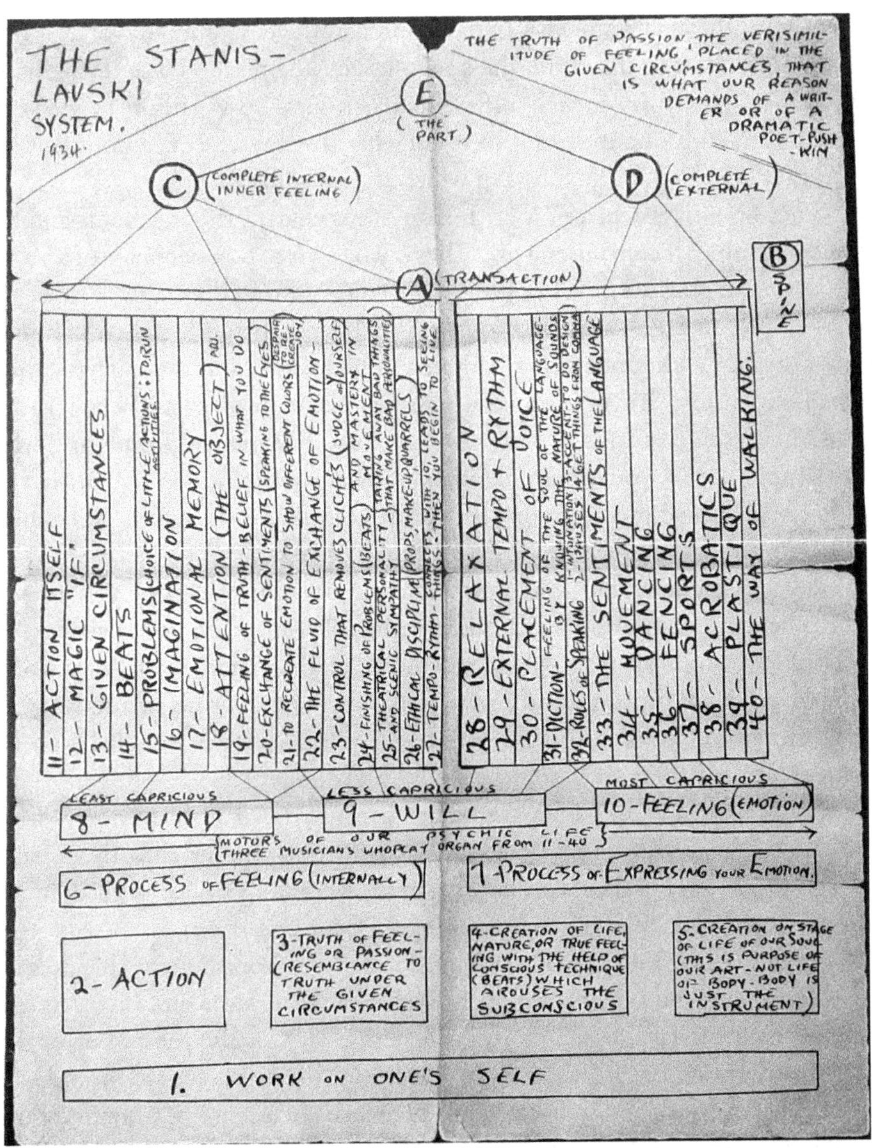

The Stanislavski System: 'Method of Physical Actions' Chart, 1934.

And hot on its heels is followed by 'the verisimilitude of feeling.' That's one of those '99 cent' words coming from the Latin word, 'verisimilitudo,' meaning a 'likeness to truth.' So, it's about art that's 'appears to be real.' 'Placed in the given circumstances.'

Years before Stanislavski used this phrase, Pushkin wanted to remind us that what we do comes from where the story is placed. So much of who we are comes from the environment we grew up in and the environment we now find ourselves in. Couple that with 'the environment' the person you're bringing to life lives in—which is entirely different than yours. So we begin to see what Pushkin is talking about. It calls to mind what Ibsen wrote: "Environment has a great influence upon the forms in which the imagination creates."

Since Stanislavski placed it at the top of his chart, I think it holds an even deeper meaning. It concludes with: 'That is what our reason demands of a writer or a dramatic poet.' So, he's pointing out you're now a 'dramatic poet' of the stage. A mantle has been passed to you. Much like a baton is passed in a relay race. Carrying with it not only the drama of high stakes but the 'carrying forth of a blazing torch.' It symbolizes the 'passing of one dream to another.' 'That is what our reason demands . . .' He's bringing up your mental powers and what they demand. Have you ever thought about what your mind seeks? Does it wish to do away with all prejudices in the world? To seek out the truth? To be more open-minded? What does your mind demand of you?

Pushkin reminds you that as a 'dramatic poet,' it's time for you to step up. To demand of yourself a clear outpouring of truth from your passion that you'll bring to others—that which resembles 'truth.' Again, I ask: why would Stanislavski place this quote so prominently at the top of his chart? Because, while everything we do on the stage 'resembles truth'—once it's filled with the truth of your passion—it becomes true.

Okay, now let's take a look at number 1. Right down at the bottom. 'Work on One's Self.' That's a great place to start on our journey into the organic process of the 'Art of Transformation,' since everything begins with that. We have to look at our Self—and that's going to require work.

Usually, when I do my 'Art of Transformation' Workshop, at this point, I have everyone stand up, and we go through a physical warm-up. If you haven't done yours yet today, now's a perfect time. Number 1. is also reminding us that there many enriching gifts that can further stimulate your creativity. Your heart. Your soul. The fiber and fabric of your existence. By spending time in nature, inside of a great novel, visiting a museum, or a trip to the zoo—all that these go hand-in-hand with 'Working on One's Self' to embellish all that you are. Certainly a 'well' to draw upon when you're working on a role. All are requiring from you a deep commitment to your over-all 'Action' as an actor—since they're all connected to number 1.

At times during your daily life, your mind may get in your way. It might make you feel self-conscious, have thoughts of feeling guilty about what others think of you. It may cloud and affect your judgment, even lead to a fear of failure, of not living up to other's expectations or approval.

When I was a child, I was supposed to play a complex Beethoven piece at a recital. But I was so scared that I wouldn't be able to do it right—that I'd let everyone down—I became paralyzed with fright. I was so worried about what others would think of me. I wouldn't leave the house to go to the recital. Nothing in the world could make me go. My parents finally relented. It did give me more time to practice for the next recital. And when I did, I aced the piece.

It's said that the first five years of your life are the most crucial for the development of who you become. Your confidence-building. Learning boundaries. Acceptable behavior. How you deal with fear. How you think. We probably don't even know what might have happened to us during those first five years. We carry around a lot with us every day, and sometimes it's necessary to sit down with yourself and 'clean house.'

Everything affects your health, your attitude, and the way you approach your work. That's why you have to take care of your body—your instrument. So that it's there to serve you and the 'other' person or persons you're bringing to life, and in so doing—serve the play. All connected to one another. One continuous stream of molecules. It means checking in with yourself every day—your physical, emotional, mental, and spiritual well-being. Look at yourself as a clean slate to be filled by all the 'wonders of the universe' every single day. Especially when you begin work on your solo play.

Now we've made it to number 2. 'Action.' One of the strongest tools you use to create life on stage. I always ask at this point: "What *is* an action?" I usually get back answers like: "Something I do." "Action is reaction." "An action makes you do something." So let's name some actions. "Reading, skipping, singing, eating, acting, and so forth . . ." All do-able actions. But do you do them the same way when you get on the stage? Remember, the stage is where there's a 'heightened reality.' And on top of it, there's more at stake—and this 'other' person is doing it. So, how and why they're doing their 'action' will be totally different from how you do it.

Well, we all know, each action carries within it its own nature and natural rhythm. An action you do on the stage is different from how you would do it in life because there's a playwright's vision behind it in the story being told. So the nature of the action takes on a deeper meaning. Plus, the audience could be a thousand feet away. So it requires courage to not settle for anything less than an action so rich, so strong, so unalterably true—that it propels you and this 'person' you're bringing to life—to the stratospheres. To do what you must do to get what you need. In a sense, we're talking about actions such as: 'to save my life' or 'to save the world.'

Adler would always say, and it bears repeating: "Talent lies in the strongest possible choice you can make." So whatever action you choose to do—living moment-to-moment—carries you forward so that this person gets what they must get. And you must complete every action. If there's something in the way, you have to make sure your action is even stronger. A lot of the times, it's referred to as an 'obstacle.' And of course, without conflict, there's no drama.

I always remind everyone when they're working on a script—to write down their 'action' for everything they're saying and doing for every line. The actions you choose always come out of the strongest needs that express who this person is—what they have to do in their 'given circumstances.' It can be a physical or a non-verbal action, but the action has to feed your imagination to generate an incredible amount of intense energy that propels you forward.

All connected to number 3. 'Truth of feeling or passion (resemblance to truth under the given circumstances).' See—that's why it's essential we continue to keep getting at a clearer sense of what 'truth in feeling and passion' means to you. Stanislavski talked about 'living truthfully in the 'given circumstances.' Of course, as we know—the stage and the setting are not real. However, through your total belief that where you are *is* 'real'—the audience will believe it.

This leads us to number 4. 'Creation of life, nature, or true feeling with the help of conscious technique (beats) which arouses the subconscious.' When Clurman in my play arrives in his apartment, where he is—is 'real'—because it's where he lives. He doesn't have to think, "Oh, now I have to do this" or "I have to do that." The same thing occurs to you when you enter where you live. You don't have to look around and start creating meaning. Everything's already filled with 'meaning' for you. But on an empty stage when there may be a few chairs—and it's supposed to be an entire apartment or a mountain vista—everything must be created and completely 'real' to you through your imagination, for creation to take place on stage.

When you look at numbers 4 and 5, Stanislavski begins with the word—'creation.' Because that's what it's all about. 'Creation on stage of life of our soul. ('This is the purpose of our art. Not life of body. Body is just the instrument.'). Well, there you have it. You are a creator. This changes the whole equation. That's why I call the dressing room—the 'Creation Room.' Because creation *is* taking place—happening in the moment you choose to become another person—bringing that person to life on the stage—living in their given circumstances inside a play.

When Stanislavski uses this word—'nature'—what do you think he's referring to? What is the nature of a human being? Have you thought about that? What makes you a conscious and compassionate person? When we take on a new role—and we look at this person—we have to ask: What is in it in *their* nature that drives them forward? That's turned them into who they are. This kind of search will bring you to a deeper understanding of your nature. Is it our empathy towards others? A lot of the time, excuses are made because of our 'human nature.' Because of the way we may behave 'badly' and the consequence of our actions.

When you're able to tap into and connect to your deepest Self, to your subconscious or superconscious, you may be able to begin to 'swim in the realm of intuition' through their subconscious. As Stanislavski referred to them, to bring forth 'golden secrets' by tapping into your limitless imagination at the creative center of your human nature.

What role does your soul play in this? When I ask students and actors all over the world in my Workshops—"Where is your soul? Can you point to it?"—they sometimes point to different places—their head, their chest, or their entire body. Where do you think your soul resides? In what way does your soul move you forward as a creative person in your life? You see, everything is connected and plays a part when you become inspired.

Now, what happens at that moment? I believe a conscious technique steps in and arouses the subconscious—accessing an overpowering and illuminating 'awakening'—connected to the totality of the universe. This is what's necessary to occur for audiences to have a transcendent experience. You and the audience joining in complete harmony—changing the molecules in the space. Creating a moment of grace.

As you go through the 'Method of Physical Actions' chart, you'll discover many other exciting tools, including the 'Magic If'—one of Stanislavski's 'gifts' to us. 'If I were this person, what would I do at this moment?' In my Workshops, I always follow it up by discussing some of Vakhtangov's re-formulations: 'If it was me, what would I do at this moment?' and 'What do I have to do to myself—to transform myself into this person?' It's all part of the 'Art of Transformation.'

Each of the tools on the chart are ways to access yourself and express your creativity in service to the role—especially when you use Relaxation, and of course, Imagination. Every one of these tools giving you a way towards your freedom on stage.

When I was at NYU majoring in acting, taking my acting classes with Stella Adler, another one of my professors, Mel Gordon, created the first year-long university course about the Group Theatre, enabling us to use some of the original Group Theatre exercises they had experimented with during their summer camps. At the same time, another professor, Richard Schechner, would lecture on environmental and ritual performance, showing us films on anthropological rituals in the Caribbean and snake-handling religious rituals in the Deep South of America.

When I'd go to the theater, I'd slip upside down into an outer-worldly Avant-garde universe of Schechner's environmental works at The Performing Garage watching Jean Genet's *The Balcony*, Richard Foreman's 'almost unexplainable' theater pieces, and Mabou Mines' experimental performances. I also experienced Peter Brook's ground-breaking re-stagings of classics plays, Robert Wilson's visionary multi-media productions, and Andrei Serban's *Fragments of a Greek Trilogy* at La Mama. All challenged my perception of what theater is, of what it's capable of revealing.

At the same time I was studying with Stella Adler—I also studied with Harold Clurman—and with Jerzy Grotowski at Columbia University, the legendary experimental, visionary Polish director, founder of the Polish Laboratory Theater, and author of *Towards a Poor Theater*.

In each session, Grotowski would examine the mythic roots of theater. We'd watch films on magical ancient religious practices and dances with drumming. Possession rituals. Trance states. The ancient role of the shaman in the Macumba religion in Brazil. Examining images deeply rooted in the collective unconscious. Communication with the divine through spirit possession.

My time with Grotowski had a profound effect on me as much as my time with Adler and Clurman. Grotowski would tell us: "The actor is a creator. The same as a poet or a painter. That all parts of the actor's instrument—the emotional, physical, the vocal part—they're all one. What happens during a performance is happening at this moment as a rite of mystery, leading us to creativity."

The actors he had trained in Poland used their entire bodies and voices in the most unusual and demanding ways. He showed us a film of his production, *Akropolis*. It was gut-wrenching to watch as if we were actually inside a concentration camp. Grotowski had taken Stanislaw Wyspianski's play, which he had first staged at the Laboratory Theatre of 13 Rows in Opole, and putting it on film, captured the incomprehensible, the unimaginable. The actors had transformed themselves to such a degree; we were no longer watching acting. We had stepped into hell itself, watching Ryszard Cieslak transform himself, along with the entire Polish company. Through a deep immersion, over months of rehearsals—the actors had let the circumstances seep into their muscles, their bones, their psyche—so there was no longer a separation between the 'person' and themselves. The physicality exposed the torment, survival, and horror.

Grotowski would talk about taking the time to experience what we see in front of us—that we live in a state of disconnection. How it's just as important to see the water flowing between the banks of a river as it is to see the flame of a candle and everything surrounding it.

I tried to bring what he said into me, what it meant. I knew he was peeling away layers and layers—in his quest towards the essence of 'creation.'

It was a path that led me into the depths to understand the eternal mysteries. Somewhere in the inner landscape between the theories of Artaud and the theater of Brecht, I went searching. For what? I wasn't sure. Grotowski and Cieslak weren't satisfied with 'performing' or 'acting like someone else.'

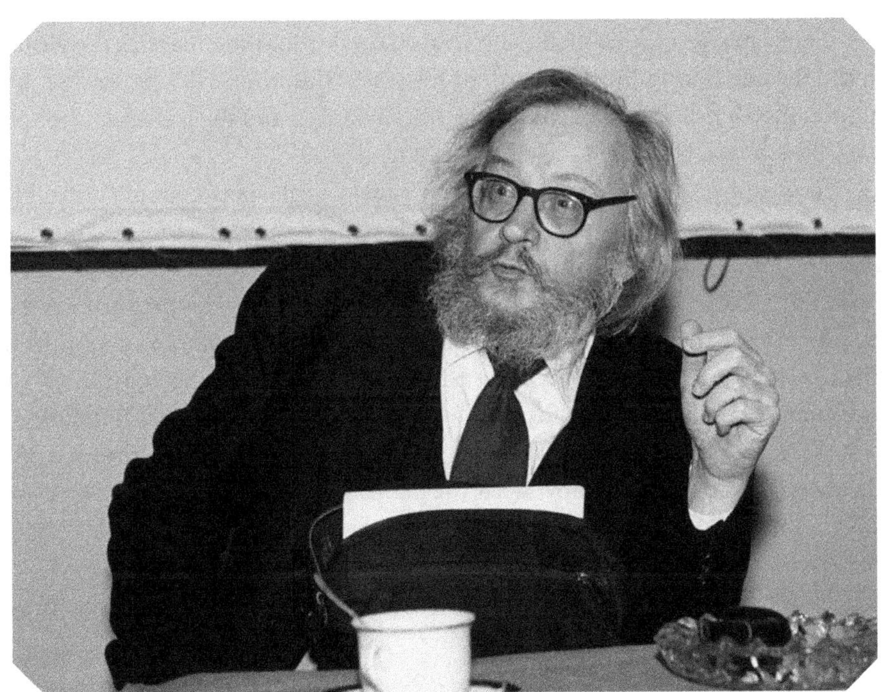

Jerzy Grotowski, 1997. (Courtesy Maciej Skawinski.)

Their process was an immersion of surrender, a constant exploration leading to create a space for the deepest expression to be laid bare. Gesture and dialogue became an unknown, unseen force that led to truth.

When I studied with Joseph Chaikin, and he directed me as Hamm in Samuel Beckett's *Endgame*, both the inner and outer landscape changed so much during rehearsal that the terrain and language required a 'stepping-off' into the unknown. Where time is no longer time as we know it, and reality imperceptibly changes into a shape that I couldn't even recognize. He kept saying: "Slower. Slower." Beckett had told him. Now he was telling me. We're always facing a crossroads with each heartbeat, with each moment of life. You decide how you want to soar. When you're ready—the energy and force necessary to create will come and fill you.

Then . . . I found out Harold Clurman was teaching. Talk about 'out of the frying pan and into the fire!' I went from one extreme to another! It was like being confronted with the fury of a full-blown two hundred mile-an-hour tornado coming straight at you, and you stand with your eyes 'caught in the headlights.' I'd check myself at the end of each class to makes sure that I was still in 'one piece.'

Clurman was another giant who banged on the door to unleash a revolution in the theater. Screaming at the top of his voice, shouting, cajoling, exclaiming in utter glee—it seemed as if the room was shaking—and the molecules bouncing off each wall took on a life all their own!

I'd sit in front of him, watching as he acted out the entire drama of his life! The entire history of humankind! Every epoch of theater! He'd describe the overwhelming importance of the actor and the artist's role in society. At the same time, I'd try not to fall out of my seat in complete laughter at his great humor, in agreement and amazement at his wizardry, his aplomb, and optimism. His unstoppable faith in everything the theater stands for and represents—as a reservoir of enlightenment for the well-being of all existence and humanity.

We're all descendants of Clurman. In the last essay that he wrote, he proclaimed: "We still do not know what theater is. How it comes into being. What it is meant to accomplish. And, consequently, how it is to be generated." Laying down a challenge for all of us to keep 'going back to the drawing board.' Of course, that doesn't mean that we don't do everything in our means to make sense of our existence through the theater.

By his actions—in everything he wrote and everything he said—he made it clear that the theater must be carried forth to the people so they can see their way forward. When you have to do what you have to do—there's no going back once you've made that choice. Everything falls into place. It may not appear that way at the moment. It may look like it's impossible. But the molecules are waiting to fly with you. That's when the world changes. Look at what Lin-Manuel Miranda has done with *Hamilton, the musical.*

Clurman would tell us, "We live in an age of amnesia. We forget everything that happened the day before yesterday." Well, if that's the case. Look at some of the greatest gifts you possess. Mindfulness. Intuition. Discernment. Listening. These are just a few you bring with you onto the stage. Keep listening to that 'still small voice' inside of you. By being an open vessel, you'll discover how all things talk to each other on this planet. Trees communicate with one another. Plants do the same. When Beethoven lost his hearing, he listened with his heart so he could hear his music. Take the time to listen with different parts of your body. Let the 'sounds of the earth' penetrate deep within your soul.

Each time I was with Clurman, it looked like he was 'shaking his fists at the Gods.' When I'd depart, it felt as if I had been picked up like the twister had swallowed up Dorothy in *The Wizard of Oz*, and around and around I'd go—and when I fell back to earth, my head was a little tilted—but it was for

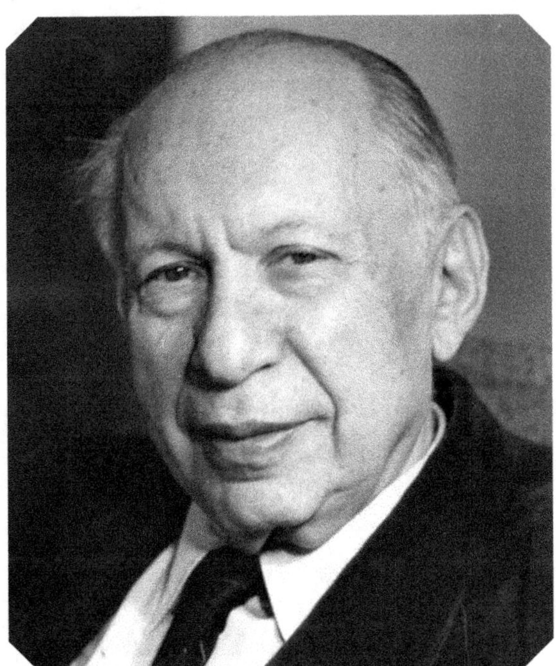

Harold Clurman, 1979. (Courtesy Mallory Jones.)

a good reason. He'd tell us that most of us are 'sleepwalking' our way through life. We don't even remember what we ate for breakfast the day before yesterday.

"Art is how we make ourselves visible," he'd tell us. "And don't forget what my good friend, Edwin Booth said: "An actor is a sculptor who carves in snow."

His passion was contagious, galvanizing. Like he says in my play: "So what if life is a struggle! So what if it's difficult! Attack it with all of your ardor! All the strength of your individuality! Because here we are—riding on this speck of dust in the middle of a magnificent, mysterious universe. And we come into it all separately. What gives us our definition? Our participation! That's what illuminates the greatest works of art. It's up to us how we shape our daily lives. We're all historical figures because we're part of all ages!"

How do you connect the dots? Everything is already there for you. It's like a magic carpet ride. Believe you can make the world a better place. Just like I did, listening to Clurman. I knew that not a thing was standing in my way. Just like nothing is standing in yours.

On and on, he'd go: "No matter what the critics say! No matter what anyone says! No matter what's been done or hasn't been done! Never lose faith in yourself! Never lose faith that the theater will survive because there are people like you who have hope! Who believe in the goodness of each other! Who believe in the goodness of life! Who believe that if you don't like what you see out there today, then go out and change it! Make it what you want it to be! Go out and change the world if that's what it's going to take! But do it through the great art of the Theater!"

EIGHT

Moments of Depth

"The world? The universe? And your position in it? This miraculous accident of being alive!" Tennessee Williams wrote these words in his one-act play, *The Case of the Crushed Petunias*. It makes you stop and think. How did you happen to be born into a 'miraculous accident' on a tiny planet that keeps taking you around in a circle, surrounded by billions of stars in the middle of a galaxy surrounded by millions of other galaxies? While beneath you, a molten outer core wrapped around an iron core is on fire as hot as the Sun. That's what you live on every day of your life. It's a miracle and a mystery, all wrapped into one at the same time. A miracle—but is it an 'accident'? Some people say there are no such things as 'accidents.' Everything happens for a purpose, a reason. Because when you come right down to it—in the span of 'all time'—your visit on this planet really happens, you might say, in a 'blink of an eye.' But that doesn't mean that you've don't have all the time you need to say everything you're meant to say. Look at what some of the most remarkable artists in history did in their span of time. They came here to do what they had to do.

Chadwick Bozeman saw his path as a way to empower others through his art in the forty-three years he was given. You have a gift. This moment. It's up to you to decide what you came here to say and put that into a solo performance.

There's something powerfully deep inside of you. That's where creating a solo performance comes into play. That what you'll create will brings us all closer to one other. Your work will bring a new meaning into the world. You'll tell us why we're alive by creating a new reality. Well, what we call 'reality.' Actually, we live in *two* worlds simultaneously. The world you see around you—and an invisible world filled with molecules. Thoughts that you can't see. But you can see what happens because of them. That's why you change the equation with everything you say and do. Hopefully, in a good way. Because we've seen the consequences when it goes the other way. We've seen pain. We've seen suffering. So what's pointing you in your direction to bring 'light' into the world? That's your gift as an artist. Giving hope when things may make no sense. Challenging us to see a new way forward.

There's no escaping the fact certain parts of our self are not perfect. Nobody's perfect. We're human. That's what makes us perfect. You're an unlimited creative force of energy. At the same time, we all carry around 'a lot of baggage' with us. It's part of what makes us who we are. All the things that have happened to us. We also have a lot of love inside. It comes down to how much you're willing to give away to fulfill your dreams to make a positive difference in the world. It's definitely going to play a large part in how you manifest your destiny. At the same time, it's also true there's a lot of aggression swimming around in each of us. Maybe you have found ways to deal with it. Maybe you haven't. You might not realize how it shows up. It can show up either in a small way or in a big way.

One of the best ways you can deal with it—is pouring it into what you create. We can't escape ourselves. That's a fact of life. It's what a lot of writers have written about. Pretty much every play, every poem that's been written, every movie, opera, dance, every song that's sung, every painting painted—everything we do as performers and storytellers—is about our human nature—trying to make us take a better look at ourselves.

Sometimes it can feel like you're in the middle of a 'tug of war,' literally. You know what you want. Yet, at the same time, life can sometimes get in the way. Or, a lot of the time, it can be ourselves. There are those times when everything's flowing in the most beautiful and perfect way. That's when some people might decide to sabotage themselves. All of a sudden, they think: It's too good to be true. Maybe I'm not what everyone thinks I am. Doubts start to creep in. Insecurities. All of a sudden, frustrations get in the way. Out of nowhere, an alter-ego can appear. Memories might spring up. Guilt can play a part. Stuff you don't want to be thinking about. Past disappointments. Expectations. Boy, it's incredible what the mind can throw at you if you let it. But that's not going to do you any good. It's not going to take you where you want to go. Keep your mind on the things you want and off the things you don't. LET IT GO! STAY IN THE MOMENT!

I know sometimes you can't. One thought will jar another. And all of a sudden—Bing! Bang! BOOM! You're not here! You're gone! You're not in the moment. Where did you go? Somewhere else. Why did you do that? You could say: My mind did it. It's what the mind does! Well, sometimes, you've got to go there to get past whatever you have to deal with. But make sure you see how easily you can fall 'out of balance.' Out of alignment with yourself. Judging yourself so much that you're not doing yourself a world of good or any favors letting your mind tell you how to think. You're in charge. Whether you want to believe it or not—it's true. So, give yourself a break—look at where you are at this moment. Look at how far you've come.

That's why the theater's been around for as long as it has. It gives us a chance to look at what we're going through. How we got to where we are. Even if sometimes it feels like it's a constant 'pushing a boulder up a mountain,' it's not necessarily true. I'm reminded of the phrase: 'This too shall pass.' Remember, when things get a bit overwhelming, we're all in the same boat together—every one of us. Every vibration you put out makes a ripple in the universe. Make it a great ripple!

Let's say you've come upon a well. You look down into it. Looks pretty deep. In fact, you can't even see the bottom, it's that deep. But this is no 'ordinary' well. It's your 'well.' It happens to be filled with unlimited treasures that are all your own. The only catch is you have to know how to draw from this 'well.' How to bring up all those 'riches.' To discover what they mean to you, how they bind you to others. Actually, they're your roots. Your heritage. Now that can mean the world to you—or they can mean nothing. We've only gotten this far because of these roots. This 'well.' Those before you who nourished your roots. They fed them. Gave them life. Without this 'well' to draw from, you wouldn't be who you are. None of us would. It's where you come from—and where we're going.

When I read Kimberly R. Fulton Orozco's words, a descendent of the Kaigani Haidi nation, in a recent article called "Inspiring Awe in Alaska," she wrote that "among the indigenous nations of Southeast Alaska, there is a concept known in Haida as 'Iitl Kuniisii'—a timeless call to live in a way that not only honors one's ancestors but takes care to be responsible to future generations."

Now your connection to your 'well' only exists as long as you 'recognize' it. No, more than that—you have to feel it. In places other than in your head. In your heart. In your soul. In your gut. In everything you do. In your entire existence. Because it's who you are. It's how you grow. It's where you'll go.

Over time, since nothing exists in a vacuum, there have been performers—actors and actresses –who have somehow connected with a force that's come into them. And in that moment, molecules have changed so much—guided by the forces of nature—that time appears to stop. A moment has arrived in all its complete richness. In its entire truth.

I call it a 'moment of depth.' A moment of revelation. A 'break-through.' An illumination. Showing us, we're more than what we're made out of. Yes, we're sinews, cells, molecules, and passion. Yet, at a 'moment of depth'—when it occurs—it can have such an effect that when you experience it—you walk out of the theater, and something has shifted. It may have been subtle. It could be life-changing. More recently, I've heard that's happened to many theater-goers who experienced *Hamilton, the musical.*

How do you draw from this 'well?' It means when you're creating your solo performance—which is akin to what the Shaman used to do around the campfire in the caves—you allow this flow to come through you. In a stream of consciousness—to come and align with you.

Creation is life-transforming. It's a matter of being in this creative state and allowing it to occur. Think about what Hamlet says: "There's a special providence in the fall of a sparrow. If it be now, 'tis not to come; if it be not to come, it will be now; if it be not now, yet it will come. The readiness is all."

During my solo play, Clurman has a moment when he's remembering—how as a child, he would hear his father's voice screaming at his mother—as he lay in the darkness, trying to block it all out. When these kinds of memories come, we may try and repress them. But in a sense, they could be considered 'a

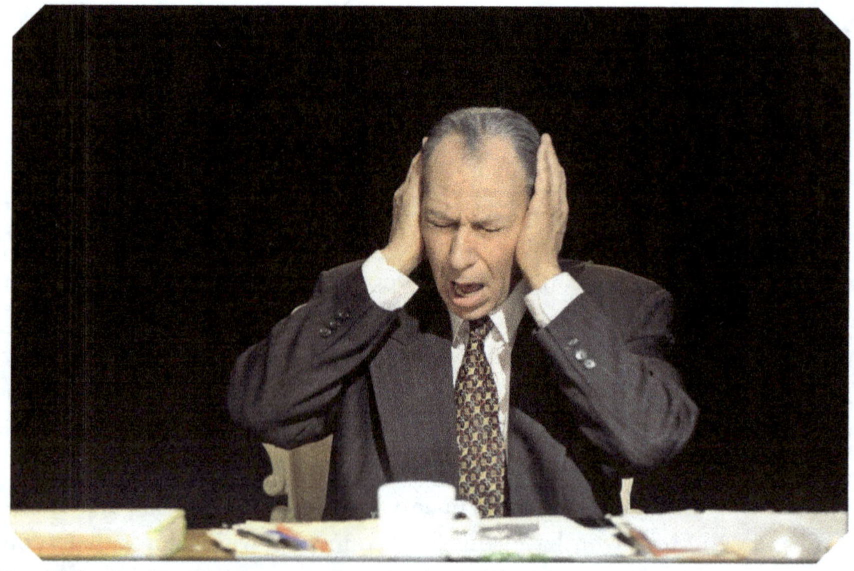

Ronald Rand as Harold Clurman in his solo play, *LET IT BE ART!* (Courtesy Ronald Rand.)

gift.' Whether we like them or not. They teach us how to cope. With pain. With loss. With everything that makes us human.

At another point in *LET IT BE ART!*—Clurman reflects on his marriage with Stella Adler. They had been together before the Group Theatre began in 1931. They remained a couple during the years of its success. Finally, they were married in 1942. After nearly twenty years, there came the point when Clurman recognized that they were like "two ships in a harbor, with no docks," as he says in my play. Then he asks: "How is it possible to land?" At that moment, he stops. He literally stops. There's a long silence. And he can't go on. The audience waits. Clurman's churning inside. In so much turmoil, he doesn't know how to go on.

At that moment—I have no idea how long it will take Clurman will recover. It's never the same. I never know what will happen. Because he has to find *his* way to cope with what's happened to him. To find how the next breath will come. After such a loss. Is there a way forward?

Every step you take leads you closer to the freedom you seek. When it comes—accept it. Transformation can come in many different shapes. It always starts with an open heart—as vast and expansive as the sky. It depends on your willingness to let this kind of creation take place.

One of my friends is a widely recognized painter of the South. His name is Tim Stevenson. He lives in Florence, Alabama. He's considered a 'Dutch master.' What does that mean? It means that his painting style is similar to how the great Dutch master painters of the 16th century painted, like Vermeer and Rembrandt. His art captures moments in the most intimate way. Stevenson told me of an experience he had—when he had entered a room at a museum in Europe—and gazed at the paintings on the walls. They were all by well-known Dutch master painters, and he was overwhelmed by what he saw. He literally felt 'weak in the knees.' These artists had been able to capture life in all its simplicity—its authenticity—its essence. It shook him to his core.

When has something like that happened to you? It makes you stop, take a moment and realize what an artist can capture. It happened to me when I stood in front of Michelangelo's statue of 'Moses' in Rome. The marble breathed. It spoke to me. There's no other way of putting it. I knew I was in the presence of a singular creation that captured me and would not let me go.

Stevenson told me that at that moment when he looked at all those paintings surrounding him, he knew that he wanted to try and say this through his art. If he could touch people in a similar way, it would bring meaning to his life.

He returned home, collected over four hundred and fifty of his 'modern' works of art, and burned them all in his backyard. He set out on a new journey as an artist. That kind of 'moment of depth' is life-changing. It can certainly have a rippling effect as it does on everyone he teaches, as well as those who gaze on his art.

A perfect example of a playwright who captured the pathos and humor in a 'moment of depth' is Neil Simon. He showed us that laughter goes hand-in-hand with great pain. In a singular 'moment of depth' in his play, *Broadway Bound*—Eugene's mother, Kate, while at the same time sharing a memory that has changed her life forever—is unable to express her anger. The deep pain she's feeling inside. As she fiercely polishes the family dining room table—in each stroke, her inner self is trying to cope with the deep pain she feels inside as she talks to her son. A 'moment of depth' such as these, when they come, can utterly shake us to the core and not immediately let us go. Or we can be turned into a puddle of laughter and barely catch our breath. It's up to you to recognize what's taking place in these kinds of moments. How an actor has brought this 'microcosm of existence' to life in front of you. When these moments happen to you during a performance, it's not wise to 'fool around with them.' They have their own organic life. You can't 'overthink' them. But when they come—they come because they reside deep inside the soul. You've tapped into that 'well.'

The theater has a rich tradition. A long line of dedicated artisans who have committed themselves through the art of acting to forge and fashion 'creation' on the stage. At times, it may appear as if a theater artist has transcended time and leaped into another realm. It's probably true. At that moment, 'they are communing with the Gods.' Or it can be a 'quiet pause in the stream.' A gentle moment. Like the morning rain.

Stories have been handed down over time. Told and re-told. Part of the folklore of theater. In every culture, in every country around the world, they each have their own traditions and legacies. When an actor or an actress had become so transformed in a performance, it was as if they had entered into the essence of the person that they were portraying, literally capturing their soul. It can happen during a rehearsal while the playwright may be watching and have no idea what actually lay inside their creation. A spirit merges with the actor's entire being—and at that moment—they become 'one' with their super-consciousness. Releasing a life force deep inside their pores. Inside their sinews. Inside their cells. Merging with this other person. Letting wondrous molecules take over to fill the space.

My friend Robert Wilson told me that when Martha Graham watched Eleanora Duse drop a letter she was holding during a performance, it was an incredibly shattering moment. She told him: "Duse didn't express the action outwardly, but inwardly felt it." At that moment, Graham said, "My life was changed forever." That kind of impact really needs no explanation. Stillness can signify something so profound that we all feel what's occurring without a single word needing to be said.

I'm sure you have also had powerful experiences in the theater or from watching a particular performance in a film. I want to share with you a few of mine.

When Cecily Tyson became Mrs. Watts in Horton Foote's play, *The Trip to Bountiful* on Broadway, she lit 'a lamp' so we could actually see inside the grace and poetry of Mrs. Watts' soul. Every one of us in the audience joined in her exuberance.

Naturally, all of Tyson's years of experience as an actress allowed her to release herself in service to Mrs. Watts' soul. But I believe it can be even more than that. When we sang with her, when we cried with her in the theater—we heard the chimes and twinkling sounds of our own soul being released. A freedom came—filling the entire space as we joined with her—and her with us.

Geraldine Page did this gracefully through her artistry in the same role in the film of the stage play. In every moment, she showed on screen what this

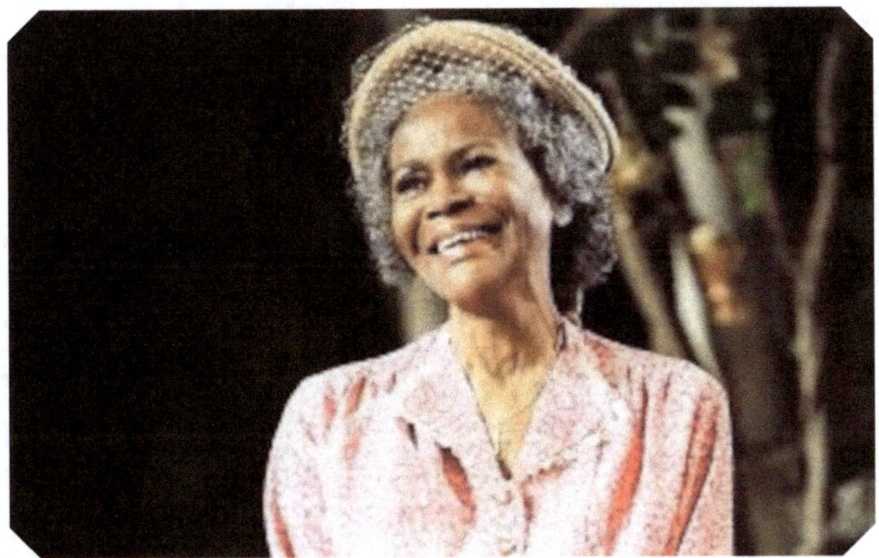

Cicely Tyson in the revival of Horton Foote's *The Trip to Bountiful.* (Courtesy Joan Marcus.)

woman was going through. It was almost as if we had an x-ray machine and could look right through her; she was that transparent. In the story, Mrs. Watts has to see her home again before she dies. When she finally travels by bus and almost reaches the town of Bountiful, she's stopped dead in her tracks. It appears everything she's done up to that point has come to naught. She couldn't have come this far only to be stopped! In that crushing moment in the film, we see Page capture Mrs. Watts' desperation—and ours as well.

Your heart is that deep, that vast. You have the power to give away what's inside. The heart is not just a muscle. It's not something we just paste on a Valentine's Day card once a year. Once you dive deep into its depth—you'll discover more about yourself than you ever thought was possible. It holds the secrets of our deepest emotions. It has a flow all its own. How willing are you to go even deeper when the time comes? You'll find your soul has more depth than you could ever have imagined. As long as you're willing to listen to it.

When Sir Laurence Olivier became Richard III on stage at the Old Vic Theatre in 1944 on opening night, he had so completely melded himself into this fiendish villain that when the curtain fell, the audience sat stunned by what they had witnessed. They felt they were actually in the presence of this 'creature,' known as Richard. So did Olivier. So much in fact that when he rushed offstage after the overwhelming ovation that went on for minutes, he shut himself alone in his dressing room and refused to come out. Olivier sat in front of the mirror, wrestling with himself. "But I don't know what I did," he kept saying over and over again to himself. "But I don't know what I did."

The Muse had overtaken him. Which is not the worst thing to happen. And when it comes—of course, there's nothing more you can do except be grateful. He knew being inspired took him to that peak, but how do you recapture it? You can't. This was his dilemma. And yours. This is why the 'Art of Transformation' comes into play—to allow you a way into creation—for it to occur time and time again. The organic process gives you the freedom you seek. Readiness is all. You have to be willing to give yourself over to the 'Art of Transformation.'

Over the years, I have watched unforgettable stage performances from Viola Davis in *Doubt*, Charles S. Dutton in *Ma Rainey's Black Bottom*, Joel Grey in *Cabaret*, Derek Jacobi in *Breaking the Code*, Christopher Plummer as Iago, Phylicia Rashad as a two hundred-and-eighty-five-year-old Ester in *Gem of the Ocean*, Jason Robards, Jr. in *A Touch of the Poet*, to Meryl Streep in Elizabeth Swados' *Wonderland in Concert*.

And when I also experienced The Grand Kabuki troupe's led by Kanzaburo Nakamura XVII, Tadashi Suzuki's production of *Medea*, Ariane Mnouchkine's Le Théâtre du Soleil's *Les Éphémères*—and Robert Lepage's *Lipsynch*—just to mention a very few. I knew what I was experiencing would be forever imprinted on my soul.

One night in 1833, the audience at Covent Garden in London clamored for the curtain to rise because they wanted to see if it was true. How could an actor named Ira Aldridge not only speak Shakespeare but even more that, dare to play Othello?! This was one of those earth-shaking moments in the theater. Facing great hostility and prejudice, he appeared. Silence fell across the audience. He spoke and brought forth one of the greatest Othello's that's ever been seen.

Not only was he the first Black actor to play the role in a setting such as that—but he went on to perform as Shylock and Lear, Macbeth—many other great roles all over the world to international acclaim. He prevailed because he knew he had to. He was born to release everything inside of him in service to the theater—to the audience. But to also say to the world—'see differently.' He knew that his task was even more significant than himself.

A little over a hundred years later, another powerful actor stepped forward to play Othello. First in London, then on Broadway, Paul Robeson, an actor of stature and a singer, understood the majesty, the power inside his soul. The son of a former slave and a preacher, he proclaimed his cause was humanity. That what he stood for in everything he did—he did in the name of "freedom, peace, and brotherhood."

When Robeson strode onstage as Othello in 1943 in front of New York audiences, all the injustices that he had suffered—all the indignities that had been poured over him—he found in Othello—and presented the Moor, that to him, spoke for "his entire People as a whole.

Each person you bring to life will be the culmination of who you are up to that point. That's why you need to be an open and willing vessel. How do you know what the Fates have decreed? We live day-to-day in a state of 'not knowing.' But that's okay. What you do know is that organic life has to occur on the stage for this kind of creation to take place. That's how you'll find out what can come through you as an artist on the stage.

With the 'Theater Gods' watching. Under the stars. Under the moon. Shining bright into his soul, James Earl Jones took on the role of Othello, first in Central Park in 1964 for the New York Shakespeare Festival. Then, seventeen years later, on Broadway.

In every one of Jones' performances I've experienced—as Troy Maxson in August Wilson's *Fences*, as Lennie in John Steinbeck's *Mice and Men*, as Othello, in his solo performance as Paul Robeson, and so many more on film, especially when he played the World Heavyweight champion, Jack Johnson, in *The Great*

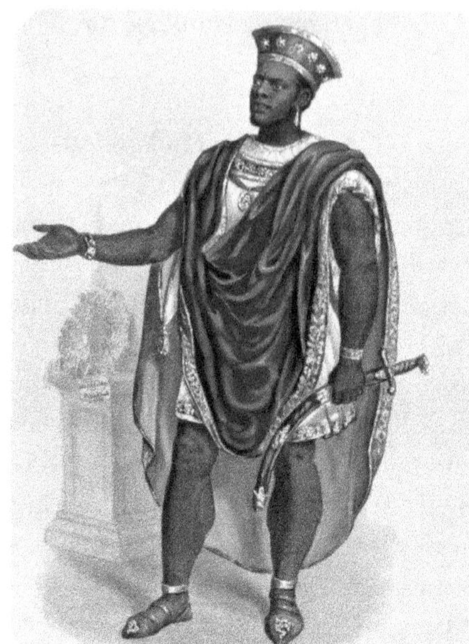

Ira Aldridge as Othello lithograph by Steindruck von Bühler, 1854. (Courtesy Folger Shakespeare Library.)

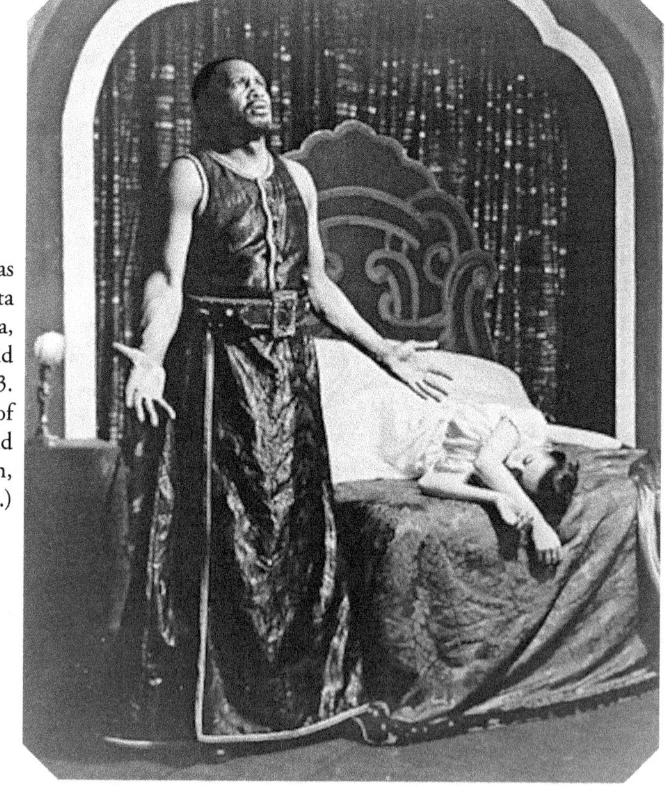

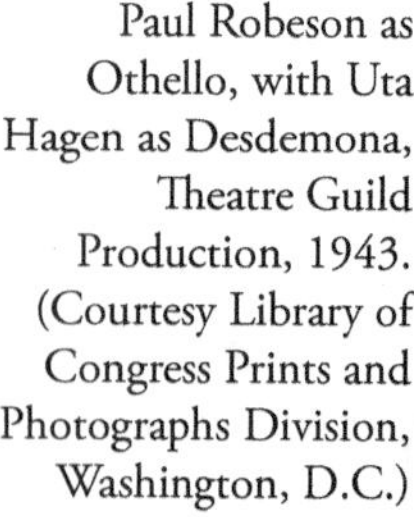

Paul Robeson as Othello, with Uta Hagen as Desdemona, Theatre Guild Production, 1943. (Courtesy Library of Congress Prints and Photographs Division, Washington, D.C.)

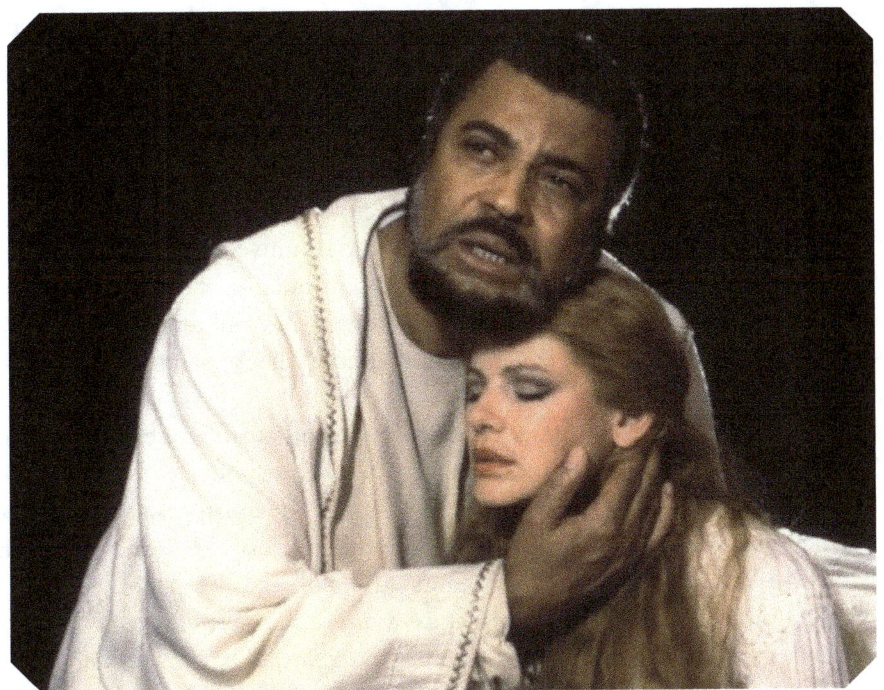

James Earl Jones as Othello, with Dianne Wiest as Desdemona, 1981. (Courtesy Martha Swope.)

White Hope—Jones doesn't rest until everything makes sense. That the truth of what the person is going through is clear and logical to him—every moment. Even to the point of telling August Wilson during rehearsals of *Fences* that "something didn't feel right, didn't add up" to help him reach the climax in the scene between him as Troy Maxson and his son, Cory, played by Courtney B. Vance. Wilson told him he wasn't going to write anything else. So what did the director do? Lloyd Richards gave Jones a chance to explore what was happening in the battle between Maxson and his son. That's what it takes. It first must make sense to you. And if you feel something's missing—you feel it in your gut—Stop! See where it takes you!

From the time Jones was nine years old, all the way up until he was in his mid-teens, he was a terrible stutterer. It's true. It was so bad he wouldn't say a single word a lot of the time. It took him several years to overcome it. He finally mastered his ability to speak without a stutter before he went off to college. He later admitted, "Once a stutterer, always a stutterer. It's stamped on your psyche." You can learn about it in his autobiography, "Voices and Silences." Jones talks about coming to grips with this particular challenge. "One of the hardest things in life is having words in your heart that you can't utter," he writes. Yet it wasn't always that way for him. He goes on to say: "When I have read great literature, great drama, speeches, or sermons, I felt that the human mind has not achieved anything greater. There is nothing more moving or powerful than the power of the Word when beautiful language is married to deep passion."

You see it in every one of his performances—how passion drives a person to do what they have to do. He refers to it as a 'universal rage.' Something that 'rages in every human being . . . a voice 'screaming in the wilderness.' For him, he says: "That's what makes acting interesting and also dangerous. Drama should always take us to the edge. We don't know what is going to happen or how far it is going to go."

When Christopher Plummer became the 'personification of evil' as Iago in *Othello* opposite James Earl Jones, Plummer showed how easily he could twist the mind of Othello, destroying all peace—showing what happens when someone like that is set loose among us. Reading the words of the theater reviewer, Frank Rich in *The New York Times* reminded me of what I experienced sitting there in front of Plummer's portrayal as a 'wizard of the dark side.'

"Mr. Plummer, a sensational actor in peak form, has made something crushing out of Shakespeare's arch-villain. He gives us evil so pure—and so bottomless—that it can induce tears. Our tears are not for the dastardly Iago, of course—that would be wrong. No, what Mr. Plummer does is make us weep for a civilization that can produce such a man and allow him to flower."

With each role we play, we have the opportunity to take our audiences to the heights of inspiration, the depths of evil, or to the 'dark side.' Playing Mother Theresa or Iago—two faces of our humanity. Still, if history has taught us anything, it's that we rarely learn its lessons. That's probably why so many of our stories are told over and over again. Writers try in their own way to bring us face-to-face with goodness and the 'face of evil.' Are we doomed to repeat the same mistakes—or draw upon our common decency, our tolerance, empathy, and love? That's part of what rests on your shoulders. There are those who see further in every generation.

This brought 'home' a personal dilemma for me as an actor. Because when I'm preparing to bring Clurman to life on stage, I can't play any one of the 'dark side.' I need to stay in a 'life-affirming' place in my soul. It's a personal choice I have to make. When I asked the Nobel Prize-winning author, humanitarian, and Auschwitz survivor, Elie Wiesel, about the possible effect it can have on an actor playing someone 'evil,' or on those watching depictions of persons of 'evil,' he told me: "I believe the actor needs to create a distance between himself and the character. What to do and how to do it remains the challenge. I don't think the acting-out of evil situations seduces those watching them. Why should a spectator be seduced if he or she realizes, if they understand, it takes place in a character in a play or in a movie, not in real life. Only those who want to be seduced will be. On the other hand, there are instances when fictional characters can have a negative effect."

At the dawn of the 20th century, an actor appeared to embody the grace and strength of the beginning of a new age. His name was John Barrymore.

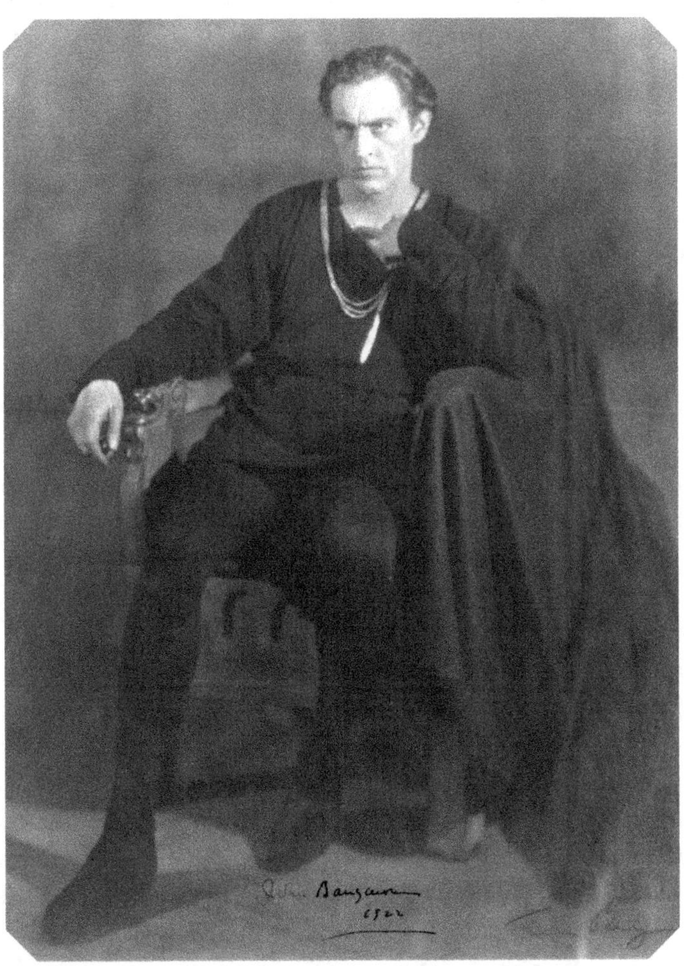

John Barrymore as Hamlet, 1922. (Courtesy Francis Bergman, Folger Library.)

At one point, he chose to take on the role of Hamlet. In a sense, Hamlet is a Prince existing inside his 'own solo world' trying to cope with the loss of his father.

Legend has it that Barrymore had a charismatic stage presence, and the scale of his voice was remarkable. He carried with him the 'stamp' of a true stage actor. During his performances as Hamlet, one stood out above all others. As the story goes, he had just begun the 'To be or not to be' soliloquy—and there was a huge laugh. That's right. Can you imagine? Of course, Barrymore was utterly shocked. Until he followed the audience's gaze to the other side of the stage. Where, lo and behold, the house cat had come out and was lingering in front of the audience. The laughter grew. What was Barrymore to do? What would you have done? He knew he had to bring the audience back into the play.

So calmly, he strode to the other side of the stage. Picking up the cat, he proceeded to deliver the entire soliloquy directly to the mischievous feline. You could hear a pin drop in the theater; it was that quiet. As Barrymore spoke the final phrase: ". . . with this regard turn awry and lose the name of action," he lightly placed his 'new-found' friend down and faced the audience. They were silent. Stunned. They had never seen anything like it. Then they rose to their feet and applauded for several minutes. In that singular moment, as Hamlet, he was shown, by his trusty friend of Elsinore castle, that the truth is always where you are. It's in the moment. It's nowhere else.

At the same time in Russia, two extraordinary actors appeared, both members of the Moscow Art Theatre. They were, you might say, in 'competition' with one another because of their unbelievable talent and genius in creating on the stage. It was a matter of: "Oh, you'll do that—then I'll do this." Michael Chekhov and Ygevney Vakhtangov. Two masters of inventiveness of 'living in the moment' as the person they would bring to life. They would spend hours and hours discovering through improvisations and different types of exercises—the essence of the person that had to be revealed. They actually both went on to become two of the most important acting teachers we've ever had. Transforming the art of acting because they 'saw' in a different way, and from their perspective—the only way forward was to create organic life on stage.

In China, Mai Lanfang, a great master in the Peking Opera, also known as the Beijing Opera, was known for specializing in playing female roles. He was the first to bring this art form to Western audiences. Introducing new ways to tell the story better, he took his audiences beyond what they were used to seeing in these kinds of performances, including creating new costume designs. "An actor should be innovative in his work," he is known to have said, " but his originality should stem from knowledge. He will not find the right means of expression if he has not studied widely and if he does not know history." Eventually, his art reflected the soul of China. When Stanislavski, Brecht, and Gordon Craig saw his innovative performances, they couldn't stop talking about them. He had an enormous effect across Russia and Europe. Even in America. Brecht actually ended up writing a famous essay about Mai Lanfang's acting and his technique.

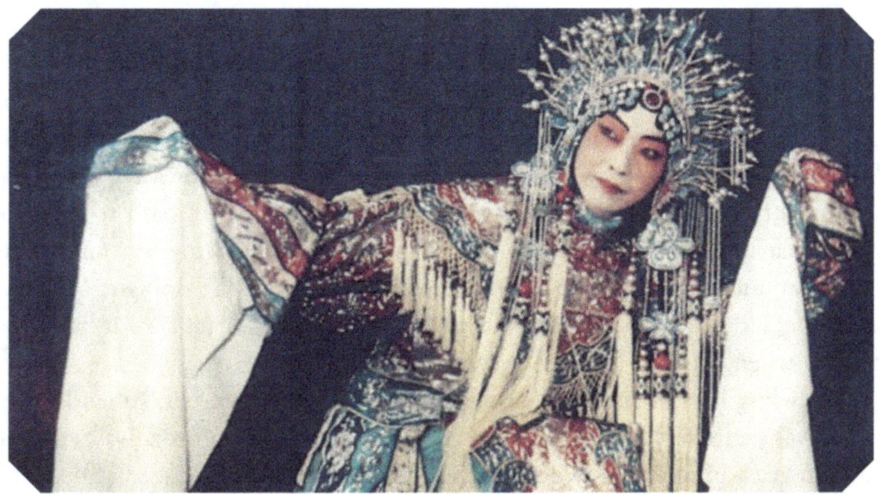

Mai Lanfang in *The Drunken Beauty* with the Peking Opera.

When you study the life of a highly skilled master of the stage such as Sir Laurence Olivier, you will also find that through his complete dedication to his 'path'—he achieved a mastery—which I think could similarly be described—as it is—in Japanese art as 'Yugen'—the highest principle of grace and beauty. Through a great deal of practice and preparation, he cultivated 'complete harmony in action' in everything he did as an actor. This exists in you as long as you're willing to cultivate within yourself this same kind of dedication to *your* 'path.'

During the 14th century, Zeami—Japan's most celebrated actor and playwright—looked deeply into art and life—and called it 'unknowable.' An emotional response that one feels so deeply, so powerfully, that it reverberates within your soul. This is how he described it:

To watch the sun sink behind a flower-clad hill.
To wander on in a huge forest without a thought of return.
To stand upon the shore and gaze after a boat
that disappears behind distant islands.
To contemplate the flight of wild geese seen
and lost among the clouds . . .

When you come in contact with a 'moment of depth' like this in your life, how can you put it into words? Life takes center stage—and the 'stage' disappears.

In 1946, a young playwright wrote an autobiographical play about his mother and his sister. It really didn't have that much a chance of getting produced. Except an 'angel' showed up. He read it and fell in love with the script. His name was Eddie Dowling. The play was called *The Glass Menagerie*. The playwright would become known as Tennessee Williams. It's hard to imagine today that nobody wanted to do Williams' play. But Dowling was an experienced producer, writer, director, and actor himself, said: "I'm doing it!" He saw what it could become. Nothing was going to stop him. That's how it has to be for you when you say: "My solo play will be done!"

Dowling had an actress in mind for the role of the mother, Amanda. Her name was Laurette Taylor. Now she had been a huge star on Broadway, starring for two years in a hit play right before World War I. But that was a long time ago. Because of the loss of her husband, she had found a new 'friend'—a bottle of gin. When Dowling finally got to meet her, he told her the role was perfect for her. But she turned him down. Do you think that stopped him? He knew she had to play Amanda. He finally was able to convince her to read the play, and guess what? She said, "Yes." Then she also told him that no one would want to produce the play with her in the part.

But Dowling was not one to give up. He was able to get a theater, the funds necessary, even directed the play himself and played the lead role of Tom, her son. After the play premiered in Chicago, they got good enough reviews to open in New York City.

Well, a few hours before the curtain went up on opening night, everything seemed to have come together. But Taylor had 'another excursion' with a bottle of gin. Somehow Dowling revived her. Got her out on stage, and as they say, 'the rest is history.' Many in the audience looked at this tired-looking worn-out sort of irritating woman playing the mother and wondered when will the famous Broadway star, Laurette Taylor, show up on stage. "Wait a minute," they said, "That can't possibly be . . . ?!"

That's how it went for everyone who came. Not only had she 'become' Amanda—seeing her performance changed the lives of numerous actors, actresses, and directors—such as Charles Durning, Uta Hagen, Martin Landau, Patricia Neal, Harold Prince, and Maureen Stapleton, who watched her over and over again, trying to understand how she was 'so natural.' She showed that acting as another person has more to do with 'living' than with 'acting.' Her Transformation was as Zeami wrote: *"To contemplate the flight of wild geese seen and lost among the clouds . . ."*

In 1959, a young gifted Black playwright came along. Lorraine Hansberry was only twenty-eight years old. But in those twenty-eight years, she had found her voice. As a storyteller, she had something to say to the world. About injustice. About who we are inside. About building your dreams. How when things are wrong, they're not right. That it was time we took a good long look at ourselves.

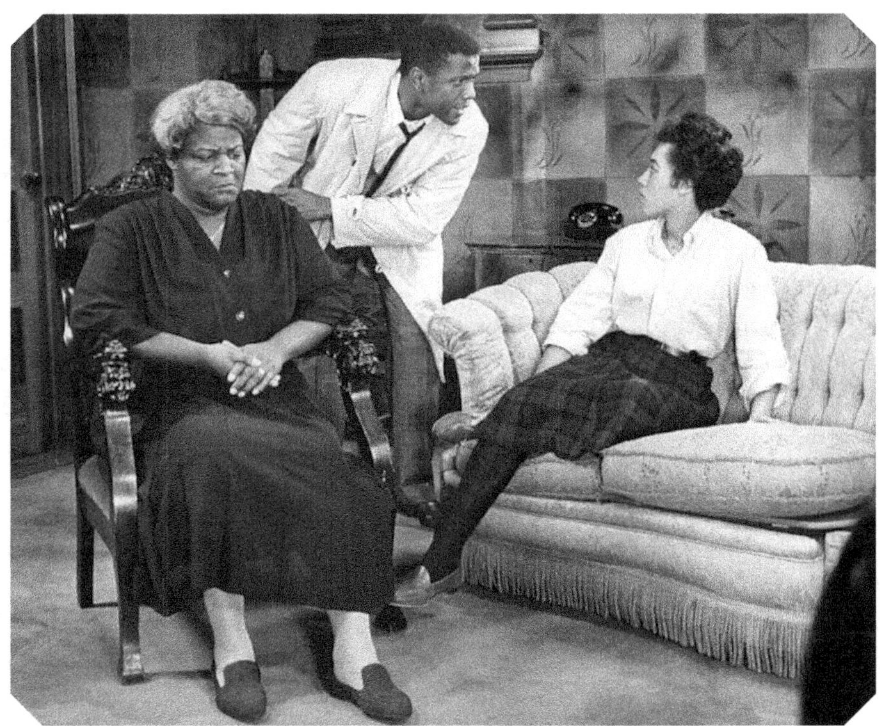

Claudia McNeil, Sidney Poitier and Diana Sands in *A Raisin in the Sun*, 1959. (Courtesy Friedman-Abeles.)

Hansberry's new play was called *A Raisin in the Sun*. No one had ever seen it before. The director, Lloyd Richards, looked around. He knew he had to have the right cast. Actors and actresses who knew the struggle taking place and had something to say from their soul. Richards knew a young actor he had spent time training in Harlem. His name was Sidney Poitier. Why did he want Poitier? I talked to Poitier and asked him what Richards was looking for, and I put it in my book, *Acting Teachers of America*.

"Richards wanted the audience," Poitier told me, to "watch life on stage. And I had to have the ability to behave as a human being in the life of the play." When he became Walter Lee, and you can see his performance in the movie, his Transformation shows us a man grappling with forces beyond his control. But that doesn't mean he doesn't deal with them. He has no choice. His mother tells him: "Become who you're supposed to be."

The play went on to change generations of theater performers and audiences and continues today. Look deep into the world. This world is depending upon you.

Almost seventy-five years ago, a play was in rehearsal. If you had been there in 1948, you'd be sitting in a small rooftop studio above the New Amsterdam Theatre on 42nd Street in New York City.

Next to you would be the director, Elia Kazan, and the playwright. His name was Arthur Miller. You'd be watching the first rehearsal of a new play called *Death of a Salesman*. Who was in front of you? There was a well-known actress, Mildred Dunnock, playing Linda, the wife of a salesman named Willy Loman, played by a large actor, Lee J. Cobb, husky in voice and stature.

Salesmen in those days would spend their entire life on the road 'selling.' If you don't know that means, it means spending every waking day trying to sell things to people, who may not necessarily know they want them, but by the time you're finished, they can't turn you down. However, Willy has lost his 'touch' in the play. He's at a crossroads.

Remember, audiences had never heard of this play before. As the days passed in rehearsal, all the actors—except for Cobb—were building their roles, learning their lines, according to the playwright in his autobiography, *Timebends*. Miller wrote: "Lee seemed to move about in a buffalo's stupefied trance, muttering his lines, plodding with deathly slowness from position to position, and behaving like a man who had been punched in the head."

Kazan tried to assure Miller that Cobb was just 'learning' his role. Miller was genuinely worried.

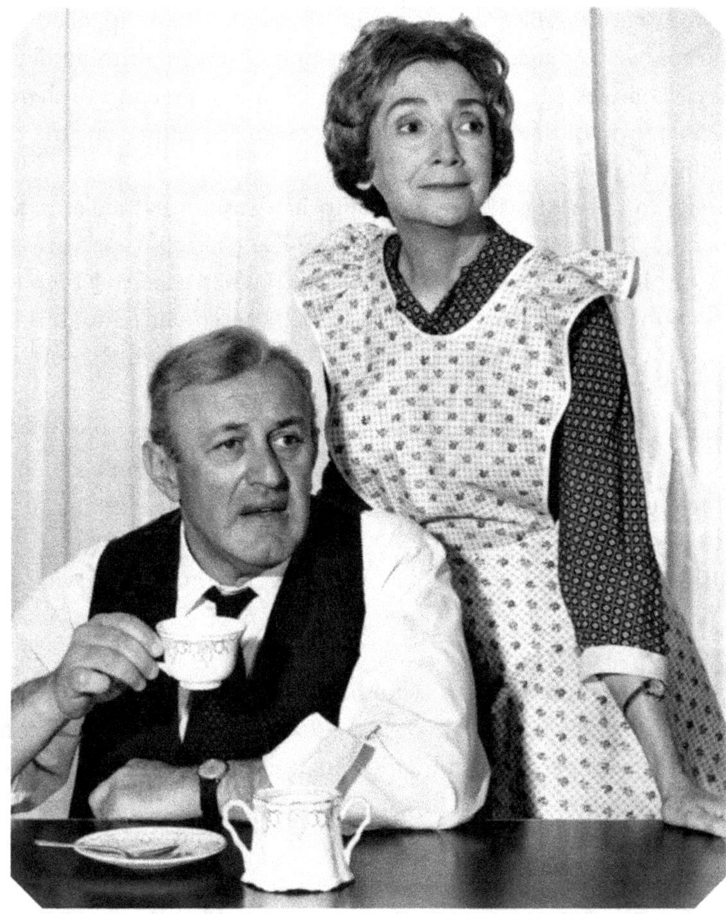

Lee J. Cobb and Mildred Dunnock in *Death of a Salesman*, 1967. (Courtesy CBS Television.)

He goes on to say in his book: "On about the twelfth day, in the afternoon, with Eddie Kook, our lighting supplier, and Jimmy Proctor, our pressman, and Kazan and myself in the seats, Lee stood up as usual from the bedroom chair and turned to Mildred Dunnock and bawled, "No, there's more people now . . . There's more people!" and, gesturing toward the empty upstage where the window was supposed to be, caused a block of apartment houses to spring up in my brain, and the air became sour with the smell of kitchens where once there had been only the odors of earth, and he began to move frighteningly, with such ominous reality that my chest felt pressed down by an immense weight."

"After the scene had gone on for a few minutes, I glanced around to see if the others had my reaction. Jim Proctor had his head bent into his hands and was weeping, Eddie Kook was looking shocked, almost appalled, and tears were pouring over his cheeks, and Kazan behind me was grinning like a fiend, gripping his temples with both hands, and we knew we had it—there was an unmistakable wave of life moving across the air of the empty theatre, a wave of Willy's pain and protest."

"I began to weep myself at some point that was not particularly sad, but it was as much, I think, out of pride in our art, in Lee's magical capacity to imagine, to collect within himself every mote of life since Genesis and to let it pour forth. He stood up there like a giant moving the Rocky Mountains into position."

How did Cobb 'find' Willy Loman? What Miller described could only be called 'genuine discovery.'

Certainly, so much of it has to do with all the experiences you have had up to that point. Something comes. Because at that moment, you become an open vessel allowing Transformation to occur. But you have to be willing to work for it. It just doesn't come on its own.

A little over twenty-five years later, a critic put into words what he experienced on opening night at another production of *Death of a Salesman* on Broadway with George C. Scott as Willy Loman.

Clive Barnes wrote: "There is nothing on earth like the magic of great acting. An actor takes off—his words fly up, image and reality become one. The actor creates a patch of humanity on the quietly empty stage. A rustle runs through the theater. A breeze of awareness. A special alertness. One of the world's few renewing miracles flickers into life. Great acting. Not just good acting, or even magnificent acting. Great acting. The kind you can never forget. The kind you tell your grandchildren about. The kind that leaves you in a state of grace, enables you to jump beyond yourself, to see something that perhaps even the playwright himself only dimly perceived."

When I saw Scott on stage, he was like an unleashed tiger on the prowl, constantly in movement—always challenging himself. You see, you come from a special breed. Once you get inside your solo play, you have to keep asking yourself: What am I seeking to find? No stone can be left unturned. Every time you perform in it, it's always as if your solo play has never been seen or heard of before.

Over the years, Miller's play has been performed almost countless times around the world, including when Arthur Miller traveled to China in 1983 to direct Ying Ruocheng as Willy Loman with an all-Chinese cast at the Beijing People's Art Theatre. I witnessed the unforgettable 1984 Broadway production led by Dustin Hoffman, Kate Reid, John Malkovich, and Stephen Lang and talked with Miller at intermission. More than twenty-five years later, as a member of the Drama Desk, I watched Philip Seymour Hoffman, whom I had worked with in the film, *The Hard Way*, step into Willy Loman's struggle wrestling with the American dream, to find out what the play meant to us after 9/11.

More than anything, *Death of a Salesman*—just as many classic plays do—no matter background, culture, or race—continues to challenge who we've become—forcing us to look at ourselves—to consider in every way imaginable what's led us to make the choices we do.

In 1972, for the first time, an entirely African-American cast brought *Death of a Salesman* alive on the stage at Centre Stage in Baltimore, Maryland. Since then, several African-American actors, including André De Shields, Charles S. Dutton, and Don Warrington, have embraced Willy Loman's struggle, transforming themselves into this 'universal' salesman. In 2019, co-directors Marianne Elliott and Miranda Cromwell decided to turn everything on its head and present *Death of a Salesman* from an entirely different perspective in a production in London, showing us an African-American family led by Wendell Pierce and Sharon D. Clarke as Willy and Linda Loman. Pierce described it by saying, "So when you see an African American family in this play, it illuminates, even more, the desperation of the situation. The more specific you are, the more universal you become."

You see, in this way, once you begin recognizing the common thread of how alike we are, you'll get a sense of how important a task you've been handed. The Transformation you go on through this art form, coupled with the Transformation in your work as a performer, will define you.

Take your time reading about Rose McClendon and Ira Aldridge, James Earl Jones, Paul Muni, Donna Murphy, Lee J. Cobb, Laurette Taylor, Sidney Poitier, and Viola Davis—about what it takes to carry a 'timelessness' of yourself and let it become infused by the dilemma of another person. Allow endless molecules to flow through you. Never rush what's meant to happen. Sometimes you have to 'wait for it.' Certain things cannot be rushed.

While there's a world of difference between what's at stake, I see a correlation in a distinct way when you listen to Leslie Odom, Jr. as Aaron Burr singing Lin-Manuel Miranda's song "Wait for It" in *Hamilton, the Musical.* In the lyrics, it's clear there will be times when you have to be willing to 'wait for it.' In the same way, the organic process of the 'Art of Transformation' has its own rhythm—its own life. You have to be willing to allow it to happen to you.

At one point, an actor came along, and by completely submerging himself into the person he was playing, he literally changed the way acting was perceived for generations to come.

This was before television was in color and every child played video games. For those who saw his performance, his fury was so explosive, so visceral—he literally left people in the audience gasping for breath. Women fainted. I'm not making that up. You thought he was going to come off the stage and 'punch you,' he was that intense. He said he 'owned the world,' and you believed him.

I'm talking about Marlon Brando as Stanley Kowalski in Tennessee Williams' *A Streetcar Named Desire* when the original production opened on Broadway in 1947. You can watch his performance in the film today. But if you had been there in that theater, it would have had an impact like no other on your life.

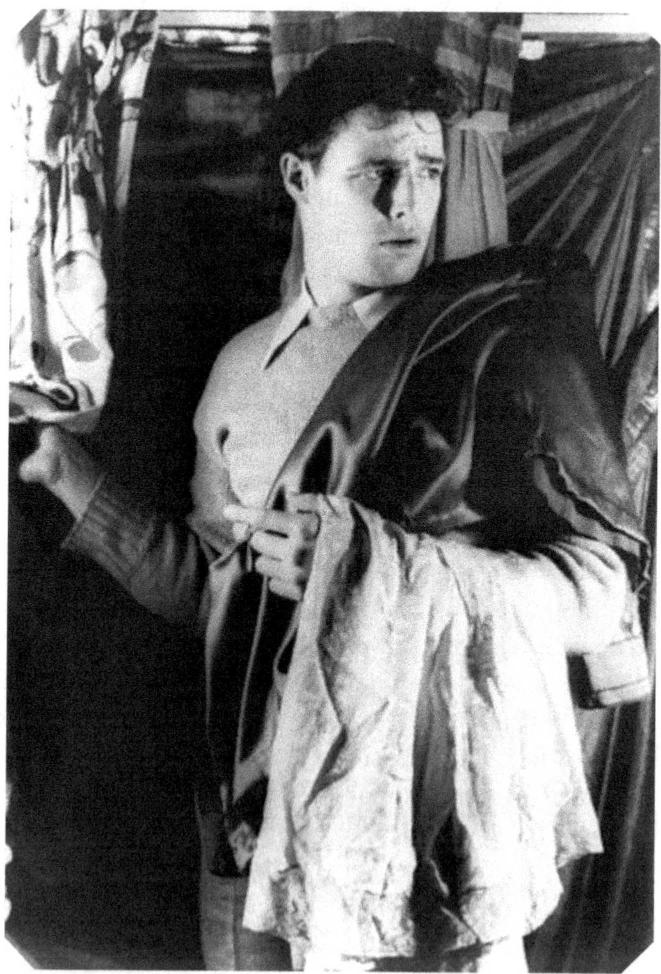

Marlon Brando in *A Streetcar Named Desire*, 1948. (Courtesy Carl van Vechten.)

However, even Brando wasn't satisfied. Something was missing, and he knew it. He was that intuitive. At the end of the second performance, there was a knock on his dressing room door. The door opened. Brando didn't move. He slightly glanced up, looking in the mirror. He saw Stella Adler, whom he was studying with at the time, standing in the doorway. Without entering, she hissed at him: "Shoes!" He still hadn't found the right shoes for Kowalski. But that was all he needed to hear. One missing element makes the entire difference between 'acting as a character' or finding the essence of the person you're bringing to life.

On a cold January evening in 1935 in the middle of the Great Depression, a night came along that changed not only the theater but millions of people's lives across the country. A benefit was being held for people down on their luck at a theater on 14th Street in lower Manhattan. Today the theater's been torn down. But back in its day, it was gorgeous. It was a famous theater. Actors like Edwin Booth and Edwin Forrest had acted on its stage. In 1926, Eva Le Gallienne, a well-known actress and director came along, and for almost ten years presented classic plays in repertory, renaming the theater after her company, the Civic Repertory Theatre.

Some say what happened that evening was an 'accident.' But remember, there is no such thing as 'accidents.' A young playwright had written a short play. It was a one-act with a couple of scenes. His name was Clifford Odets. The play was called *Waiting for Lefty*. It was supposed to be in the middle of the benefit between some songs and dances, but instead, at the last minute found its way to become the finale. Several members of the Group Theatre were in the cast. Odets and Sanford Meisner had directed the one-act.

Clurman was in the audience with Stella Adler. He wrote about what happened that evening in his book *The Fervent Years*. In my solo play, at one moment, Clurman brings it alive.

"In the audience, there were doctors and lawyers, taxi drivers on strike, mothers, young people like yourself. First scene starts, and it's like a tidal wave sweeps over the audience! They start laughing, talking to each other. To the actors on stage! The actors aren't acting any longer! They're being carried along by an exaltation I had never witnessed before! The actors and the audience become one! Line after line brings applause, whistles, bravos! And at the end of the play, the character yells out: "Well, what's the answer?" The spontaneous roar of "Strike! Strike! Strike!" becomes a birth cry! The audience becomes delirious. They start stomping, clapping, screaming! They storm the stage! They lift Clifford onto their shoulders! They don't leave the theatre for hours! They're stunned! They're dazed! They're happy! A new awareness has entered their souls, and their lives will never be the same!"

At that moment, people rose up and said: "Enough!" Strikes broke out across the country wherever the play was done. Every major city banned *Waiting for Lefty* but did that didn't stop actors and directors from putting on more and more productions everywhere they could. They were even beaten up, but they still went ahead. What did Odets tap into? Theater became a searchlight showing us what's wrong. That it's a time for a change. When that happens, you can't hold back the tide.

What did Jackie Sibbles Drury's 2019 Pulitzer Prize-winning play, *Fairview*, tap into? *Slave Play*? The theater keeps showing us—turning away is no longer a viable option.

Look at the works of writers like James Baldwin, Amiri Baraka, Alice Childress, Pearl Cleage, Guadalís Del Carmen, Lydia R. Diamond, Owen Dodson, Randolph Edwards, Larissa Fasthorse, Monet Hurst-Mendoza, Michael R. Jackson, Suzan Lori-Parks, Mary Kathryn Nagle, Lynn Nottage, Marisela Treviño Orta, Paz Pardo, Randy Reinholz, Mónica Sánchez, Alexis Scheer, DeLanna Studi, Douglas Turner Ward, William Yellow Robe, Jr., to mention a few.

They say to us it's time to peel back the 'skeletons in the closet.' Confront who we are. But it takes artistic directors who are courageous. Playwrights willing to challenge us with the poetry of theater to say there's no other way forward—unless we step forward! Actors like you—unafraid—daring us to look at ourselves.

As I write these words, the theaters on Broadway are shut down in the face of the 2020 Pandemic, and we're watching actors act on a small screen on computers. I appeared in a new play about King Midas by Bernard Pomerance in the same way. Still, nothing can replace watching live actors perform in front of you. That's what makes it 'theater.' I know this will all pass, and we'll enter into a new 'normal.' But nothing can replace our losses. So much of our life as a stage artist depends on a 'live' audience breathing with you.

This is what you're a part of and what you're responsible for. To make us see who we are and what we can become.

NINE

Restoring the Balance You Need

The breath of life flows through you. You're the amalgam of all existence. With each breath you take on the stage—you breathe for the audience. The world's in a constant state of flux. You restore a balance in their lives by what you bring on the stage—and once you let the molecules come and guide you, they'll bring you a greater sense of ease—a heartfelt feeling of harmony—that you'll be able to draw from to create in every single moment of your solo performance.

Maya Angelou reminded us: "If you don't like something, change it. If you can't change it, change your attitude." There's a lot of things you'll need to do the work you must do. Good health, good friends, spending time in nature, making peace with your family—all of these are critical, leading you to your greatest satisfaction in what you do every day of your life. When you rest your head on the pillow at night, the dreams you'll need to dream will come helping to change the world for the better.

Does that mean everything's going to be 'all right' all the time? No, there's no question at some point; life will throw you some curves. How do you keep yourself in alignment? That's the challenge we all face. I know—it's easier said than done. However, the key is to know that no matter what—you will find a way through.

A lot of artists have been drawn to meditation, yoga. Why? They give you an opportunity to relax your mind. To strengthen your inner core. To put yourself in a state of ease. They're valuable practices in achieving a balanced state of harmony. If you're using them already—great. If meditation and yoga aren't something you're comfortable with, there are other different types of exercises that can bring you the same kind of ease and strength you need. A simple physical and relaxation combination exercise every day will help you stay centered. Allowing you to go forward, letting go of any tension you may be feeling. Always try and spend time in a peaceful place every day, preferably surrounded by nature.

We know that there's a 'collective unconscious' we're all connected to. Once you spend some time reading Carl Jung, you'll come across the phrase: 'Collective unconscious.' Find out what it means. Why it's helpful to allow Transformation to occur. Some things appear to be beyond our control. Like I had mentioned before, some coincidences just seem to happen. So, if that's the case—there must be a reason. It's almost like our 'invisible antenna' is able to pick up a deeper vibration. But it's only able to do that when you're open to receive. When you step inside the flow that's occurring—it's like a natural rhythm—like the wind moving through the branches. Like the birds passing by. Like how your breath comes when it needs to. It has its own rhythm. So much of our work depends upon tapping into this seemingly unconscious vibration. Your willingness to align yourself with this—by being an open vessel—will bring you the balance you're seeking. Finding this kind of balance is essential in the work we do, whether you're working on your own solo performance or in collaboration with other actors.

When I listened to Christopher Plummer in an interview, he described how thrilled he was to work with Elia Kazan in the early part of his career, playing Nickles in a play called *J.B.* on Broadway opposite Raymond Massey. At the beginning of rehearsals, he said "I came in to the rehearsal with as much 'Method' realism as I could. I was determined to be 'real' with every word." He had worked himself up so thoroughly that he was going to show how intense he could be. Out of the darkness, he heard Kazan's voice yell out from the back of the theater: 'Sixty percent!"

You see how important it is to find the right balance you need—whether it's in rehearsal or in performance. The truth is in the balance that *already exists*. It doesn't need something added to it. It's what it is, and you slip into it. If you add too much, you're out of balance. How do you find that? We all have a natural instinct for certain things. For some, it can be an infinity with music. Others are graceful in sports. Trusting your natural instincts will lead you to the confidence you need—but also to this kind of 'knowing.' Yes, at times, others will recognize when you're not in sync. You have to be willing to listen—and to accept—and to invite another flow of molecules to bring you this kind of clarity. This kind of ease. This kind of balance. Something brought you to read this book. Was it a desire to grow? To see further? To keep learning as much as you can and see how far you can go?

Where's one of the best places to start? With humor. Laughter. Spontaneity. Surprising yourself. Just smile, and let it take off and turn it into a laugh—and not just a laugh. An uproarious bellowing laugh. Once you let go and have fun—let exuberance fill your entire being—and all of those around you. Fall down. Pick yourself up. Fall down again. Let the world spin! Everything's topsy-turvy! Keep laughing out loud! Tell yourself corny jokes. Watch a lot of comedy. Fill your heart full of joy. Sing! Dance to your heart's content! Restore and balance your bloodstream. This is what your body's hungry for. LOTS AND LOTS OF FUN! Your body's constantly reacting to everything it hears every day. Everything it comes in contact with. It listens to everything you tell it. So why not embrace the unexpected and continue to reach for the stars every single day with laughter.

When I performed in Chelyabinsk, Russia, in front of a packed audience that, for the most part, only spoke Russian—and they followed along, reading the translation on a screen that was right next to me on the stage, while I spoke in English. The flow that began occurring was a 'give-and-take' both ways. Laughter broke out, and it never stopped. Clurman's passion captured their imagination and coupled with their 'willing hearts'—delight and exuberance vibrated in every molecule flying around the theater. When this occurs—the 'Art of Transformation' is occurring at its higher vibration. An energy is set loose. There's no longer a separation between anyone in the theater. A harmony is flowing into everything, giving you the permission to go even further. When that kind of freedom comes—welcome it! Open your heart completely. Take the moment and let what's occurring—occur.

When you're creating your solo performance during rehearsals—allow one moment to lead into the next. All in balance with one another. You can only find this kind of balance by letting it take you where it has to go. Finding the right rhythm of what this human being has to say and do.

We have to accept certain things may be beyond our control. But when you're willing to be open enough, they bring you an invitation for a different kind of rhythm to occur. A new kind of balance to take place. Make the most of every moment that's being handed to you.

One of the greatest things you have going for you is the creation of a 'mastermind.' It occurs when two or more minds come together—recognizing the 'path of least resistance'—showing you what's necessary to make the impossible possible.

"Life is like riding a bicycle," Albert Einstein reminded us, "To keep your balance, you must keep moving." Even when you're in a deep state of relaxation or meditation, you're still in a state of movement. Especially when you're sleeping. Your eyes are constantly moving. Your body is shifting to countless positions. Certainly, your mind is in motion. It's a matter of acceptance—and remaining open to the mystery and awe surrounding you. Every day, you're transforming just a little bit more. When you're working on your solo performance, you're fulfilling your life's meaning. Each impulse bringing you closer and closer to the 'voice' that has to speak from deep inside of you.

When I've brought my solo performance around the world—this kind of sharing, I believe, brings a balance into the world. Peace is not an abstract thought. It happens when we step outside of our comfort zone and elevate others' spirits through our life task. Vibrations—ever-widening molecules—creating a ripple in the universe. Invisible though it may be, it has an impact that's life-changing. Is it something you can feel and see and touch? Absolutely. We're always stepping across 'fragile stones.' As if the bridge has fallen, and we're finding another way to cross. You are—at the same time—the stones and the bridge. Because when you allow this kind of force to come through you, to enter you—and you share it with others—you're creating through the art of solo performance—an opportunity to create a shift in the heart of all of those experiencing everything you are.

How do you keep enlarging your ability to allow this to happen? By listening to the eternal melodies. Letting them fill you. Listen to silence. Listen deeply to the sounds in nature. It takes a lot of guts to fall from the sky, but that's what links you with every creature on the planet. We have the ability to rise again. What will restore you and bring you the freedom that you desperately need? So much of the time, your own body will tell you. There are eternal imprints within you. Let them show you how to move and express yourself.

Let me ask you: What fascinates you in life? What gives you your greatest joy? Every day you have the opportunity to discover more about yourself. That's why curiosity is your greatest ally. It's certainly one of the blessings you've been given. The stage is as wide as you make it. It becomes a new world when you bring this kind of unlimited freedom into what you're creating. But it takes practice. I'm not going to tell it doesn't. It takes years of learning, discarding, listening, discovering all over again. But the more you decide to let nothing stand in your way. Let nothing hold you back—a new 'calm' will come. A confidence will take over. You'll become even more daring. More fearless. Yes, there's this kind of strength inside you—a simplicity in motion. It has its own natural rhythm—and you'll discover it as long as you're willing to breathe into the balance you're seeking. It's waiting to be released in ways you never thought possible.

That's why the theater—the art of telling stories—is a visible truth. When the audience comes—they find their balance in the world through you.

Take your time to experience and listen to Maya Angelou reading "On the Pulse of Morning," the melodies of Mozart's *Symphony No. 41*, W.C. Handy's "St. Louis Blues," tribal dances at an indigenous community Powwow, study the brushstrokes of Faith Ringgold and John Singer Sargent, the free-flowing lines of Elizabeth Catlett's sculpture and Zaha Hadid's architecture, the movements of Bill T. Jones, and the notes flowing through the air of "Amazing Grace" sung by Jessye Norman.

These are just a few timeless gifts of wonder inviting you to flow with the eternal. As you experience them, let them come into your cells, your sinews, and move you physically. Give yourself over to the muse within you. Once you decide to release all obstacles in your path—you'll discover what's drawing you forward to allow you to become all that you're meant to be. The balance you seek is like opening the palm of your hand and letting molecules rest gently inside.

Achieving this kind of balance is what allows creation to take place. It's a necessary part of what occurs in the 'Creation Room'—bringing forth the deepest humanity inside yourself. In that instant, the flow of nature in every molecule and all eternal life surrounds you—and you bring it with you onto the stage—and it surrounds you every single moment.

When you're doing the work you love, you're most in balance. That's where you'll find the faith you need. The confidence in 'knowing' you're bringing more 'light' into this world.

TEN

Telling the Story

How far can you see? How high? How deep? When Michelangelo stood before a block of marble, hammer, and chisel in hand, beyond logic, he held an unconquerable faith in his ability to look into the stone. When he did—he saw the figure of Moses. All Michelangelo had to do was bring him into being. He began chipping away until he appeared. His gift of storytelling lay in how facile his ability was to allow his natural gifts to merge with his craft. The story he had to tell came to life, and his fingertips followed. Every one of his instincts obeyed—allowing molecules to fly. They knew exactly what to do. The flow was all in sync with every stroke he made.

What makes a story worth telling? What makes a story worth listening to? So many stories are told every day. Ultimately, it's how well it's told that makes you remember it, that you want to hear it again and again. Stories come from many different sources and hold within them an idea that captures the imagination. The heart. The soul. They can be about redemption, perseverance, courage, sacrifice for country, the power of love, right over wrong—and so much more. They hold the secrets of the universe. Revealing a truth we can no longer turn away from.

How do stories come? They whisper to you. They tell you what must be told. They hide in your dreams, and when they come, they linger in your subconscience, marinating. They come to tear away the 'mask' that hides each of us from one another. Remember, storytelling's not about repeating 'what we already know'—but drawing your audience into a journey of Transformation—tapping deep into their imagination.

Sometimes a writer's written a solo play, and they need a performer to perform in it. Other times, the performer and writer are one and the same, or the performer has adapted another's creation and created a new one. When you choose to tell your story—the stronger the reason, the stronger it will resonate. And it'll be told again and again. Cascading into the mind and the body of the audience—staying in their memories—touching the deepest places within their heart. Sometimes it'll go even deeper into the inner recesses and climes of their gut. Deep into their soul. Illuminating and transcending all time and space.

What makes you remember a story? Was it the way it was told? The performer acting in it? The writing? Or a combination of all three? What images captured your imagination that you've never forgotten? These are things you need to think about. You see, a pattern emerges in storytelling—a wave takes the action further and further. One of the most beautiful things about creating your own solo performance on stage is how far you can take the audience to so many different places on a journey they'll never forget. Having them meet many interesting people. Because the eye, the ear, the heart of the audience is open—willing to go with you. Joining together to go wherever you're willing to take them.

During my solo play, when Clurman sees bridges crossing the Seine river and the sky above him in Paris—so does the audience. When Stella Adler meets Stanislavski—they want to find out what's going to happen next. Stories are spoken images becoming visible in the moment because you bring them to life. That's your gift. At that moment, they see what you see.

During my play, Clurman is constantly telling stories. It's the same as it is with you—it's in our DNA to tell stories. Clurman grew up reading and hearing stories told to him. So have I. Many of us have. That's why storytelling's a part of our everyday existence. Clurman gets an intense enjoyment from telling the stories he does. He also knows that if these stories are *not* told—there will honestly be something missing in the world. The need is that great.

As a storyteller, once you let the organic process flow through you—turning your thoughts into action, into behavior, into language—you let loose a genuine impulse—as natural as the wind blowing through the forest. The wind's invisible, but you can certainly see the effect it has everywhere it travels. Your solo performance will have that same kind of effect. It's a collaboration between you and the audience happening because of the human connection taking place.

That's one of the reasons I thoroughly enjoy performing to audiences around the world who have different histories and cultures than we have. For many of them, they practically have no idea who Clurman is or what he's come to say. That's why the moment holds so much promise. I'm not there to tell them how to think. That's not why I've come. But to let the molecules go where they will—and a lot of the time, they're picked up in the most-subtlest ways. It becomes an unspeakable bond ushering in a 'heart' connection. Touching the core of everything we share in common. As fragile as the strand of a spider's web or as tangled as a beehive.

Even if it's been claimed there are only seven basic plots—a quest, voyage and return, rags to riches, rebirth, defeating evil, comedy, and tragedy—we're who we are because of our shared stories. In reality, I think it's even more than that. It's our desire to hear them over and over again because they keep adding to our collective memory, teaching us how to live from day to day.

Is it true that a lot of good stories begin with a question? A 'what if'? They could just as well begin with a discovery, a loss, or something bizarre. Remember, a story is just as important as who the storyteller is and why it's being told. That's one of the biggest questions you always have to address. While it's true that a lot of stories have moral lessons within them, what's at stake makes all the difference.

What's your personal feeling about what words mean? How important are they to you? Can one word change a story just as much as two? Think of the images that immediately come to your mind with just one word, whatever it happens to be. You see, our mind is an 'image-maker.' We can't help ourselves. We're constantly throwing images at ourselves. Memories. Thoughts. All day long. All night long. Take a day and consciously try and hear every single word that comes out of your mouth. Take notice of the words that you write down or type out. The words you read. Examine why images and the words you hear in your dreams come to you. You'll begin to see how powerful words are transforming you every single day.

Of course, words can have a double or even a triple meaning and mean something entirely different from one culture to the next. And where would we be without the words we hear in songs. Of course, there's always the meaning behind a word. Take at a simple phrase like: 'the pursuit of happiness.' That can mean so many different things when you consider what the word 'happiness' means.

Herbert Kretzmer, the librettist of *Les Miserables*, said: "Words have resonance within a culture; they have submarine strengths and meanings." It's apt that he uses the metaphor of a submarine because, in a sense, words travel through many different layers, down different paths, and all of a sudden, everything changes. That's the effect words have when they hit us in places in our viscera—in our consciousness. We've also seen the destructive power of words throughout history—and how transcendent and life-giving words can be used to help change the world for the better.

So much of the expression of a word is communicated physically. Watch people from different countries like Italy, Russia, or India—words are always accompanied by a hand gesture or a head movement. A lot of the time, we 'act' like we know what a word means. But most of the time, when I ask an actor what a particular word means, they come up with another word without getting to what it really means to their being. When you're not sure, take the time to look up the meaning of a word and find out what it really means to you. Notice how a word changes completely when it's given a certain stress. How a stream of words sound when they're coupled with a rhythm changing the entire dramatic impact—especially when a strong emphasis is given to a particular syllable.

A perfect example is the way Lin Manuel Miranda expresses himself as Alexander Hamilton in *Hamilton, the musical*, or how Lucky speaks in *Waiting for Godot*. Two entirely different individuals but the need to say what they have to creates an unstoppable rush of dialogue. Each word building on top of the next, leading to a climax. Be aware where there's a need for loudness or softness. A high or a low pitch. Every thought we have colors the meaning and the way we use words.

Watch what happens when a flow of words stops and begins again during a pause or a silence. A shift like that can create a dramatic tension changing the momentum. Notice different nuances and intonations that solo performers use with their voice and body. When they're 'in love'—telling another person how they love them—every word is coated with the bliss they feel inside—almost occurring unconsciously. Recognize how extreme emotions play upon a word—stretching it—shaking it beyond recognition. See how far words are carried through the air, literally vibrating—scattering in every direction or like a laser-focused in a steady stream.

Even if there are probably seven thousand languages in the world today, solo performance is a language all its own, giving us a way to reach each other. Look how humor affects how words are spoken, especially when they come from comedians and comediennes through the art of telling a joke. So much of it has to do with timing. Watch how the story is set up. Look at the storytelling by John Leguizamo, Bill Irwin on stage, or Charlie Chaplin in film. How they use their body to tell the story is an entire language of its own.

It's been said some actors have an 'ear' for a particular dialogue. The creator of M*A*S*H, Larry Gelbart, in my book *CREATE!* talks about how a performer can pick up a script and know exactly how it should be delivered. He says:

"When I write, I'm hearing the dialogue in a specific way, and when I'm reading what I wrote, I also hear it in a specific way. Now I have had actors, to name a few, like Alan Alda and George C. Scott, with whom I shared the same 'ear.'" What is that exactly? An 'ear' for dialogue? It's a 'learned' craft. A sensibility that comes into an actor or an actress who's developed their instrument over many years of practice and performing—and can immediately identify with the intention and rhythm of what individual's ideas are expressing in their action.

Listen to the way Phylicia Rashad speaks as Aunt Ester in August Wilson's *Gem of the Ocean* or André De Shields in *Hadestown*, Stephen Lang in *Beyond Glory*, Tovah Feldshuh in *Golda's Balcony*, or Christopher Plummer in *Barrymore*. Examine how they fill the inside of a word. Feel the power of their voice. Sometimes it may seem as if the dialogue they're speaking carries within it something so personal, and yet, at the same time, connected to all the ages.

Take the time every day to read poetry. Make it a practice. If you're already doing it—good for you! Couple the experience of reading poetry with reading a new play every day. Constantly feed your talent—your soul—allowing it to flower into all it's meant to be. Understand how carefully certain words have been chosen when you read great poets. How they string words together like chimes making the most perfect notes, causing the reader to step into another world through their heart. Of course, poetry was planted in our subconscious over years and years by our teachers reading to us rhymes as a child, contributing to the development of our own natural rhythm and creativity. In grade school, I began writing poetry bringing me into a deeper realm of consciousness, expressing the wonder of life.

Take a leap and write a haiku. If you haven't discovered what a haiku is, learn about its beauty and simplicity. I'm sure you may have your favorite poets you read. Study the use of imagery by reading poets such as Maya Angelou, Gwendolyn Brooks, Billy Collins, Lawrence Ferlinghetti, Eduardo C. Garza, Federico Garcia Lorca, Toni Morrison, Pablo Neruda, Edgar Allen Poe, Adrienne Rich, Rumi, Shakespeare, Carmen Tafolla, Apriana Taylor, Sir Derek Walcott, Walt Whitman, and Yevgeny Yevtushenko. Take a look at many of the young poets writing today like Sandra Beasley, Wendy Chen, and Donte Collins. Each voice like no other. Showing you how language can be a window into the soul.

Like a shower of leaves falling from out of the sky—new phrases are born every generation. New expressions. New words. Changing the way we tell stories. This is how Virginia Woolf approached words asking: "How can we combine the old words in new orders so that they survive so that they create beauty so that they tell the truth? That is the question . . . Undoubtedly, they like us to think, and they like us to feel before we use them; but they also like us to pause, to become unconscious. Our consciousness is their privacy; our darkness is their light."

Where someone's born makes a huge difference in how they express themselves. For example, Clurman grew up on the lower East Side in New York City, but then his family moved to the Bronx. Definitely impacting how he spoke the rest of his life, how he enunciated his words. Some people grow up speaking one language—and then learn another, it clearly affecting the way they speak. Stella Adler assumed a regal and precise way of speaking. So much, in fact, people thought she was British. She'd politely correct them: "Oh no dear, just affected.

Listen to the arching rhythms of Martin Luther King, Jr. How he builds phrase after phrase, sweeping you up because his words fly into a natural rhythm joining with how you hear them, taking you higher and higher. Watch Amanda Gorman, the youngest inaugural poet in American history, as she reads her poem, "The Hill We Climb," especially how she punctuates her phrases with life-asserting energetic gestures.

Be aware of where someone's voice is located. Is it in the mask of their face? Some people speak, and the sound stays close to their mouth, and they barely move their lips. Others, it's in their nose. Most people don't take a full breath, which affects the tempo and the number of words they speak.

Of course, as someone ages, it will also have a distinct effect. Watch and listen to Hal Holbrook as Mark Twain in *Mark Twain Tonight!* How the tempo and sound of his voice change when he tells a story as a young Huckleberry Finn. Stephen Lang transforms himself into eight different veterans in his solo play, *Beyond Glory*—each with an entirely different and distinct persona, and he's created an authentic voice for each person.

During my solo play *LET IT BE ART!*—Clurman is seventy-nine years old. However, when he goes back in time and gives a Talk during the Great Depression, he's thirty years old. So, his tone, body gestures, and energy changes back to how he was at that age. However, he's still seventy-nine telling the story. Several individuals come alive through Clurman's telling of his life story, such as Stella Adler, Robert Edmond Jones, Alfred Stieglitz, Lee Strasberg—even Jacqueline Kennedy Onassis. Each existing as real as Clurman is.

Clurman's boundless energy and volcanic passion at his age of nearly eighty were unforgettable. This is essential to keep in mind, especially if you're becoming someone who's different in age, demeanor, and temperament than yourself. This is where your power of observation comes in. To take in how people of all ages, whether they're one or one hundred, behave and change to communicate what's inside of them.

At times you may notice how certain phrases or the same words are repeated over and over again in a song or in the dialogue of a play. Through their repetition, patterns emerge from the words themselves into harmonies and melodies. You can especially hear it in drumbeats. When these words or phrases come at you, over and over, it's referred to as 'semantic satiation.' Meaning our mind's now hearing sounds, not necessarily the words themselves. So what's occurring is we're becoming part of the repetition, almost unconsciously. Everything building on what you just heard the moment before. Unconsciously, you become 'transformed' through this repetition.

We're living through an extraordinary moment. Several theater-makers have chosen to create life-changing dramas by adapting real-life documents—using words found in transcripts from actual events that have occurred, transforming them into what is referred to as 'documentary' plays. Familiarize yourself with how the stories have been shaped. Powerful works by Anna Deavere Smith, Dael Orlandersmith, and V (formerly Eve Ensler), are a direct line stretching back to the Ancient Greeks, wrestling with the same issues we face today. That all human beings have certain unalienable rights. Is there a way past injustice? Can we free ourselves from our deep-seated fury and prejudices that lead us to war? How do we come to terms with what tears us apart as human beings?

It was a revelatory experience watching *The Exonerated* by Jessica Blank and Erik Jensen, not only because injustice was laid bare, but it painfully asked each one of us: How does society correct a wrong done to a human being? Blank and Jensen created another play, *Coal Country*, using riveting accounts by surviving miners and their families about the mining tragedy at the Upper Big Branch mine in West Virginia in 2010.

When Moises Kaufman and members of the Tectonic Theater Project staged *The Laramie Project* about the 1988 murder of Matthew Shepard in Laramie, Wyoming, we, in the audience, became witnesses on a shattering journey of evil, acceptance, and forgiveness. Powerful experiences like these performed before us by living, breathing human beings teaching us at the moment to look deeper at ourselves. You have the power to choose to either go in that direction through your solo performance or to choose another way of storytelling. It's all entirely in your hands.

When I've experienced plays created by artists from different countries at international festivals—a vast majority of them are done with a few words and sometimes even none—performed in masked pieces, mime, and dance. One of the most powerful 'word-less' performances I've experienced was a play, *Andre & Dorine,* created by Spain's Kulunka Teatro. Using only large sculptured life-sized masks and their expressive bodies, Jose Dault, Rikarte Insausti, and Edu Carcamo told the entire story of Andre and Dorine's love—without the use of words. Everything they did on stage tells us the story of their relationship and how aging and the creeping effect of Alzheimer's disease changed their lives. Leaving everyone in the audience uplifted by their storytelling. Transformation—in the truest sense of the word—sweeping us into another time and place.

With every breath you take—every heartbeat—you're given a new day to transform the world. Every experience you have is constantly adding up to who you are at this moment. A lot of the time you may not even be aware of the change occurring. That's why it's necessary to make a conscious effort to shed old or bad habits. Listen carefully to every word that comes out of your mouth. Always invite the 'Law of Attraction.' Shake up your spirit! Unleash all your molecules! That's your gift as a storyteller. Yes, it's a responsibility and a blessing. But it's yours! Through every discovery process you go on—through every rehearsal—in every performance—creation is taking place. Pulsating. Breathing through you. Allow it to come through the organic process of the 'Art of Transformation. It will be both illuminating and life-changing. How far are you willing to go!

Allow yourself every day to be nurtured by the gifts of nature. Keep finding newer and newer ways to tell the stories that mean the most to you.

ELEVEN

Having the Vision to Fly Solo

In this chapter, you're going to hear from twenty-two performers who chose to perform in a solo play in their own words from interviews that I personally conducted with them. About their commitment to the craft. What shapes their work. How they transformed themselves. Each performer chose to bring to an audience an opportunity to step into a world we would never experience, except through a singular life-changing solo performance.

ADRIENNE BARBEAU
SUSAN CLAASSEN
BILLY CRUDUP
OLYMPIA DUKAKIS
KAREN ETEROVICH
HERSHEY FELDER
MARGA GOMEZ
SPALDING GRAY
JULIE HARRIS
ANITA HOLLANDER
STEPHEN LANG
TONY LO BIANCO
LAURENCE LUCKINBILL
ANGELICA PAGE
CHRISTOPHER PLUMMER
RONALD RAND
SABERA SHAIK
LIBBY SKALA
ELIZABETH VAN DYKE
V (FORMERLY EVE ENSLER)
JEAN-CLAUDE VAN ITALLIE
BEN VEREEN

ADRIENNE BARBEAU

Ms. Barbeau has starred in numerous films, television shows, concert performances, musicals, and plays. A best-selling author and recording artist, she received a Tony Award nomination and a Theatre World Award for her creation of Rizzo in the original Broadway production of *Grease*. Off-Broadway, she played Judy Garland in a one-woman show written by Billy Van Zandt, *The Property Known as Garland.* In 2015, she played Berthe, Pippin's grandmother, in the National Tour of *Pippin*. Ms. Barbeau made her Broadway debut as Tevye's second daughter, Hodel, in *Fiddler on the Roof.* She played Beatrice Arthur's daughter, Carol, in *Maude*. Her other television appearances include *A.J. and the Queen, Carnivale, Criminal Minds, Drew Carey, Revenge, Sons of Anarchy, General Hospital, and Grey's Anatomy*. Ms. Barbeau's film appearances include *ARGO, The Fog, Escape From New York, Creepshow, Swamp Thing, Cannonball Run, The Chain, For the Love of Jesse, Unearth,* and *Eagle and the Albatross* with Dan Lauria and K-Pop star Amber Liu.

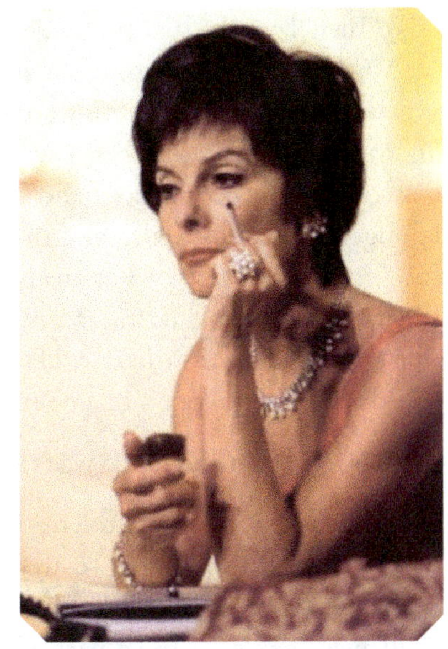

Adrienne Barbeau as Judy Garland in *The Property Known as Garland* (Courtesy Danny Sanchez.)

▪ **Why did you want to play Judy Garland?**

"I didn't want to play her initially. I began by listening to tapes Judy had recorded about her life. She was making notes for a proposed autobiography. It was just about her darkest hour. When I listened to them, I thought a play about this isn't something I want to do; it wouldn't make for a fun evening as an actress. So I put it aside. But when Billy finished writing the script and I read it—it was totally unlike what I had anticipated; it was great material for an actor."

"Well, when we did a workshop production of the play for four performances because Billy wanted to hear what we had and to see how the audience would respond—those performances led to people saying they wanted to invest in the show."

▪ How did you begin to work on the role?

"I read everything I could find, and there's a lot of material, all the biographies, and Lorna Luft's autobiography. I watched Judy's movies, and most importantly, her television appearances. I really drew from the videos of her appearances on various talk shows with Mike Douglas, Johnny Carson, Merv Griffin, Jack Parr. I tried to get my sense of her as much as possible."

"Then I worked with a dialect coach. Judy Garland was trained to speak by MGM, with a mid-continental way of speaking; I wanted to capture that as much as I could. I wasn't doing an impersonation. I didn't watch everything with an eye toward imitating her. I was trying to represent the way she moved. She was very physical with her hand movements, her body movements. They were strong, sharp, and specific, and that's not me, so I had to work on those things."

"I also discovered what an incredible sense of humor she had, what a wit she had. She was a fantastic raconteur, a fabulous storyteller. That's a quality you don't find in a lot of women when we think of movie stars from the 1940s. She could tell a story like no one else. That fascinated me."

▪ What kind of a challenge was it playing Judy Garland?

It was a challenge finding the reality of it, fulfilling it. The added challenge was knowing people knew her so well and expected certain things; they expected her to be a certain way. The way she uses herself, her mannerisms. That was a challenge, making those a part of myself, so I wasn't thinking of them when I was performing."

▪ How did you prepare before you came on stage?

"Because I drank a lot of juice on stage, I went to the bathroom before I came on stage! It's supposed to be wine, but it's cranberry juice. They were playing 1960s tunes in the theater, so I was usually dancing as the lights in the theater went down. I took a nap when I got to the theater. I needed all the energy I could get for when I got out there on stage."

▪ What did you want to get across to the audience in telling her story?

"That she was a survivor; that she had an incredible spirit. She was not solely the tortured soul we all think of as Judy Garland. She continued on, in spite of what was thrown at her, in spite of what happened in her life. She loved her audiences more than anything in the world; from there is where she drew her strength."

SUSAN CLAASSEN

Susan Claassen has been the Managing Artistic Director of the Invisible Theatre in Tucson, Arizona, for over fifty years. A versatile actress, she has performed as Edith Head in *A Conversation with Edith Head*, a solo play co-written with Paddy Calistro, around the world in over five hundred performances, including London's West End, Russia, Belize, the Republic of Georgia's GIFT Festival, across America at the Carrie Hamilton Theatre at The Pasadena Playhouse, North Carolina Stage, New York City's National Arts Club, and at many festivals and art centers. Ms. Claassen received an LA Stage Alliance Ovation nomination and a San Francisco Bay Area Critics Association nomination.

■ **How did touring *A Conversation with Edith Head* begin for you?**

"The opportunity to create a theatrical performance based upon Edith Head has been a dream come true. I first got the idea when I was watching a biography of Edith Head; I literally did a 'double-take.' My physical resemblance to her seemed uncanny. The more I watched, the more I knew there was a story to be told. My research indicated that no theatrical production had ever been done on her, so I contacted The Motion Picture and Television Fund, and they

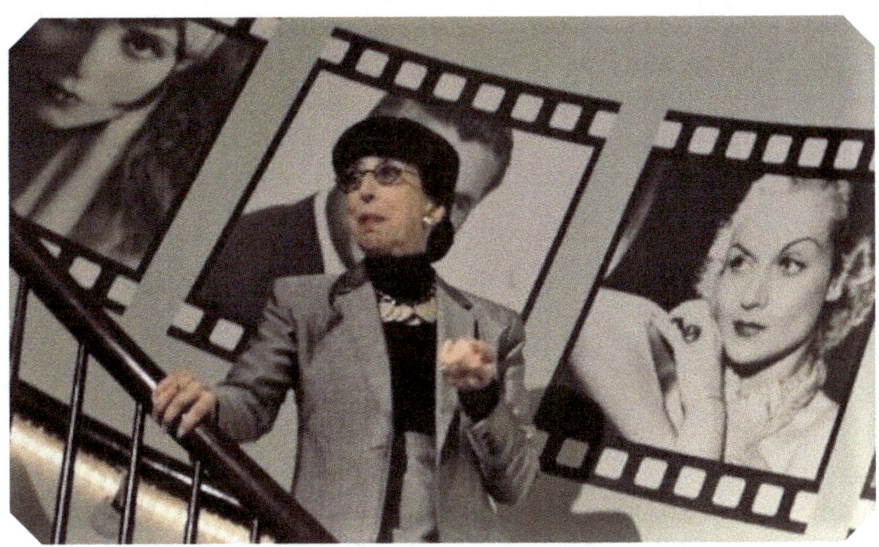

Susan Claassen as Edith Head in *A Conversation with Edith Head.* (Courtesy Susan Claassen.)

granted me permission to pursue the project. I read anything I could find, and I read Paddy Calistro's *Edith Head's Hollywood.*

"I located Paddy in Santa Monica, placed a phone call, and it was kismet. At our first meeting, we knew the connection was right and agreed to collaborate. Paddy had inherited thirteen hours of taped interviews with Edith Head—it was truly a gift from heaven.

"*A Conversation with Edith Head* is based upon the words and thoughts of all of her 'Edith-isms.' In her six decades of costume design, she worked on 1,131 motion pictures, dressed the greatest stars of Hollywood, received thirty-five Academy Award nominations and an unprecedented eight Oscars."

▪ **How has the audience played a role in your performing?**

"What's wonderful is I'm never alone on stage—the audience is my partner. I'm able to improvise and personalize each performance depending on the audiences' questions and the locale. Some of those who come to the play really think I'm Edith Head until they calculate how old she would be! It's a privilege to keep someone's legacy alive. In this case, I like to think of it as a perfect fit!"

▪ **What continues to make performing such an integral part of your life?**

"My passion for what I do. I don't equate success with where you choose to live but rather with how you choose to live your life. Tucson has provided me with an extraordinary quality of life, both personally and professionally.

"Ralph Waldo Emerson said, "A friend may well be reckoned the masterpiece of nature." Well, my life has been graced by having the opportunity to work with so many masterpieces. Their talent, passion, and compassion never cease to amaze and inspire me!"

BILLY CRUDUP

Billy Crudup appeared on Broadway receiving the Tony Award for the first two parts of *The Coast of Utopia*. His other Broadway appearances include *Waiting for Godot* with Sir Ian McKellan and Sir Patrick Stewart, receiving Tony nominations for *The Elephant Man*, *Arcadia*, and *The Pillowman*. Among his many appearances Off-Broadway include playing nineteen characters in David Cale's one-man play, *Harry Clarke*, receiving a Drama Desk Award and an Obie Award, *The Metal Children, America Dreaming*, *The Resistible Rise of Arturo Ui*, and *Measure for Measure* at NY Shakespeare Public Theatre. Mr. Crudup's film and television include as Cory Ellison in *The Morning Show*, receiving the 2020 Emmy Award and Critics Choice Television Award, Jack in *Hello Tomorrow*, Eric MacLeish in *Spotlight*, *Jackie*, *Jesus' Son*, *Without Limits*, *Princess Mononoke*, *Almost Famous*, *Mission Impossible III*, *Public Enemies*, *20th Century Women*, *Gypsy*, *Youth in Oregon*, Russell Hammond in *Almost Famous*, and Will Bloom in *Big Fish*.

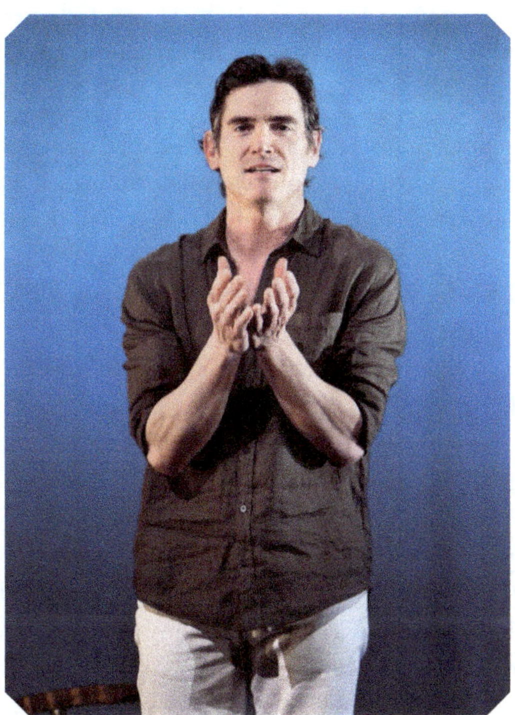

Billy Crudup in *Harry Clarke* by David Cale.
(Courtesy Carol Rosegg.)

▪ **What makes it especially rewarding and also challenging being an actor?**

"It is a privilege and a meaningful experience to have a chance to find a creative voice in one of the performing arts, with the potential to expand the human experience and the reception of it. I feel extraordinarily grateful. One of the things I realize, as I get older, which is so worthwhile, is the aspect of collaboration and impressing on your creative boundaries of articulating the human experience.

"As an actor, I'm most interested in how I interpret the material that's been created, and I gravitate to these source materials that exceed my own intellect and capacity, at the opportunity to expand my own understanding, my creative limits, and my personal growth. And that through that understanding and the experiences you're going through, you realize you're occupying different spheres in your life. You go from someone who's in an entry place, moving to someone with a bit more experience, to someone who has become a veteran from all of their experiences. You become a father, a citizen in the community; you're becoming a different person. As a performer, I feel quite blessed that I've been given the opportunity to explore my own incarnations."

▪ **How have you learned to lessen the 'critical' or 'judgmental' voice we all carry within us, to be in the moment for an audition—in your meetings with directors?**

"One of the primary oppositional forces to people trying to be self-aware is what happens when self-awareness makes you becomes self-conscious. Because of your own self-expectations or what other people will think of you. You have to confront these experiences through a proactive approach. For me, it's been one of mindfulness—and mediation has been a huge tool because it's all about not becoming attached to those thoughts.

"When I have an audition, I always bear in the mind that this is my chance to play the part. I give it my best effort and use the tools I have. Of course, there's not a whole lot that you can do to the outcome. At that moment, your career may not be going as well as you'd like, or the casting director doesn't know you, there could be a million reasons, or maybe it's something you couldn't possibly know about why you may or may not get the role. Challenging yourself with any kind of self-conscious thoughts can seriously hamstring you. I focus on what I have. I let my mind be busy concentrating on my breath, embrace the opportunity, whatever the circumstances are, to keep my feelings off of any self-doubt."

▪ **Are there certain things you've discovered in the art of collaboration with a director and the cast?**

"Absolutely. I'm always bearing in mind certain things in the rehearsal process. If I'm in a room of five people and you know you'll be working together for several weeks, you know the stage manager, the assistant stage manager, you begin to recognize features inherent in the collaboration. You will notice a shift that may turn out to be monumental to the rest of the cast and the play. It usually happens in a subtle way over time, as we keep whittling away at the play, and all of a sudden, the character comes into view. It's as if you were taking a sledgehammer to a block of stone, hoping something miraculous would happen. It's also rare that a lot of what you come up with really has a lasting impact. That being said, all those ideas you keep coming up with during the process are really important because they keep you asking questions. That's one of the greatest requisites I learned from working with Ron van Lieu at NYU. Questions are one of the actors' most profound tools by the time you get to the third week of rehearsals.

"It's during the first day of rehearsal you have all this energy of invention. As you continue through the first week, you're answering questions that are pretty obvious, and your mind goes to certain references, but you're still working in a superficial way. By week three, you're actually getting to the specificity of what you're doing, leading to the re-creating of a human life.

"There was a line in *Oedipus*, which I did with Frances McDormand, to the effect: "If I had two thousand years to explain what was going on in my head, I wouldn't be able to do it." It's true; there are a thousand ways towards specificity. It's up to the actor to take the time to refine behavior, to keep asking questions. It's a matter of persistence to keep coming up with ideas or watershed ideas that may change the entire tone of the piece that are fundamental to its outcome. The momentum of a production has a life of its own. You must continue being inventive and working with a good director, and they'll give you the opportunity to discover the things that become important to you. But it's all not just an ongoing creative expression—everything always has to be in service to the play."

▪ How do you keep yourself centered?

"Rigorous exercise. I have to exercise, and most of the time, handling being a father keeps me both driven and well-centered. It can be so hard under any circumstances, but being involved in the community is really important. We're not telling stories in a vacuum. It's important to be in the world, to know that you're going to try to influence, whether to entertain or to attempt to influence the cultural landscape—to know it's your responsibility to be engaged with who the audience is that you're making an influence on."

OLYMPIA DUKAKIS

On Broadway, Olympia Dukakis had starred in a one-woman play, *Rose*, *Who's Who in Hell* and *Social Security*. Her film and television appearances included *Steel Magnolias*, *Moonstruck* receiving an Academy Award, *Sinatra*, *Mr. Holland's Opus*, *The Cemetery Club*, *Cloudburst*, *A Life for a Life*, *The Event*, *In the Land of Women*, *Mighty Aphrodite*, *Joan of Arc*, *Jane Austen's Mafia!*, as Anna Madrigal in *More Tales of the City* receiving an Emmy Award, and starred in and executive-produced *Montana Amazon*. Ms. Dukakis had written her best-selling autobiography, *Ask Me Again Tomorrow: A Life in Progress*, in 2003. A documentary of her life, *Olympia*, was released in 2018.

- **You gave a memorable performance in Martin Sherman's solo play, *Rose*. What were some of the challenges you encountered?**

"It was an incredible challenge for me as an actress. First: the memorizing! I said: "I didn't think I could do it." Then I said: "I don't think I can do it," which developed into "I can't do it," into "Nobody can do it!" I kept taking small bites. I had to trust my sensibilities, my instincts and put my willfulness behind me. Second, figuring out how to do it. A one-woman show I never aspired to do,

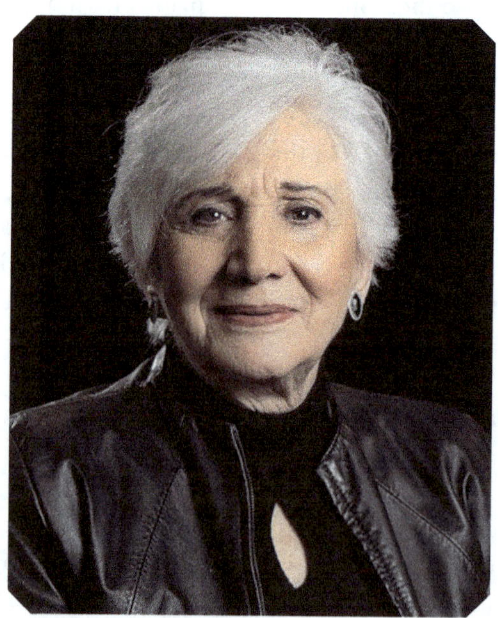

Olympia Dukakis. (Courtesy Neil Grabowsky.)

neither did the director or the writer. We all found our way. I divided the play into seven sections. It felt like the seven gates in the Sumerian myth, pretty mystical. Third, holding it all together. You have so much information in your body. All I was able to do was drink water and eat yogurt. It was Rose's effort to know who she is in the world. What happens to her as a result of a telephone call.

"Everything is evoked in her—the past, the present is rattling about. She's a woman who never felt in any one place; she felt separate, apart in her own family, whatever she was, in Warsaw, and later when she was in the Holocaust, and in America."

- **Who was the audience to you?**

"They were a group of people who came together and knew everything I knew. I counted on their knowing, on their coming with their feelings, their attitudes, their humanness, on their being informed. As a result, there's a tremendous permission to be intimate: what the evening is going to be about, what I'm going to do, where we might go."

- **You have said: "To be open-hearted, you have to trust or be willing to trust—but trust with open eyes. You have to look at the reality of things. Sometimes there's darkness and pain."**

"That's part of life, too. It's about knowing yourself—and what it is to be human."

- **Throughout your life, you've worked with some of the greatest writers in the theater.**

"I've never let go. I'm always wanting to act on the stage. I love acting. I love the process. I don't love the traumas that await me, but one doesn't happen without the other—the dark and the light, the chaos and the order. I'm excited by the ideas, the depth of the characters, the writer. The people I'm going to work with; it's about collaboration. With the right people, something lively is going to happen. I love to go back to a play a second or a third time. You become more informed by life. Your vulnerability to the play deepens your willingness to take in the play. We defend ourselves against the depth out of fear of failing, wondering if we're going to land on her feet. I did Hecuba twice at A.C.T. and went on to do it a third time. Theater can be a way of evolving if you want it to be."

KAREN ETEROVICH

Her play, *Love Armed: Aphra Behn and her Pen*, has toured across America and internationally, including performances at The Bedlam Theatre during the Edinburgh Fringe Festival. She has also performed as Jane Austen in her solo play, *Cheer from Chawton*, at the Players Club presented by Ronald Rand, at the Mission Theater in Bath, England in 2006, 2010, and 2019, in Jane Austen Festivals. Both solo plays were performed in repertory in Bath in 2007. Her New York appearances include Lady Catherine in *Pride & Prejudice*, Gertrude in *Hamlet*, *The Three Musketeers*, and *The Importance of Being Earnest*, all with the Hudson Warehouse. In regional theater, she has appeared in *Twelfth Night* with the Kings County Shakespeare Company, *Great Expectations* at Indiana Repertory Theater, *The Rover* and *The Cherry Orchard* as part of Cornell University's Resident Professional Acting Company, and the Shakespeare Theater's production of *All's Well That Ends Well* in Washington D.C., directed by Michael Kahn. Ms. Eterovich is currently a founding member and Artistic Associate at the First Flight Theatre Company.

▪ **How did it come about that you wanted to create a play about Aphra Behn?**

"I had seen a number of solo plays produced by Cosmic Leopard Productions Womenkind Festival at the One Dream Theatre in Tribeca. Cosmic Leopard was a collective of female solo artists presenting plays from all over the world, and we helped each other. When I watched solo shows in the festival, good or bad, they were all inspiring. I wondered what makes a solo play work? In 1992,

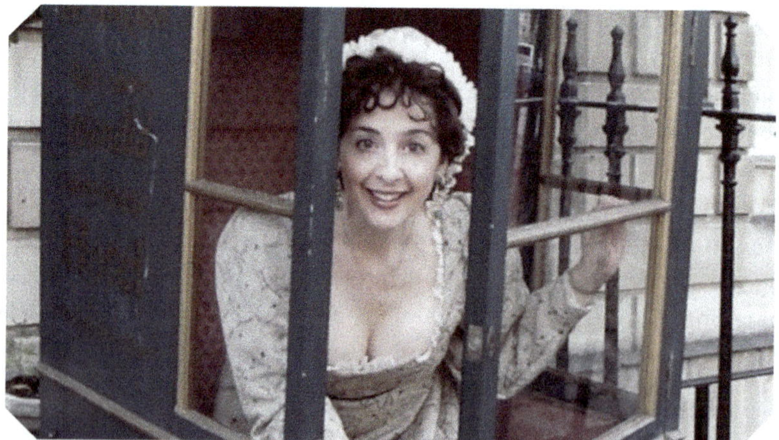

Karen Eterovich as Jane Austen in *Cheer from Chawton*. (Courtesy Karen Eterovich.)

I was cast in a production of *The Rover* by Aphra Behn in Cornell University's Resident Professional Acting Program. At that time, I thought Aphra Behn was a guy; I had never heard of her.

"Since it was a Restoration play, I began to do research. In learning about her, I found out she broke every rule in the 17th century. She was born in 1640 and died at forty-nine years of age. She's considered the first professional English woman writer and originator of the novel in its modern form. People think it was Daniel Defoe, but her "Oroonoko" predates "Robinson Crusoe" by seventeen years. I thought she would make a fantastic one-person show. The first thing I had to ask was: Where's the conflict? Reading more about her, I discovered she had a live-in bisexual lover for nine years. She had been employed by Charles II in the secret service in the Netherlands and had been thrown into prison many times for her debts and her politics. I also read her many poems, and that gave me a window into how she thought. I've been doing the play now for more than twenty years."

■ **In what way did *Love Arm'd* begin?**

"Originally, I had created a five-minute audition piece for the Womenkind Festival. When I met the producers, they asked me how long the play was—I told them it was twenty minutes long. So, I had three months to write the other fifteen minutes! The play was first performed in March of 1994. At the time, people were very excited and wanted to know more, so I did further research and found her 'spy' letters in the library at the University of Louisville. I read most of her plays and all the biographies available. In 1995, for the Womenkind Festival again, *Love Arm'd* grew to forty minutes, and a year later, it was sixty minutes long. In 1996, I was approached to go to International Fringe Festival in Edinburgh, Scotland, so I raised money and went a year later."

■ **What have you learned about performing alone on stage, and how has that changed over the years?**

"In the beginning, it was the fear of 'going-up.' So I forced myself to focus on my objectives. Now I go through a certain process before each performance. Of course, my nerves still get to me, and I ask myself: "Why am I doing this to myself?" I think about the first beat, and I tell myself that I don't know what will happen next. I tell myself to breathe and remain open, to allow the space and the audience to work on me. I've been reading Clurman's *On Directing*, and he states the audience is an implicit collaborator. You can't know what to expect. Every single audience is a living organism, and they'll feed me differently. Grasping this has been frightening but ultimately freeing!"

▪ What do the responses you receive after a performance mean to you?

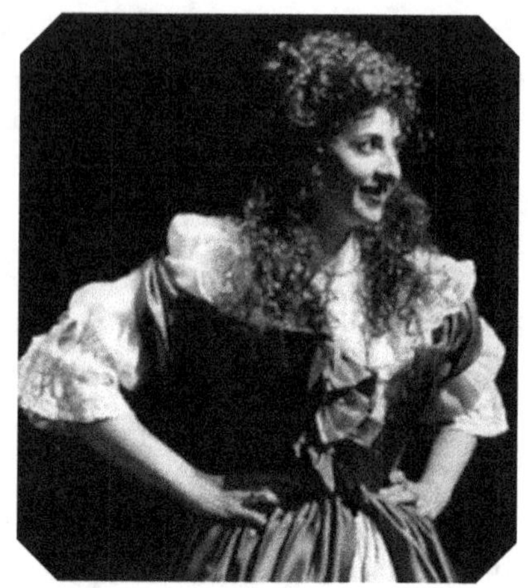

Karen Eterovich as Aphra Behn in *Love Arm'd: Aphra Behn and Her Pen*. (Courtesy Karen Eterovich.)

"I usually have a Q & A period, and most audience members have no idea who Aphra Behn was. It's encouraging to see how they become excited about language. That has always been one of my goals. I feel I've succeeded if they want to learn more about her and read her novels, plays, and poems. I look at Aphra as a heroine. When I've listened to women playwrights being interviewed, many times they'll mention male writers; it's rare to hear them mention a female writer.

"I feel much of our history is lost to us. Aphra Behn wrote more than seventeen plays, more plays than any other playwright in the Restoration period. The only writer as prolific was the poet laureate John Dryden. She was influenced by Shakespeare's plays and the plays of her English contemporaries like Etheridge and Wycherly, as well as by Moliere and Italian Commedia. Communicating Behn's complex Restoration language has been one of the biggest challenges and the poetry in French and Italian. I feel audiences experience emotion on another level when they hear a language they may not be familiar with."

▪ What kind of a transformation do you have to go through to bring Jane Austen to your audiences?

"I usually spend the better part of a day getting ready to perform. Most times, it's easier to put make-up on where I am staying and then go to the theater. To support my voice, I do at least a half-hour of vocal warm-ups. After that, I run the whole play or sections of the text that I want to investigate before the show. I run the dance, and I set my props. I enter her world. I think about what might have happened to her on that day—and what she feels about the approaching night with her family might bring to her. The play is set on the eve of Jane Austen's birthday—December 1816—so she's anticipating a good time. Making the entire audience members of Jane Austen's family adds to the excitement and intimacy for me. Jane's been a part of my life since 2005, and I feel I know her."

HERSHEY FELDER

Hershey Felder has played over 6,000 performances of his self-created solo productions at some of the world's most prestigious theatres. His shows include *George Gershwin Alone* on Broadway and West End's Duchess Theatre, *Monsieur Chopin*, *Beethoven*, Leonard Bernstein in *Maestro*, Franz Liszt in *Musik*, *Lincoln: An American Story*, *Our Great Tchaikovsky*, *Puccini*, Sholem Aleichem in *Before Fiddler*, Claude Debussy in *A Paris Love Story*, and Sergei Rachmaninoff in *Anna & Sergei* and as Irving Berlin. His compositions and recordings include "Aliyah," "Concerto for Piano and Orchestra," "Fairytale, a musical," "Les Anges de Paris," "Suite for Violin and Piano," "Song Settings," "Saltimbanques for Piano and Orchestra," "Etudes Thematiques for Piano," and "An American Story for Actor and Orchestra." Mr. Felder is the adaptor, director, and designer for the internationally performed 'play with music,' *The Pianist of Willesden Lane* with Mona Golabek, producer and designer for the musical, *Louis and Keely: 'Live' at the Sahara*, directed by Taylor Hackford, and writer and director for *Flying Solo*, with opera legend Nathan Gunn. He created *Live from Florence*, performing in his many acclaimed solo productions. Mr. Felder has been a scholar-in-residence at Harvard University's Department of Music and is married to Kim Campbell, the first female Prime Minister of Canada.

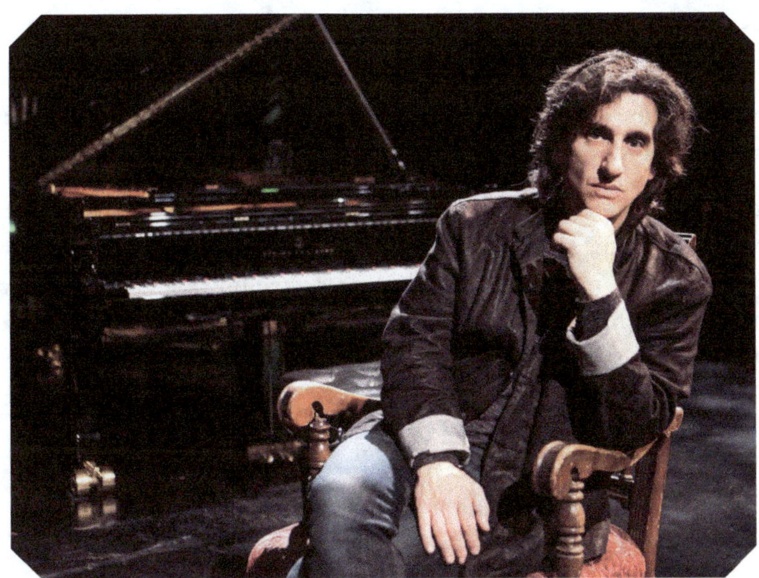

Hershey Felder. (Courtesy Hershey Felder.)

- **Naturally, the music of these great composers speak to you. Why do these particular composers mean so much to you—and how do you begin to allow them to join with you before a performance?**

"While the composer-characters are not the only characters and plays I perform, they have made up the bulk of my performing life, naturally, because as a musician as well as a writer/producer/actor, I am drawn not only to great music but to the process of understanding how great music is created, what makes for 'great music—if there were a specific recipe so many of us would be great composers. Why does some music have staying power, and some not, and above all—I am drawn to humanizing these icons, in that someone like Beethoven was not made of his 5th or 9th symphonies, or many of the other great works, but he was a man who made these great works.

"What of this 'man?' The 'man-part' is of great interest—and so these pieces developed. That said, I am not of the 'hocus-pocus' school of performing, as you say, allowing these 'spirits to join with me for a performance.' I am of the school that knowledge is the only route to creating illusion. The more one knows, the more one studies, the more one rehearses, the more one prepares—the more one will be able to create the illusion of embodying a real person on the stage for that brief two hours. Of course, there is the fact that every word and note must serve to create the full artist—and that too takes a lifetime of study and choice, but it's all part of the process. There is no magic in it—only hard work. The magic comes once the hard work is done, and a character can live and breathe based on preparation."

- **What were some of the most exciting secrets you discovered by stepping into Tchaikovsky and his music at this time in your life?**

"Tchaikovsky's secrets were more heartbreaking than they were exciting. The music is extremely exciting, so brilliantly crafted, such tunes—and an endless well of singable, enjoyable, moving, brilliantly constructed music—is Tchaikovsky. The hard part was learning about the man and the depths of his despair concerning his own sexuality and how it affected his life and by extension—his music."

- **How do you prepare and continue to allow yourself to be open and strong enough for what needs to come through you?**

"It's all about preparation and study. Spending a life as a musician and an actor—always studying and practicing and learning, always working, and again—knowledge, knowledge, knowledge. The only way for a character to come 'through' a performer, or as the case may be the character of the composer coming through the character of music—is to be on an endless journey of discovery—and never stop studying, crafting, shaping, editing, not for one minute."

"Naturally, one has to have the fundamentals, if one is a pianist—one must be able to play, and all that that entails. If one is an actor, one must be able to speak lines, be heard, and communicate—and all that that entails. But once the fundamentals are somewhat in order, it is all about knowledge and exercise—just like the great artists themselves, and then maybe, what one does might hint at what it means to be an artist."

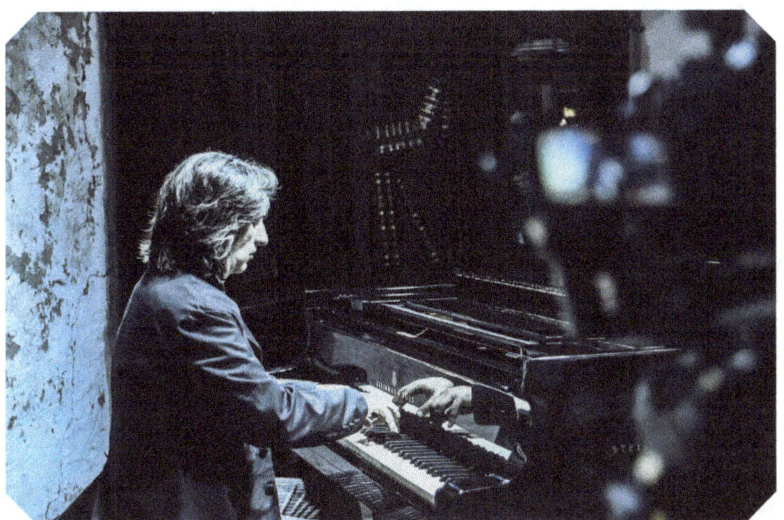

Hershey Felder as Beethoven in *Live from Florence, Hershey Felder Beethoven.* (Courtesy Hershey Felder.)

MARGA GOMEZ

Marga Gomez is a comedian, teaching artist, and writer/performer of thirteen solo plays that have been presented nationally, internationally, and Off-Broadway. Selections from Gomez's work have been published in several anthologies, including *Extreme Exposure*, *HOWL*, *Out Loud & Laughing*, *Contemporary Plays by American Women of Color*, *When I Knew*, and *Out of Character*. Her performances include Off-Broadway and national productions of *The Vagina Monologues* with Rita Moreno. She can be seen in season two of the Netflix series, *Sense8*. At the start of the 2020 pandemic, Gomez pivoted to adapting and presenting her work for live streaming. She has been featured in online theater festivals from New York to San Diego, as well as a five-week virtual run for Brava Theater Center in San Francisco, where she is an artist-in-residence. She is a GLAAD media award winner and recipient of the 2020 CCI Investing in Artists grant. Ms. Gomez teaches how to create a solo performance for the virtual audience to groups and individuals. She was born in New York City to entertainers in the Latino community.

- **You have drawn a great deal from yourself and your family to create your solo plays—plus, you also draw from everything that's happened around you. How have you learned to shape your shows, and what makes the best stories to tell?**

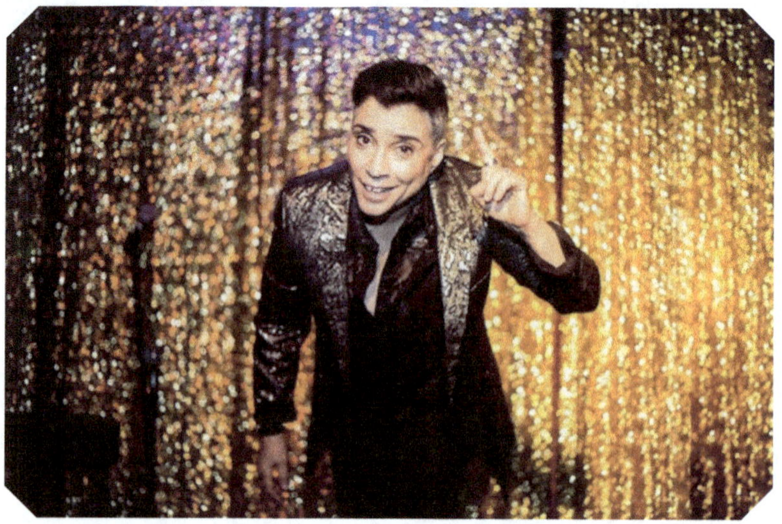

Marga Gomez in *Latin Standards*. (Courtesy Fabian Echevarria.)

"My first solo play, *Memory Tricks*, was written after my mother was diagnosed with early-onset Alzheimer's. Her younger days had been fabulous. *Memory Tricks* was my homage to her in good times and bad. In 1990, I was living in San Francisco, where solo performance was gaining popularity via a venue called "The Marsh." I was working as a comedian and in need of a way to process losing a loved one. I found myself in the right place at the right time, with a pressing need to begin a career as a solo writer/performer. For most of my solo plays, I work with a director who doubles as a dramaturg when it comes to building the structure and finding new meaning in my own life stories.

"For me and my audiences, stories with action, tension, and lessons are the most satisfying. I'm not too interested in excessive or flowery verbiage."

- **You've said your solo play, *Latin Standards*, is a father-daughter story. Were you surprised by what you discovered and what it taught you when you actually performed it?**

"*Latin Standards* was the second solo play I wrote about my dad, who is my greatest influence. I went back to the father-daughter 'well' because it is so deep. His life ended badly and too soon as a result of his demons. I chose to center *Latin Standards* on the most glorious day we ever had together. The process of creating that piece taught me to go towards the light and the win for the story and myself."

- **What have you learned about the ingredients it takes to communicate the passion and humor floating around inside of you, and the simplicity of memory to an audience?**

"Humor is like breathing for me and my family. I need a little irony or satire baked into even the heaviest drama, or I look for the exits. Memory is as complex as present-day and harder to process because there are no second chances. How do we store that data? How do we let go of the baggage? By trying to distill one day from the past into a 70-minute transformative show—you need to be a tough editor.

"As storytellers, we are in community with our audience. Many come to see us for the same reason some go to church. We should be rigorous in creating our pieces as a way to respect the audience—our theatre partner. Before I begin a new solo project, I ask myself: What did I learn, and how can I share it?"

SPALDING GRAY

Spalding Gray was known for the autobiographical monologues that he wrote and performed for the theater in the 1980s and 1990s. His monologues included *Swimming to Cambodia*, receiving a National Book Award, adapted into a film by Jonathan Demme; *Monster in a Box*, directed by Nick Broomfield as a film; *It's a Slippery Slope* at Lincoln Center Theatre; and *Grey's Anatomy*, directed by Steven Soderbergh as a film. His film and television appearances included *Beaches*, *Buckminster Fuller: Thinking Out Loud*, *Kate and Leopold*, *Saturday Night Live*, and *The Nanny*. In 1970, he joined Richard Schechner's experimental troupe, The Performance Group, and he helped co-found the theater company, The Wooster Group. Mr. Gray appeared on Broadway in *The Best Man* and as the Stage Manager in *Our Town*. His books include *Sex and Death at the Age 14* and *A Personal History of the American Theater*. In 2011, *The Journals of Spalding Gray* was published. Steven Soderbergh made a documentary film about Mr. Gray's life, *And Everything is Going Fine*.

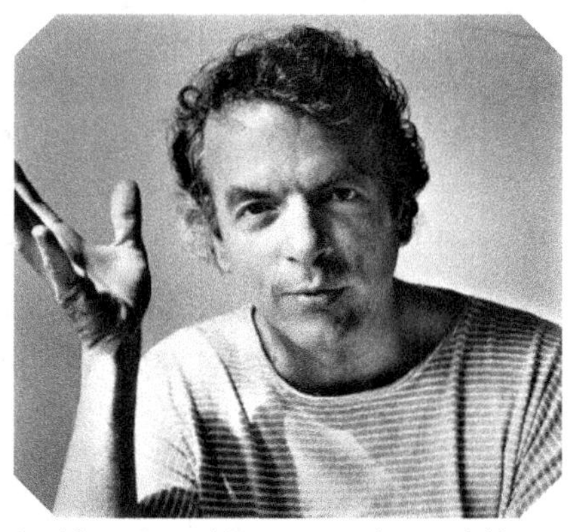
Spalding Gray. (Courtesy Hali Brindel.)

- **How did you develop your rare gift of storytelling with the articulate and powerfully moving capacity to touch the nerve of the audience?**

"I think I began doing it around the time I was in Emerson College. I became more aware of it when I came to New York. I was in a job situation at a secretarial school. I started talking about my day to dishwashers, the Irish cooks, and they enjoyed it. So I naturally fell into it. While I was living with Elizabeth LeCompte in the city, we had no television, and I would do the story of my day to her. It was a natural thing at that time as we were being influenced by Grotowski and Artaud. I became extremely attracted to The Open Theatre, and I also took Joyce Aaron's Workshop. I was open to 'jamming,' a technique where you'd voice a stream of consciousness. I brought in 'the story of my day,' and Joyce asked me, "Who wrote it for you?" I knew I had done something special. This was in 1959. Then The Wooster Group encouraged me. They'd transcribe what I'd say, and they became texts."

- **Julian Beck said: "We have to be a lot like Columbus—to go out and discover and take our audiences on a voyage." Who is the audience for you?**

"Being in front of audiences for thirty years is like a second home. Originally they were like a mother to me; I was 'infertilized' by them. They're such a diverse body, from the age of six like my son to ninety! I've had ethnic mixes and Puerto Rican audience members who would yell out in the middle. There's this dynamic 'happening' occurring, a dialogue of understanding."

- **I'm reminded by what Joseph Chaikin said: "We're made to cherish things we don't even care about and to give up things we fundamentally cherish." How did *Swimming To Cambodia* come about?**

"One could connect all of reality and our sense of reality to a certain transience in all of us. Life is change. We have this tremendous anxiety. We can't find our center. The quest is to find this feeling of silence in the middle of the motion. We labor with that in our material. When I went to India in 1976, I started to keep a journal. I continued writing in it for seven years. *Swimming To Cambodia* was a good example of left-over energy. I was completely full of regret that I had to leave. I was haunted. These images would come up and grow out of it. When I came back to America, I sifted through my imagination, my fascinations, endless dreams. It was a real epic piece, a most complicated piece. It had to be."

- **How do you find a way of maintaining a balance between becoming discouraged and, at the same time, remaining open to finding new ways to express yourself?**

"I think I have found it. Twenty years ago this September, it began. It led me to concentrate on producing good work. It's actually a discipline, a form of meditation, of feeling less threatened, of continual exploration. When I was doing research for *Gray's Anatomy*, I saw these psychic surgeons in the Philippines. Because of my research, I was able to see things I wouldn't normally have seen. That's the kind of openness that's necessary."

- **Why did you decide to confront mortality so deeply in your pieces?**

"It's so much in our conscience. It's denied so much of the time throughout our lives. It's the ultimate task of the poet, what any shaman's or priest's role should be. I like to hope I'm a poet, and I strive to combine it in a way that's not morbid. If my pieces are successful, they're hitting all the chakras, with chance endings that have been built into them. To talk about death is what makes life so poignant, exciting. I wonder who doesn't think about death and how we avoid not thinking about it. After all, it's the 'bottom line' reality. We should give ourselves permission to accept our neurosis. Culture is ultimately neurotic."

JULIE HARRIS

Considered the 'First Lady of the American Theater,' Ms. Harris' many memorable performances on Broadway included Emily Dickinson in *A Belle of Amherst, The Last of Mrs. Lincoln, A Shot in the Dark, Marathon 33, And Miss Reardon Drinks a Little, Forty Carets, The Glass Menagerie, Lucifer's Child, The Lark, I Am a Camera, The Gin Game,* and as Frankie in *A Member of the Wedding,* directed by Harold Clurman. Her film and television work included *East of Eden* opposite James Dean, *I Am a Camera, A Member of the Wedding, The Last Mrs. Lincoln, Harper, Victoria Regina, A Doll's House* with Christopher Plummer, and *Knots Landing.* Ms. Harris won five Tony Awards, three Emmy Awards, a Grammy Award, and an Academy Award nomination. She was awarded the National Medal of Arts, a member of the American Hall of Fame, and a Kennedy Center Honoree.

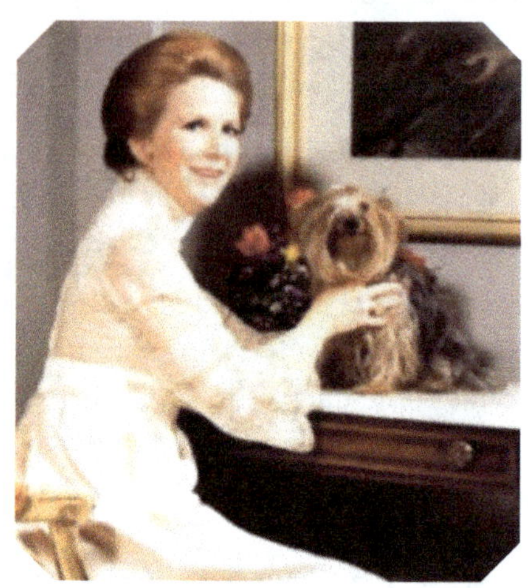

Julie Harris as Emily Dickinson in *The Belle of Amherst.* (Courtesy Stuart-Rodgers Photography.)

- **I think it's fair to say you're a living reflection of a true artist of the theater. What makes your art all the more amazing is how connected the audience becomes to your acting.**

"It's the storyteller's job—the involvement of what you have to be for that time on the stage. It's become more and more important to me as time has gone on to become increasingly simpler and simpler. I strive for that simplicity in my work."

- **I thoroughly enjoyed your inspiring performances as Emily Dickinson in *A Belle of Amherst* and Isak Dinesen in *Lucifer's Child.* What attracted you to want to play them?**

"It was their perception of life. Emily Dickinson led a very sheltered life while Denison's was sophisticated, and she fell in love with a white hunter. Their spirits talked to me. Talking about what they accomplished, and it was the beauty of the writing in the plays. I see the theater as a place that can re-awaken our humanity. That's why it's so important for me to tour with the shows I'm in. The theater has the power to reconnect us back to life."

ANITA HOLLANDER

She has performed across America, Europe, and Asia as an actress, singer, composer, lyricist, director, producer, and teacher. Ms. Hollander premiered composers and playwrights new works at Carnegie Hall, Playwrights Horizons, and New York Shakespeare Festival, where she sang original works of Philip Glass. She received a Helen Hayes Award nomination for the Olney Theatre premiere of *The Fifth Season* and originated the title role in *Gretty Good Time* at Kennedy Center. As a two-time cancer survivor, Ms. Hollander has negotiated over half of her almost six decades performing career on one leg, enlightening the world about disability and as the *National Chair of SAG-AFTRA Performers with Disabilities,* promoting greater visibility and employment for performers with disabilities. The Kennedy Center presented her original one-woman musical, *Still Standing: A Musical Survival Guide for Life's Catastrophes,* and she won the Audience Award at the United Solo Theatre Festival. *Still Standing,* published in an anthology *At the Intersection of Disability & Drama*, has been presented at The White House, Off-Broadway, Disney World, and throughout the world. Her new solo musical, *Spectacular Falls*, premiered on 42nd Street in 2019.

▪ **You began acting professionally when you were quite young—**

"Yes, I had my first professional role at eight years old. I didn't lose my leg until I was twenty-six years old, and then I opened in a show four weeks later. It was

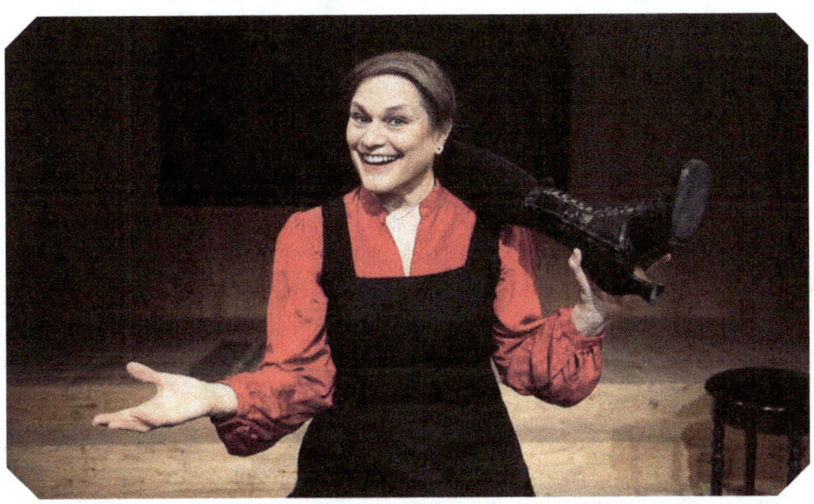

Anita Hollander in *Still Standing.* (Courtesy Andrew Brilliant.)

never a question of whether I would continue singing and acting. Before my amputation, I performed on a brace in Europe as Laura in *The Glass Menagerie* and Evie in *Stop the World I Want to Get Off.* People say I was 'born in a trunk' because nothing seems to be able to stop me from getting on a stage!"

▪ **What was the impetus to create *Still Standing*, and how did you shape it?**

"There were two driving factors. In 1977, while on chemo & radiation, I sang at a coffeehouse while I was a senior at Carnegie Mellon University. The next day, my teacher, Merry Conway, said: "It's nice hearing Joni Mitchell, James Taylor, and others' music, but the audience didn't learn anything about you or what you're going through."

I jokingly asked, "What? So you want me to write my own songs?"

To which she replied: "Yes. That night I wrote what I believed to be the most depressing song in the world, 'The Choice,' just to show her what a mistake her advice was. But instead, she loved it. It became the cornerstone of what—over the next sixteen years—would turn out to be *Still Standing.*

"But my solo show wouldn't have turned out to be *A Musical Survival Guide for Life's Catastrophes,* if not for the death of my dear friend and brilliant Richard Rodgers Award-winning composer, Michael Devon, in 1991. When he was diagnosed with AIDS, he asked me: 'How did you get from *there* to *here*?' Meaning how did I survive cancer. I was tongue-tied.

"After his death, the show became my answer to him and to anyone struggling to survive. Each of the sixteen songs represent a 'tool for survival'—and it became even more relevant during the pandemic than it ever was in twenty-seven years performing it."

▪ **How has your performing the show evolved over the years?**

"The show started out as a traditional-style musical with a full cast and narrative story, entitled *Here I Stand,* performed in a series called *Broadway Tomorrow.* But a musical about someone surviving cancer wasn't popular with producers—so I rewrote it as a solo show with backup voices and performed it at Primary Stages Theatre and at the cabaret, 'Don't Tell Mama.' I recorded the music and took the show out-of-town—sending the tracks ahead online and carry nothing with me—which is terrifically convenient traveling on one leg, especially to places like South Korea and Russia.

"The show evolved even more when I performed for audiences of all ages at Naval bases, a girls' prison, teaching hospitals, temples and churches, schools and colleges, VA Medical Centers, Rehab centers, and film festivals. Adding my sister, Rev. Rachel Hollander, an American Sign Language Interpreter, broadened my audience to deaf and hard-of-hearing people, and more depth of meaning to the show."

▪ **What led you to create your second solo musical, *Spectacular Falls*?**

"I started noticing a trend in my songwriting that I thought might lend itself to a new solo musical: the opposite of standing—falling. Falling is a big part of my life. But I never fall in an ordinary way. I fall spectacularly. Backflip over a turnstile. Crutch falls through a manhole cover on Fifth Avenue, taking me with it. I trip over my own crutches while entertaining my toddler. I fall into a garbage can on my way out of an audition.

"When I fell and broke my hand in front of *Ripley's Believe It or Not* in 2015, I knew I was ready to write *Spectacular Falls*—a show about the many meanings and uses of the word—'fall.' Falling in love, falling apart, falling into place, Twin Towers falling, immigrants falling through the cracks—and my favorite season when leaves fall.

"All these true stories are in the second song, 'Banana Peel Away,' expressing how everyone is just a banana peel away. The big fall in front of Ripley's broke my hand and robbed me of my ability to walk for twelve weeks—but I still got a job at the Goodman Theatre. My life hands me gifts in the form of stories that beg to be told in song. And the bonus prize is that people relate to them.

"After I spent time at SPACE on Ryder Farm—and at The Wheelhouse & Millrose Music helping me solidify the writing, arranging, choreography—*Spectacular Falls* premiered in the 'fall' of 2019. Perhaps the third show of the trilogy will be called *Balance*. The show will begin with me falling off a piano!"

▪ **As the National Chair of SAG-AFTRA Performers with Disabilities, have you seen more opportunities for disabled actors like yourself performing in solo plays?**

"There has been progress. In the last five years, we broke barriers on Broadway, Off-Broadway, and regional theatres across the country. More theatres are hiring Performers with Disabilities. The Goodman Theatre, Williamstown, Public Theatre, and especially Kennedy Center have hired Performers with Disabilities for several years—and there's now a National Disability Theatre.

"That's one of the reasons I put myself out there so much. I see fear and then interest when I'm working with non-disabled inner-city kids with Boston's Urban Improv. They're afraid of me when I take my leg off. But after an hour, when I'm ready to go, they won't let me leave; they have so many questions.

Those kids will never look at a disabled person the same way. I feel that by performing in my solo plays, by doing this work, the children of this generation will look at us differently.

"Golde, Grizabella, Fraulein Schneider, Gorgeous, and Shirley Valentine are just a few of the roles I've played on one leg, or an artificial leg, with absolutely no problem for the audience. I feel that it's all about using what you have and not hiding it. Doing what you can do because no one else can. Being unique enhances and enriches a live theatre audience's experience."

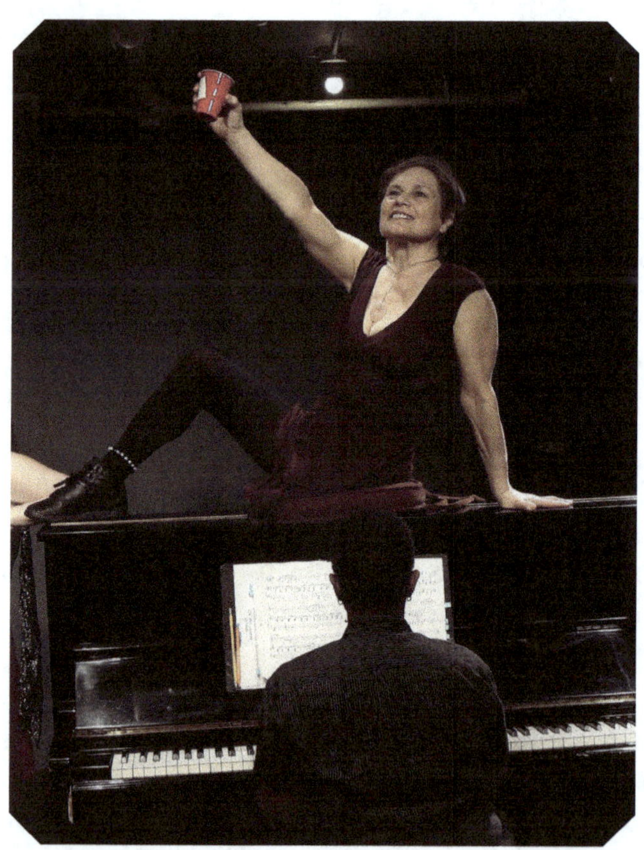

Anita Hollander during a performance of *Brecht on Brecht*. (Courtesy Carol Rosegg.)

STEPHEN LANG

Mr. Lang is widely known for his roles as Colonel Miles Quaritch in *Avatar* and *Avatar 2*, Major General George E. Pickett in *Gettysburg*, Thomas Stonewall Jackson in *Gods and Generals*, The Blind Man in *Don't Breathe* and *Don't Breathe 2*, and his one-man show, *Beyond Glory*. On Broadway, he played Colonel Nathan Jessep in the original production of *A Few Good Men*, (Helen Hayes Award), *The Speed of Darkness* (Tony nomination), and was Happy in the 1984 revival of *Death of the Salesman* opposite Dustin Hoffman and in the television movie. Off-Broadway, Mr. Lang played Colonel Littlefield in John Patrick Shanley's play, *Defiance*, and in Arthur Miller's last play, *Finishing the Picture*, at Chicago's Goodman Theatre. He has performed his one-man show, *Beyond Glory*, presenting stories of valor of veterans from World War II, Korea, and Vietnam, for troops deployed overseas and across America, receiving a Drama Desk nomination and a Lucille Lortel Award. His film and television work includes the title role in *Babe Ruth*, *Manhunter*, *Last Exit to Brooklyn*, *Tombstone*, *Public Enemies*, *The Men Who Stare at Goats*, *Conan the Barbarian*, *Crime Story*, *The Fugitive*, *In Plain Sight*, *Into the Badlands*, and *Mid-Century*. Mr. Lang was Co-Artistic Director of The Actors Studio from 2004 to 2006. He was profiled on CBS *Sunday Morning* about *Beyond Glory*. He is the author of *The Wheatfield*, a story of Gettysburg for young people and adults.

- **What led you to take on *Beyond Glory*, a solo play adapted from Larry Smith's book, portraying eight Medal of Honor recipients?**

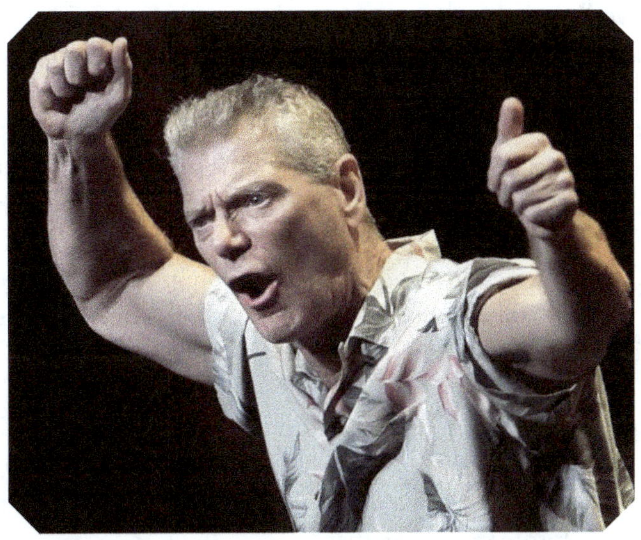

Stephen Lang in *Beyond Glory*. (Courtesy Diane Williams.)

"I wanted to take full responsibility for my life and my career. I felt the time had come to utilize my entire self. I wasn't at all sure I could do it initially, and that was part of the allure. It's both a confidence-builder and a leap of faith.

"In the play, I play an eighty-nine-year-old Nisei, Senator Daniel Inouye, and seven other diverse and complex men: all eight characters requiring all my resources as an actor. The experience of going through what these men faced at these defining moments, again and again, in all states of exhaustion is energizing and thrilling, and humbling.

"I allow the material to operate on me, and I've been surprised by what it takes to give it its full life and experience. I'm stirred, inspired by the lives of these men. It's truly exhausting, but there's nothing more satisfying for me and for those who come."

- **Have you found you share a healing experience with your audiences?**

"Absolutely! Theatre is a shared experience, and I've been approached so many times by veterans and families speaking about how deeply the show touched them, in many cases providing insight into experiences never discussed within the family. There is a healing factor for the vets themselves as other men articulate feelings that have been long buried. It is catharsis, pure and simple.

"For me, *Beyond Glory* demonstrates the raw power of the theatrical experience."

- **How would you describe how you transform yourself into a character and the effect it has on your own growth?**

"I do whatever is necessary to enter into them completely. There are no rules, and everything is up for examination. I want to be open to the worlds of possibility that exist within each character.

"Daniel Boone is reputed to have said: 'Just because I don't know where I am, doesn't mean I'm lost.' I love exploring or inhabiting that territory. The older I get, the whole phenomenon of 'becoming' becomes all the more important for me. It's the only way I know to go about it.

"T.S. Eliot defined poetry, and I may be paraphrasing, as a 'state of complete and utter simplicity,' costing not 'less than everything.' I like to believe that my own direction and growth as an actor and as a human is embodied in those words.

"Simplicity and honesty achieved through hard-fought improvisation and imagination: rocky roads, tangled paths, dead ends, blind alleys that are to be explored, which will finally bring me to tranquil fields and shores of clarity and understanding. Or something like that."

TONY LO BIANCO

He has appeared in over a hundred films, television programs, and stage performances, both on-screen and off, as a writer, director, and producer. Off-Broadway, Mr. Lo Bianco won an Obie Award in *Yanks-3, Detroit-0, Top of the 7th*. For his memorable performance as Eddie Carbone in Arthur Miller's *A View from the Bridge* on Broadway, he received a Tony Award nomination and the Outer Critics Circle Award. He received an Emmy Award for *Hizzoner! The Life of Fiorello La Guardia*, bringing him to life in his acclaimed solo play, *The Little Flower*, and received two Emmys for *Just A Common Soldier*. His film performances include the five-time Academy Award-winning *The French Connection* with Gene Hackman, *The Seven-Ups* with Roy Scheider, *The Honeymoon Killers, God Told Me To, Bloodbrothers, City Heat* with Clint Eastwood, *Nixon* with Anthony Hopkins, *The Juror, F.I.S.T.* with Sylvester Stallone, *Kill the Irishman*, and *The Engagement Ring*. On television, Mr. Lo Bianco starred as the undefeated heavyweight champ Rocky Marciano in *Marciano*, the remake of *The Rocky Marciano Story*, the mini-series *Marco Polo*, Franco Zeffirelli's *Jesus of Nazareth*, he co-starred in *La Romana* with Gina Lollobrigida, *The Last Tenant* with Lee Strasberg, and starred in the television series, *Police Story, Palace Guard and Jessie*.

- **Why did you want to play Mayor LaGuardia in your one-man solo play *The Little Flower*?**

"I admired LaGuardia's mind, his larger dream, and the kind of person he was. Politically, LaGuardia was a 'fusion' candidate. He took the best from both sides and logically used it for the betterment for the people. His biggest strength was his common sense. He was a dreamer and a doer, a mayor for twelve years, and

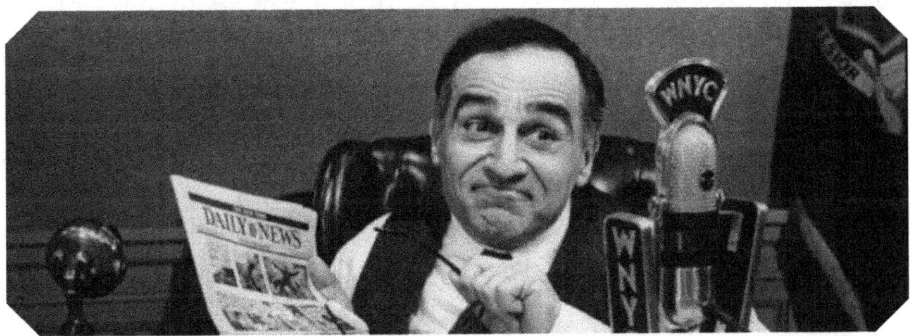

Tony Lo Bianco as Fiorello La Guardia in *The Little Flower*. (Courtesy Tony Lo Bianco.)

together with Robert Moses, his master builder, they built tunnels, bridges, parks, so many building projects across New York City, everything you could imagine."

▪ **Why is it important to you to share the play with young people today?**

"There's a lack of education occurring in our schools and our universities. They are teaching new social opinions as fact, denying and throwing away history that doesn't fit into their political agenda. It seems by pressing a button, we've forgotten how to build something with our mind and hands—what it takes to dig a ditch, what it takes to build a handmade piece of furniture. We look for fast answers. We've become a 'throw-away society.' With a TV clicker, people think of themselves as the master of the universe. LaGuardia was a man of sacrifice. When he became mayor, he cut his salary in half. He did everything for everyone else; that's what life is about. I want college students to be inspired, to be engaged, to understand that kind of sacrifice it takes. After I perform the play, I talk with the audience and students. They don't know about this man, what he did, and that he gave so much of himself. I'm eager to learn what their understanding is of what they just witnessed. I believe by giving people examples that there is a more compassionate way of thinking about life, you can make the world a better place to live in."

▪ **How did you meet Arthur Miller, which eventually led to your originating the role of Eddie Carbone in *A View from the Bridge* on Broadway?**

"I went to the Dramatic Workshop for two years. It was across from the Winter Garden at 50th Street on Broadway, where the Capital Theatre used to be. Lindy's Restaurant was on one side, and Jack Dempsey's was on the other. I made a commitment; I wanted to understand and learn everything I could about acting—from costume, make-up, directing, lighting, mopping the stage—what it requires to put it all together. I'd do plays on the weekend—Bernard Shaw's *Overruled*, Tennessee Williams' *Mooney's Kid Don't Cry*. My first play was *Waiting for Godot*, and my first paying job was with Jerry Orbach in *The Threepenny Opera* in 1959. My whole idea was to stretch as an actor. To me, that's what acting is all about.

"When I was in acting school, Arthur Miller came and spoke. He had written a one-act play, *A View from the Bridge*, and a scene from it was presented in class. Well, when I saw it, I said to myself, "I have to play the role of Eddie; I will do that play someday!" Some years later, I went to do summer stock and did a production of *A View From the Bridge*, which was very successful.

"In the early 1960s, an Off-Broadway production of *A View from the Bridge* was being cast. Somehow I was able to be seen and met Arthur Miller. I said to him: "I want to play Eddie." He told me: "You're too young to play Eddie, play Marco. " I told him I didn't want to play Marco. I want to play Eddie." Needless to say, I didn't play either. Then Arvin Brown came to see me in *Yanks 3 Detroit 0 Top of the Seventh* at the American Place Theatre. He asked me what I'd like to work on. I told him I'd like to do *A View from the Bridge* and play Eddie. So we did it together at the Long Wharf Theatre. A lot of people came to see the production—Dustin Hoffman, Paul Newman, and Arthur Miller. He thought the production was quite good. Some years later, we did it on Broadway. I was the first actor to play in *A View from the Bridge* on Broadway as a full-length play. Doing that play was like a religious experience to me. It is what we want to do as actors."

- **Your performance has never left me. What compels you to make your next performance even richer than the one before?**

"It's how we want to communicate with the audience. I loved meeting the people who come after a show. They say things such as: "How did you understand those emotions, those feelings?" or "That's my life. How do you know it so well?" I'm curious, to say the least, and challenge myself to be better each time. It's what you strive for. If you hit one performance that is sublime out of a hundred, you're a success. Everything has to be worked on."

- **You were also in Harold Clurman's midnight acting classes.**

"Harold was a great storyteller, a 'foundation of human earth,' with a simplicity of complication. That is—if you were wise enough, you'd understand the purpose of the stories he told."

- **What kind of preparatory work do you do for a role?**

"That depends on the character and the playwright. I have been trained to work from the outside in and from the inside out. When I read the script—I read the character—I know the person I'm going to play—it's not me. So how do I have to become this person? My job is to transform myself, whether I do it by inner molding or costumes, from the outside in, or through body language—which will dictate my voice, or through a combination of all of them."

- **You have a great love for acting—**

"I love acting because it's a way to share insights into either political or social realities. I hope what I do will inspire, enlighten and hopefully change someone's viewpoint. I'm not interested in fame or fortune. I'm trying to communicate with people. Whether I'm acting or not, I feel our purpose as humans is to be examples—ambassadors for our community, our country, and an example that my mother and father can be proud of. I believe in Arthur Miller's words: "Attention must be paid." We mustn't destroy what's beautiful just because we have the right to.

"As an actor, you're able to make your eight performances a week a demonstration of what you believe in—and to keep demonstrating an ideal. That's what's so rewarding. In the 1930s, the Group Theatre put on plays about social issues, plays for the people, because they felt they'd make a difference in the world. Odets was pounding away about the class struggle and injustice. It's a big fight, but we're able to bring something to those who want to believe in a better world. That's why I continue performing, teaching, producing, directing. It's why I'm compelled to do what I do because of what I believe in."

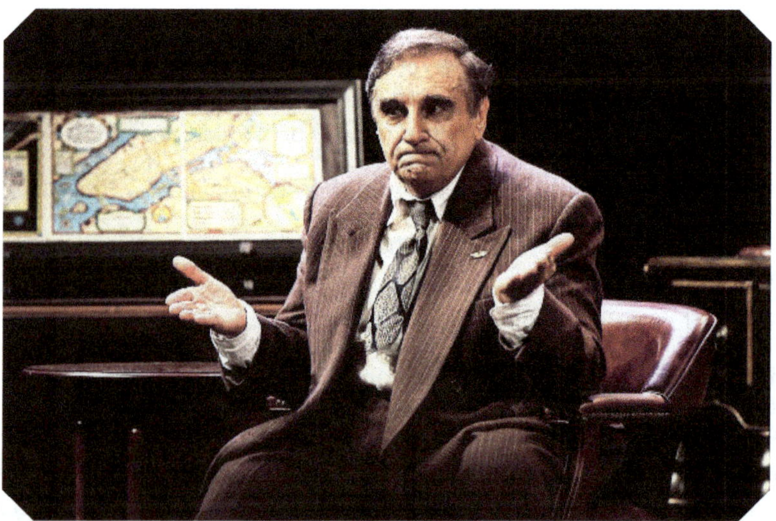

Tony Lo Bianco as Fiorello La Guardia in *The Little Flower*. (Courtesy Tony Lo Bianco.)

LAURENCE LUCKINBILL

Best known for creating and performing his memorable one-man shows, including *Lyndon* as President Lyndon Baines Johnson, receiving an Emmy nomination on PBS, *Clarence Darrow* Tonight, receiving a Dramatists Guild Award nomination, *Teddy Tonight* as Theodore Roosevelt, and as Ernest Hemingway in *Hemingway.* Mr. Luckinbill is well known as Spock's half-brother, Sybok, in the film *Star Trek V: The Final Frontier.* On Broadway, he appeared in *A Man for All Seasons* with Paul Scofield, received a Tony Award nomination for *The Shadow Box,* the original production of *The Boys in the Band,* the first American production of Joe Orton's *What the Butler Saw, Chapter Two, The Electric Map, Poor Murderer* and as Bertolt Brecht's *Galileo* with his own company, The New York Actors Theater. Mr. Luckinbill's many television appearances include *The Delphi Bureau,* starring in James Ivory's *The 5:48* and *Ike.* He appeared in the films *The Boys in the Band, Such Good Friends, Messenger of Death, Cocktail,* and *Moonwalk One.* His book, *TEDDY,* was published in 2021.

- **What compelled you to write, direct and play Clarence Darrow in a solo play?**

"It's been a transforming effort over the years. I was invited to play my solo performance as Lyndon Johnson in Boulder, Colorado, for a Eugene McCarthy celebration, and I looked around for a 'liberal' to write about and came up with Clarence Darrow, the famous criminal lawyer. It piqued my interest, so I dug deeper into *The Story of My Life* by Clarence Darrow. I learned that he had actually come to Pueblo for the Ludlow Mine Massacre trial.

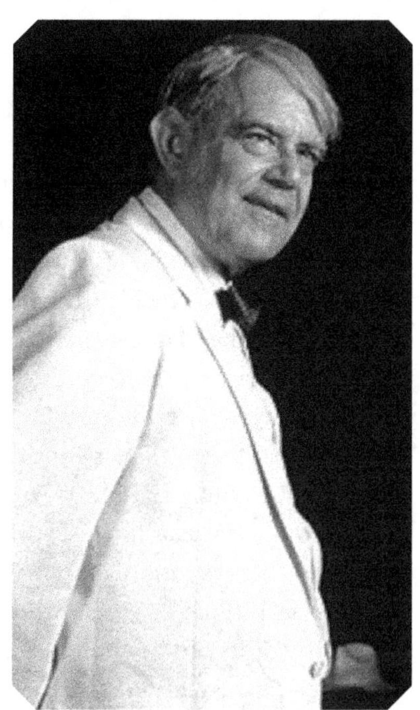

Laurence Luckinbill as Clarence Darrow in *Clarence Darrow Tonight.* (Courtesy Laurence Luckinbill.)

"In Boulder, I ended up meeting a 100-year-old gentleman who actually had attended the trial. I was worried that he would be critical of my performance since he had been at the trial where Darrow appeared as a witness for the defense of the murdered miners. But afterward, all he said was, 'You were wrong about one thing!' I said, 'What?' He said, 'Darrow never wore a white suit!' I actually was wearing a rented suit from the Mark Taper Forum in Los Angeles, which had been worn by Christopher Reeve when he did *Summer and Smoke*.

"The theme of my play, *Clarence Darrow Tonight* is 'What is justice?' Toward the end of his life Darrow, who was not a rich man, went out to speak for small fees on the town Hall and Chautauqua circuits, enduring long, hard train journeys to bring his message to those who would listen. He was often called 'The Great Satan' for his agnostic views, which were intolerable but fascinating to Americans stuck in Victorian moral codes and racist attitudes. He lectured on justice as a scientist, scouring his own experience to find out if it actually existed in this world or not.

"Darrow was also called 'The Defender of the Damned'—those who were seemingly indefensible, like Leopold and Loeb—or too poor to afford a lawyer. His passion was to find out the truth of why crime exists, believing that to understand 'why' is to begin to be able to able to change society for the better. I think he was our greatest humanist."

- **What are some of the greatest lessons you've learned from being on stage alone in a one-person show?**

"I've written my own shows, so I'm responsible for the stories I'm telling based precisely on the person's life. I call the series of the four shows: *Great Americans*. Each man I've chosen—or, who somehow chose me—stood across his time as a Colossus. Each had ideas and beliefs about the nature of life, politics, and humanity that had to be dealt with by those in their time and today in our time. The struggles they faced were giant challenges, and their responses against the odds were thrusts towards greater justice and a better world for all to live in. They were witty, wily fighters, at ease in the constant conflicts they inherited. And each has been a great inspiration and a teacher of how we must make a better civilization.

"Second, it was a huge surprise to find out that these shows, one by one, were going to free me from sitting by the phone waiting for some agent or producer to call me. I wrote, produced, and directed myself—and as time went on, I learned how to book myself everywhere I played. I was responsible for my own career. It turned out to be a thirty-year odyssey with infinite possibilities.

"Being alone on stage is always a problem; it could be lonely. So, I chose men who would and could interact with those they were speaking to and built-in places in the script for that to happen. I eliminated distractions for the audience. I made bare evocative sets, isolated them in space, and was drawn into light or darkness as the story demanded, leaving only my voice and the words of these great men to guide them. I found that the audience can be a tremendously powerful force pushing the story along. The imagination of a theater audience, once drawn into being by the actor, creates a collaboration. It becomes a great tango in which every move instantly engaged, led, or followed. Audiences have told me for years that they forgot about 'the actor' on stage and believed totally that I was 'him,' whoever 'he' was. A great gift to an actor."

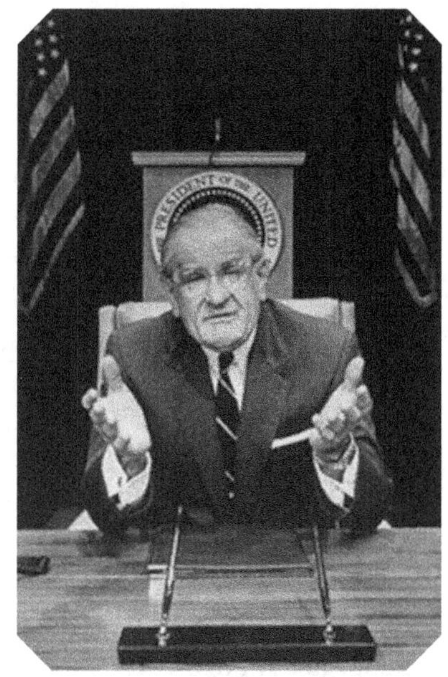

Laurence Luckinbill as President Lyndon B. Johnson in *Lyndon*. (Courtesy Laurence Luckinbill.)

- **What have you learned about creating a role from performing as many roles as you have?**

"I'll tell you a secret: in a long-running show it takes 6 x 8—six weeks times eight performances a week, like on Broadway, until you're actually alive on stage—really listening, really breathing—really thinking and feeling what the character is thinking and feeling. You exist, but as an adjunct to the character—as a facilitator. There is no difference between you and him. He is you.

"In a one-man show, you rarely get a six-week run. It's often one-night stands. So, you rehearse, rehearse and rehearse. You do it for your family or friends, for anyone who will listen, so you'll be prepared to give it the best you have 'on the night.' The secret is the real joy that comes in giving it away! Only when you can play it, as if it is a free gift to the world in every performance, only then, in that purity, have you become the actor you have always wanted to be."

ANGELICA PAGE

Angelica Page starred on Broadway in *The Best Man* and recently toured in a new solo play, *Turning Page*, about her mother, the legendary actress Geraldine Page. She mounted a production of Eugene O'Neill's *Anna Christie,* playing the lead role, directed by Wilson Milam. Ms. Page garnered an Outer Critics Circle nomination as Sylvia Plath in her solo play, *Edge*, and toured across America, Australia, and New Zealand. She received the Helen Hayes award in the Tony award-winning *Sideman* at Kennedy Center, after its Off-Broadway and Broadway runs. Ms. Page received a Helen Hayes Award nomination for her performance in Tracy Letts' *August: Osage County* on its national tour. She has appeared on many television shows and in several films, including *Nobody's Fool, The Sixth Sense, The Contender, You Were Never Here, The Turner Exhibit, The Hungry Ghost,* and her own film, *Lucky Days*, receiving the CIFF Best Feature Award and Worldfest Gold Award.

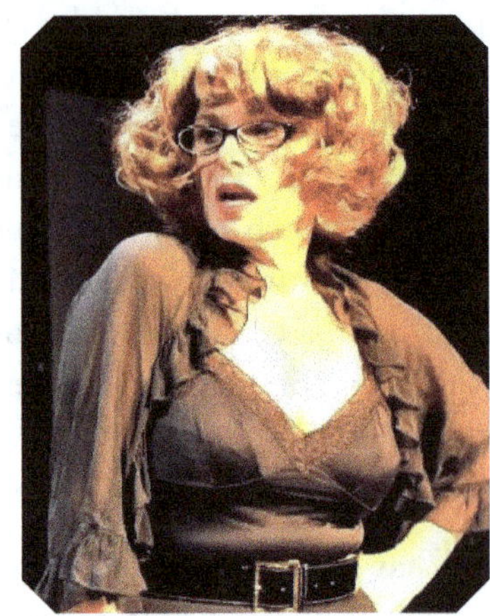

Angelica Page as Geraldine Page in *Turning Page.* (Courtesy Ty Donaldson.)

- **What led you to take on transforming yourself into Sylvia Plath in *Edge*—and how has it changed?**

"When I was a freshman in high school, I was introduced to Sylvia Plath in the school library. I was playing hooky during English class and got caught trying to cut class early for lunch. My teacher told me I had to go back and pick out a novel to check out before I could leave. I saw behind her a book with an interesting cover and asked if she would pass it to me. It was the novel *The Bell Jar* by Sylvia Plath. I checked it out without any intention of reading it. I ended up reading it five times. It completely changed my life and my attitude toward literature. I wanted to give her something in return. The experience of playing Sylvia hasn't changed that much over time. It's like picking up with an old friend you haven't seen in a while."

- **What have you learned as a Solo performer—and from the response of the audiences?**

"The level of concentration is different. In a play with other characters, I can put all of my attention on the person or people I'm playing opposite. Solo shows are

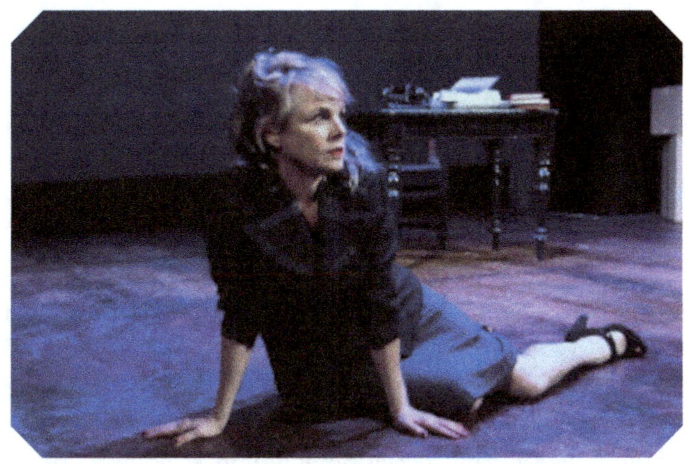

Angelica Page as Sylvia Plath in *Edge*. (Courtesy Yael Gezentsvey.)

really challenging because I have to carry all the attention and generate all the content. The audience becomes the other character that I'm on stage with, and as a collective being, they change so much from performance to performance.

"In a solo play, there's much more that isn't nailed down. It doesn't necessarily have to be; other actors aren't relying on you to give them the same cue each show. The tech team calling cues for me need to be sharp on their toes, as I do have a more playful fluidity naturally when I'm solo.

"I have become more and more comfortable with being on stage, and in turn more and more comfortable with audiences, which lends for a greater sense of communion and spontaneous magic that is only possible with live performance."

- **You also have brought to life your mother, Geraldine Page, in a solo play. Why was that important for you, and in what ways has it added to your growth and fulfilled you as an artist?**

"It's so interesting . . . I always found my mother to be the most enigmatic person when I was growing up. A complete mystery. I didn't start acting until after she died—she made me promise to "try it." What brilliant parting words. By pursuing acting, I not only began to understand more of myself, but I began to also understand who she was—just from the perspective of finally understanding what she was so busy doing all those years! Now with performing a play about her and actually playing her . . . becoming her . . . that just takes my understanding to a whole other level of a 'wow' factor. She never ceases to amaze me. She's a bottomless cup. I'm sure I'll find another part I will want to play someday, but Geraldine Page is a tough act to follow."

CHRISTOPHER PLUMMER

A lifetime in the theater on both sides of the Atlantic Ocean and well over a hundred motion pictures have made Canadian-born Christopher Plummer one of the most respected actors of his day. He had been a leading member of Britain's National Theater, The Royal Shakespeare Company, and in its formative years, Canada's Stratford Festival. Back in movieland, he had received the Academy Award for *Beginners,* an Oscar nomination for his Tolstoy in *The Last Station*, plus an Oscar nomination for his J. Paul Getty in *All the Money in the World.* Mr. Plummer had received Tony Awards for *Cyrano, the Musical*, and for his John Barrymore in *Barrymore.* A long list of Broadway plays has earned him seven Tony nominations. His television appearances go back to live television which earned him two Emmy Awards and six nominations. His many films included from *The Sound of Music* to *The Man Who Would Be King*, *Waterloo* as Wellington to *The Insider* as Mike Wallace. More recently, *The Exception* as the Kaiser and the very popular *Knives Out.* Apart from the Golden Globe, British Academy Film Award, and other honors, Mr. Plummer was invested into America's Theatre Hall of Fame, Canada's Walk of Fame, and in 1968, he was made a Companion of the Order of Canada, the country's highest civil honor.

- **What was the greatest challenge for you in bringing John Barrymore to life in *Barrymore*?**

"The greatest challenge wasn't playing him as much as giving the piece some substance. Bill Luce and I worked a great deal on creating depth in the play. It

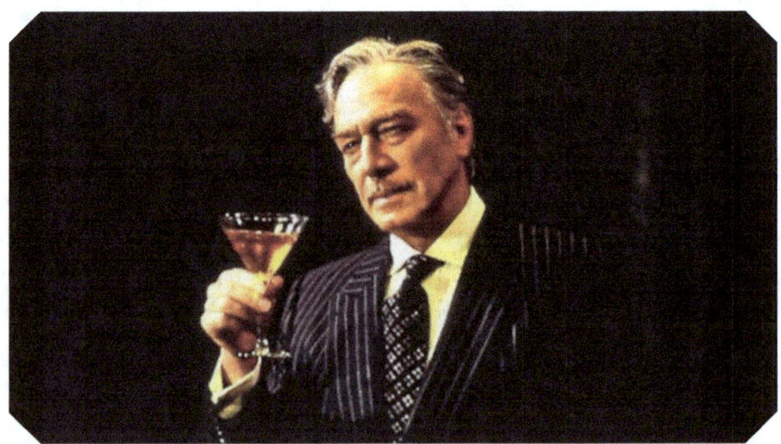

Christopher Plummer as John Barrymore in *Barrymore.* (Courtesy Cylla Von Tiedemann.)

was hard to find the pain he was in and put that on the stage. We both knew he never showed it, but it was always evident. He was not an indulgent or self-pitying creature.

"We went as deep as we could to find the serious side of Icarus. I think we were successful; we worked hard on it."

- **You had the extraordinary opportunity to work with several fine directors, among them: Elia Kazan, Tyrone Guthrie, and Theodore Komisarjevsky. What did you learn from each of them?**

"They all had the same attitude. Guthrie's attitude was the theater is like a three-ring circus, which had a large canvas on which he loved to work. He had an enormous sense of humor.

"Kazan was a different fellow. He was wonderful at political drama, and he had his own set of immigrant background that spurred him on. They were all very exciting to work with—their great energy; Guthrie had more fun. They had the passion to get to the truth burning in them. None of them were infallible. They admitted their own mistakes; they were self-critical.

"When I worked with Komisarjevsky, he had the other view—opposite than Stanislavski—in his way of working. They all had basically the same passion for the theater but just worked at it in their own different way."

- **What makes acting on the stage so important for you?**

"I put it in my book; I make my case. It's always been a place to go and hear ideas, but today, unfortunately, not enough people want to think. We are unable to understand or appreciate the nuances and humor in language.

"It's a tough road for the theater today. Eventually, the actor comes back to the theater because he discovers he needs to experience this kind of work. It's where the imaginary forces work. And that is what the theater offers us.

"Today, you have everything spelled out for you in film, but when you work in the theater with an audience, they have to imagine what they don't see. That is the magical force. We need it. It will never go away. And also because the writing is so wonderful. We have the best writers and poets writing for the stage. There is always less dialogue in film.

"I go back to the theater because I love the music of the words and the poetry. And it isn't always the theatre for me. I adore painting and music and the beauty of nature. But I'm not pleased with what we're doing to it as a human species. But I still have hope, though.

"There's an optimism boiling up inside of me. I want to do so much more."

RONALD RAND

As a Goodwill Cultural Ambassador, he has brought Harold Clurman to life, the 'Elder Statesman of the American Theatre,' in his solo play, *LET IT BE ART!* in three critically-acclaimed productions Off-Broadway, representing the U.S. at the World Theatre Olympics in India. Touring for over twenty years in his solo play to twenty-five countries, five tours across India, he performed at Nairobi's National Theatre and at over a hundred theaters, universities, and colleges across twenty U.S. states. Mr. Rand created two other solo plays, as Charles Dickens in his own adaptation of *A Christmas Carol*, and as Helen Keller's father, Captain Arthur Keller. He has appeared in several plays Off-Broadway and regional theater, in more than a hundred films and TV shows, including *The Royal Tannenbaums*, *When in Rome*, *In & Out*, *Family Business*, *Saturday Night Live*, *A Marriage—Georgia O'Keefe and Alfred Steiglitz* with Christopher Plummer, *Homeless* with Yoko Ono, *and Quiz Show* with Ralph Fiennes and Paul Scofield, directed by Robert Redford. An international director, his production of *LUV* was performed for over eight sold-out years at Sarajevo's Chamber Theatre 55 with Zana Marjanovic. Mr. Rand is the Librettist of *IBSEN*, the first opera about Henrik Ibsen, the Founder and Publisher of *The Soul of the American Actor* newspaper for over twenty years, and author of *Acting Teachers of America*, *CREATE!*, and *Solo Transformation on Stage*.

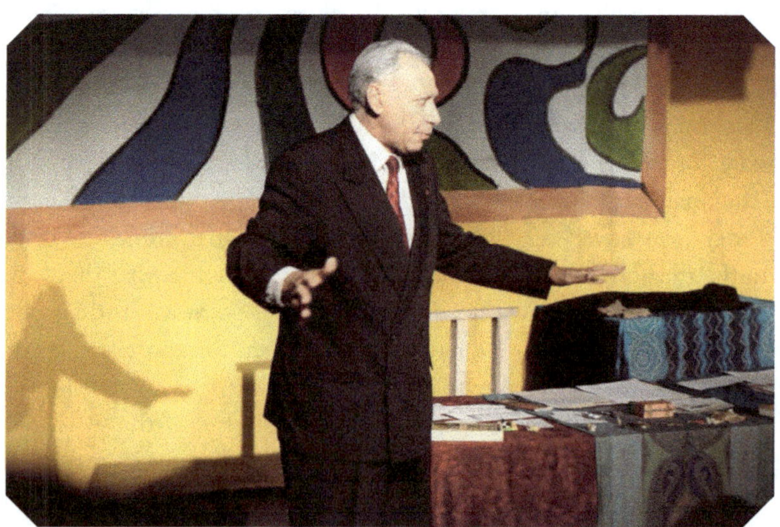

Ronald Rand as Harold Clurman in *LET IT BE ART!* at Nakuru Players Theatre, Kenya International Theatre Festival. (Courtesy Ronald Rand.)

▪ Why did you decide to bring Harold Clurman to life in a solo play?

"I believe he 'chose' me. I studied with Harold Clurman right out of high school. The impression he made on me was life-changing. I certainly had no idea I would ever write a play about him and bring him to life. As the 'Elder Statesman of the American Theatre' and the theatrical conscience of his time, Clurman is someone everyone needs to hear, especially today. Once his passionate ideas grab you, they don't let you go. He 'lays it all out on the table.' In class, he would tell us: "Stop sleep-walking your way through life! Look around! Be aware of everything you see! Feel for everyone! Give all of yourself to make this a better world for all of us to live in! Do it through the great art of the theater!" Of course, it's one thing to say, "I'm going to bring Clurman to life." It's another to find the right way to tell his story. It took a while to discover where Clurman is in the play—*why* he has to say the things he has to say—who he's talking to. Three of the most important requirements for making a successful solo play."

▪ When did *LET IT BE ART!* begin to evolve into a solo play?

"Actually, it was after I had read Stella Adler's foreword to Clurman's book *The Fervent Years*. For her—and for a lot of us—he was the greatest American theatre individual of the 20th century. She wrote she feared his legacy might be lost. When I read that, I thought that would be a great injustice because of everything he had accomplished and spoke about. I felt this generation desperately needs to hear his ideas, to feel his life-changing passion. Something took root. I thought back to my time when he was in front of me, and this great stream of passion flowed toward me. So I wrote to Stella Adler and told her I was considering writing a solo play to bring Clurman to life. She wrote back: 'Oh no—no one can play Harold.' It was probably because his energetic life force was so enormous in size. But then she added: 'If you have to—go ahead!' I began re-reading everything Clurman wrote—his books, essays, reviews—spending a great deal of time doing research on his life at the Library of the Performing Arts at Lincoln Center. Interviewing members of his family, close friends, well-known actors who had studied with him. Studying him in videos, pouring over notes I had taken in my classes with him. I had also played Clurman in several staged readings of my play about The Group Theatre. But one day, I stopped. Put everything down. I sat quietly—and asked Clurman: 'What do *you* want to say?' I listened to what 'he told me'—and I wrote it all down."

- **What makes performing your solo performance as Clurman such a necessity for your life?**

"I firmly believe theater and storytelling are essential for who we are as human beings. Having brought my show to so many different countries for over twenty years, I see how time and time again, Clurman's passion immediately breaks down all barriers of language. Opening up bridges of understanding and compassion for all of us to walk across together—especially when I've performed in countries like Belarus, Zimbabwe, and Colombia. Clurman galvanizes all those who come as they listen to every word he says. Through my process, I become a vessel for his passion to flow through, re-igniting the audience's 'love of life' at that moment—like 'a burning flame of hope.' Especially at a time like this, as he put it, when we 'live in an age of amnesia.' It continues to a great blessing!"

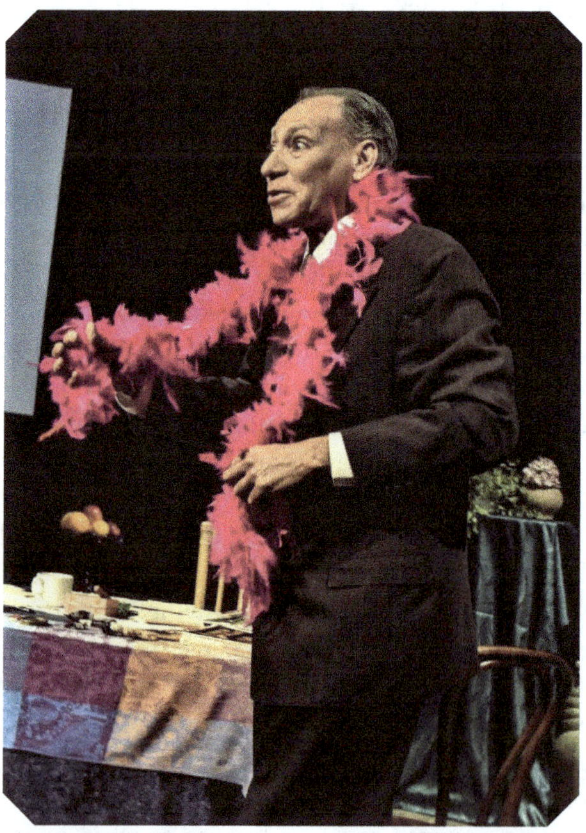

Ronald Rand as Harold Clurman in *LET IT BE ART!* wearing Josephine Baker's boa in Paris.

SABERA SHAIK

Considered one of the most versatile actresses in Malaysia, Sabera Shaik has toured extensively with her two solo plays, *Lady Swettenham* and *Puteri Saadong*, directed by Tage Larsen of Denmark's Teater Laboratorium, to New Delhi, Pune, Mumbai, Jaipur, London, Brasilia, South Africa, across Malaysia to Penang and Kuala Lumpur. A prolific director, Ms. Shaik produces for her own theater company, Masakini Theatre Company, including the productions: *My Bollywood Summer*, *Naga Women*, *In the Name of Love* by the acclaimed dancer Ramil Ibrahim, Alan Bennett's *Habeas Corpus*, and *Happy Days*. Ms. Shaik is the first practitioner of Malaysia's contemporary shadow theatre, directing *Wayang* with Chi Azim, and *The Story of Kuala Lumpur*. She also conducts workshops for actors and marginalized communities.

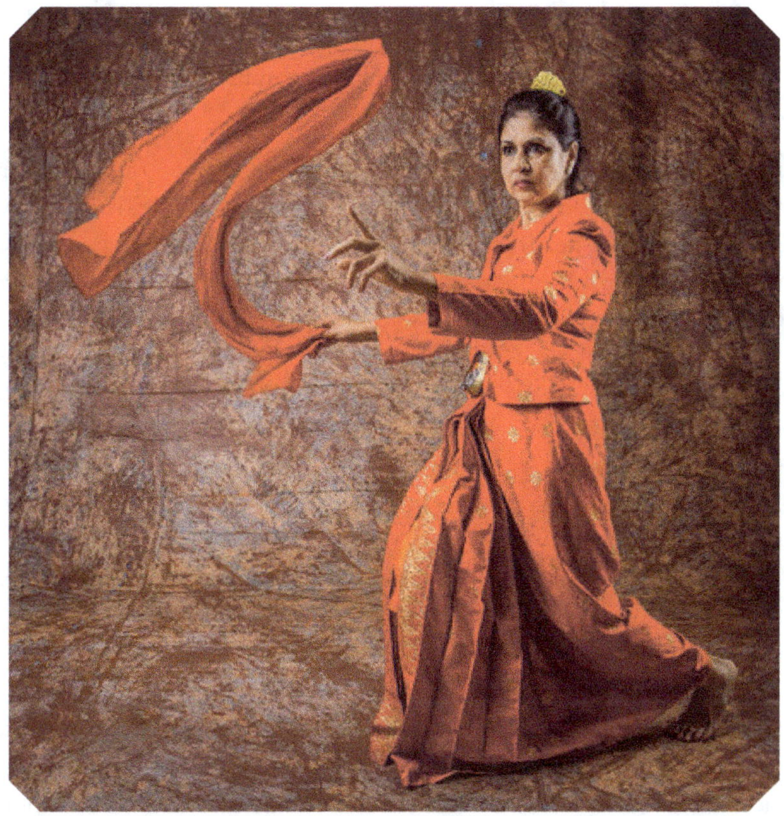

Sabera Shaik in *Puteri Saadong*, directed by Tage Larsen. (Courtesy Sabera Shaik.)

▪ How was the solo play *Lady Swettenham* you've been performing created?

"*Lady Swettenham* was first written in 1995, but it wasn't until 2009 that it evolved into a solo performance. *Lady Swettenham* came out of a chapter of Henry Barlow's book, *Swettenham.* A friend and a talented actor and director, Ramli Hassan, told me about this woman who was rather misunderstood and mistreated by her powerful and well-respected husband. We found her life fascinating, so we'd sit together over several weekends while drinking copious cups of tea and white wine, to plot it out and write the script.

"In 2009, itching to take *Lady Swettenham* on a solo journey, I asked Tage Larsen of Odin Teatret in Denmark to direct me. He gasped when he saw the forty-page script. We eventually pared it down to twenty pages. Within two weeks, we had the whole play worked out. I worked hard, sometimes alone in the Red Room at Odin from 8 pm till four o'clock in the morning. Some nights would find me falling asleep only to be woken by the creaking of the huge tree near the door. The October wind howling outside made my imagination run wild."

▪ How did you create the script for your memorable performance in *Puteri Saadang*?

"I had only one sentence to work from—'The queen of the 17th century who killed her husband with her hairpin!' Legend? Myth? Truth? However, there is a mention of her in the ancient annals of Kelantan, where she ruled and where I was born. Numerous depictions of her have been performed by different theater groups, but never a solo piece. In Kelantan, I spent numerous hours in the library in Kota Bharu, the capital of Kelantan, mulling over the history of that period. It was a time of high trading activities. Puteri Sadong's mother, the Queen, had her own female army and devised the Mak Yong as entertainment for the female members of her palace. It was not a period where women were subservient to men, as some historians would have us believe. I let my imagination run free—immersing myself in her character. I began to write about a fifteen-year-old princess who marries an older man she loves. Creating 'real' rather than 'dreamlike' sequences.

"Some days it sounded good, some days, it was awful. Many drafts later, with Tage Larsen's help, the final script was born. But one day, after two performances in Penang, I wrote to Tage: "I'm changing the whole piece into something of my own. Tage wholeheartedly agreed. I ended up 'borrowing' a few sentences from Aeschylus and Shakespeare, attributed to them—incorporating their words into the script—and I was utterly happy.

"At the same time I write, I imagine the music. Music is integral to my crafting a character. For *Puteri Saadong,* I felt the soulful call of the rebab—a three-stringed traditional instrument with a bow. It became my partner in conceptualizing her character. Tage suggested that the musicians be characters in the play. It turned out that I also wrote the lyrics for the songs to be sung by the musician, lady in waiting, palace official, and the naughty boy. They played the role of the narrator in a seamless way. When I hear music, I try all ways of speaking it through my body. I found a sort of dance mode between the interplay of 'keras' and 'lembut'—with 'a tension and release'—becoming the rhythm of her whole being. She is both flirtatious and unyielding. Silat—our martial arts—with its myriad of moves, became a daily exercise routine.

"I spent two weeks in Denmark with Tage. Then he came to Kuala Lumpur for another two weeks, incorporating the musicians and completed directing the play. At that stage, the full Transformation of me as the character took place."

- **I thoroughly enjoyed your performance. How do you go about your process and Transformation before the performance?**

"Although the costume may not yet be the real one, I'm already costumed from day one. So my movements are already set by the limitations or freedom of the dress—and when the music is included—it's all precision, precision, precision. Before going on stage, I prepare meticulously. In the morning, I make sure all parts of my costume, right down to the last pin, are in place. My make-up, wig, and other paraphernalia are checked and re-checked. Two hours before I go on stage—I'm alone, and I run the whole performance in my head. I re-read the script and imagine the stage.

"As I put on my make-up, I begin to feel differently, and by the time I have zipped up my costume—I am the character in my mind and under my skin. I wait for the signal to start, and I begin to panic. I think I have forgotten my lines. At that point, I always tell myself: "It's all right. Just get out there and do what you have rehearsed." Every performance of *Puteri Saadong* is exhilarating but tiring, too."

- **What gives you your greatest joy being a storyteller?**

"I love solo performing. Any character I read about, I see with an eye for a solo performance. The greatest joy is when audiences come and listen, laugh at the right places, and are engaged, even though they may not understand the language I'm speaking. Then I know my acting can tell the story with only physical movement and sound. It gives me great joy to watch audiences open up, to give them a feeling of freedom, to expand their vocabulary. I believe that every solo performance evolves over years. This particular solo work has evolved into something traditionally Malay, yet with some western elements in it.

"I'm currently working on a new solo piece, *Breakout*, written by a Malaysian writer, Jennifer Rodrigo. I play a lesbian woman who has been forced by her manager to become a drag queen because she can make money that way. However, she wants to break out and sing in her own voice. Every day, I work alone in my studio. Physical exercises, vocal exercises—and every day, my voice gets a little deeper—yet more 'girly.' I work on my walk, the way I cock my head, how I listen to my manager. A myriad of gestures. This is the hardest piece I have ever worked on because the truth has to exist on so many levels—from my physicality to my speaking voice, my singing voice—my anger at all the manipulation—and finally, the strength to change. I again seek music as the basis for my work. Putting together a whole production gives me the greatest pleasure. Yes . . . it's always worth the sweat and agony."

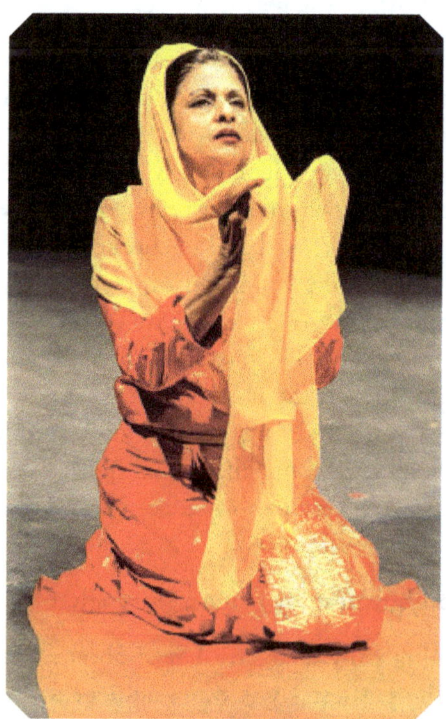

Sabera Shaik in *Puteri Saadong*, directed by Tage Larsen. (Courtesy Sabera Shaik.)

LIBBY SKALA

Libby Skala was best known for creating and performing in her critically acclaimed solo play, *LILIA!*, about her Oscar-nominated actress and grandmother, Lilia Skala, produced Off-Broadway at the Arclight Theatre by Mirror Repertory Company, at Los Angeles' Groundlings Theatre presented by Gary Austin, in Seattle, Toronto, Winnipeg, at Vancouver's Pacific Theater, Edinburgh Fringe Festival, in Germany and Georgia, and in London. Her second solo play, *A Time to Dance*, about her great aunt, Austrian modern dancer and award-winning dance therapy pioneer, Elizabeth Polk, won the Best Solo Performance Award at the London Fringe Theatre Festival and was performed at the Saint Lawrence Shakespeare Festival. Ms. Skala collaborated with her husband, musician Steven May, to create her third show, *Felicitas*, about her great aunt, Felicitas Sofer, an Austrian baby nurse. Her last solo play, *Irene Sendler: Rescuing the Rescuer*, premiered at the London Festival Fringe.

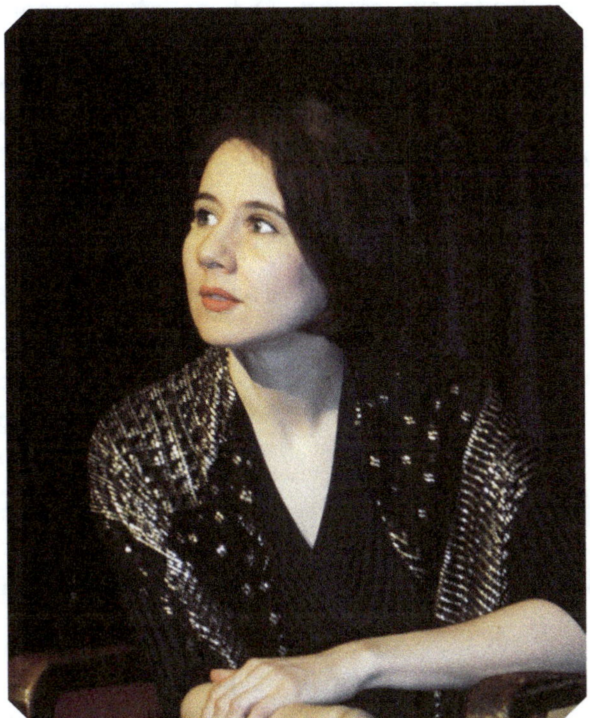

Libby Skala in *LILIA!*. (Courtesy Doug Minor.)

■ **What initially happened that made you begin writing *LILIA!*.**

"After my grandmother passed away, I was living in Seattle and took an improvisation workshop taught by Gary Austin. Gary asked each of us to talk for five minutes about a real or fictitious person who we found to be "interesting, compelling or fascinating." I spoke about my grandmother and described her as an immigrant who had difficulty adjusting from the high-profile life of being the first female architect in Austria to being a penniless factory worker in America. He immediately put me into an improvisation scene, in which I played her working in a New York zipper factory after her arrival as a refugee in 1939.

"After class, another student mentioned to Gary that my grandmother was nominated for an Academy Award for her role in *Lilies of the Field* opposite Sidney Poitier. When he heard that, he told me that I had to write a one-woman show about her life. Gary has this profound sincerity, which made me listen and trust him. It was really his encouragement and inspiration that prompted me to begin writing. But I had no idea how to go about it. So he said, "Go home and write down everything she ever said to you." So every night before I went to bed, I would listen for one sentence. And one sentence would lead to three pages. Certain stories my grandmother had told me, and certain experiences would come back to me. In class, I would act them out as improvisations. That's how the play was born. It stepped up to a work-in-progress, as I'd put segments of it in presentations with Artistic New Directions, which Gary directed."

■ **What has been the greatest challenge in performing as many performances as you have in *LILIA!*?**

"Naturally, it's always a challenge doing a play so many times and keeping it fresh. I was always conscious of the fact that the audience was hearing the play for the first time. I love thinking of the word—'rehearsing'—as 're-hearing.' If I ever found myself on 'auto-pilot,' I quickly did something to surprise myself—by playing more with sound or movement or taking breaths in unexpected places. But the foundation of my inspiration came from the deeper insights I kept getting from my grandmother and from acting itself."

■ **In the play, we see your grandmother's faith as something extremely important to her.**

"Very much so. She would talk about her religion on the radio and in television interviews. Everything good in her life she attributed to God. She felt strongly that everyone's talents come from God. The bus driver's 'talent of courtesy.' The garbage man's 'talent of reliability.' The 'actor's talent to take a character off the page and breathe life into it. Everything she did in her profession proceeded from her sense of utilizing what God gave her. Once a young starlet said to her: 'Oh Ms. Skala, you are so talented!' And she replied: 'Yes, I am. Thank God!' In a way, her reply could have been perceived as arrogant, but she felt her talent came from a universal source much larger than herself. Faith, to her, was something practical that you carry around in your heart. I'm learning that talent doesn't originate with me. As I become more conscious of the infinite nature of 'source,' I become capable of giving more and more because it's not about my personal ego."

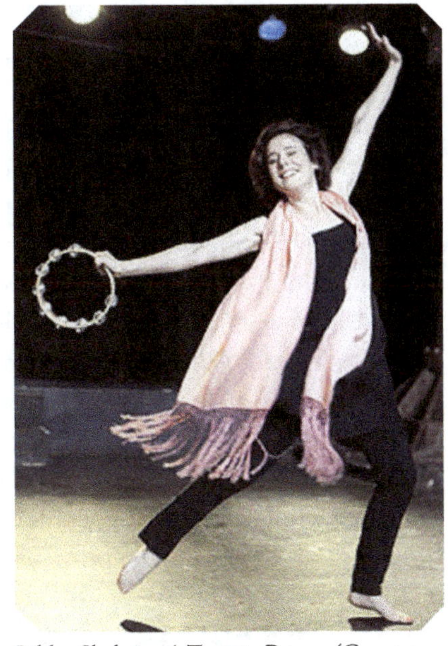

Libby Skala in *A Time to Dance*. (Courtesy Michael Nagle.)

▪ **What kinds of other insights have come from performing in *LILIA!*?**

"I remember my grandmother saying to me: 'Stop going about your career the way the world tells you to do it. You have your own path that God will show you. Do you see what I did? Use all of your God-given talents. You have a talent for writing, so write!' Since this show came along—it's finally dawning on me; we all truly do have unique gifts and talents that no one else possesses. I could go to a thousand auditions, but no one else could write and perform this particular play from the perspective of Lilia's granddaughter. These unique gifts are actually already in the hands of each one of us. We just have to have the courage to recognize it. *LILIA!* has become a spiritual journey, not unlike my grandmother's."

V (formerly EVE ENSLER)

A Tony Award-winning playwright, activist, performer, V wrote the theatrical phenomenon, *The Vagina Monologues*, which has been performed in over 140 countries, published in forty-eight languages, and received the Obie Award for Best New Play. She is the founder of V-Day, a twenty-year-old global activist movement and violence against women and girls. V created *That Kindness: Nurses In Their Own Words* with help from James Lecesne. Her plays include *Necessary Targets*, *OPC*, *The Good Body*, *Lemonade*, and *An Emotional Creature*. An acclaimed author, V's books include *The Apology*, *Insecure at Last: A Political Memoir*, *I Am an Emotional Creature*, and her critically acclaimed memoir, *In the Body of the World*, which she adapted and performed at the American Repertory Theater (A.R.T.) directed by Diane Paulus.

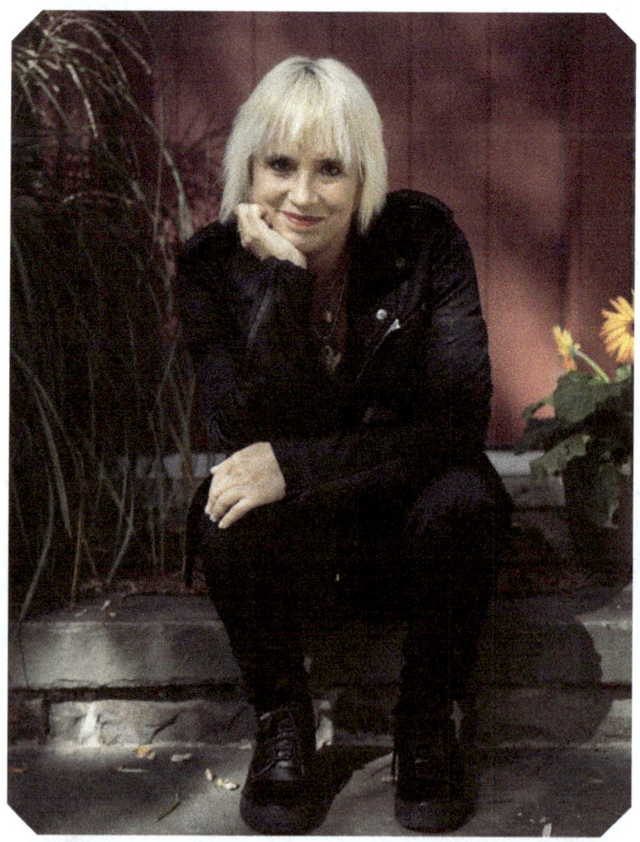

V (formerly Eve Ensler). (Courtesy Paula Allen.)

- **What gave you the greatest joy in performing *In the Body of the World*?**

"Doing *In the Body of the World* at A.R.T. was a profoundly joyful experience. There was such an incredible synergy of all these different artists coming together to create this piece. It was at once—metaphysical, political, personal, ecological—and very beautiful. And the making of the work was joyful. I think everyone felt it—the producers, the director, the designers, everyone who did the outreach, all the speakers who came and spoke at the end of the show, and of course, the audience. Even though the material is difficult, there was an underlying joy. It is so rare that everyone is in sync and lifting each other higher. It had a lot to do with Diane Paulus, her energy, her care, her trust, and her direction."

- **Creating a theater piece from your book, *In the Body of the World*, with Diane Paulus as your director must have also been quite stimulating collaboration.**

"It was magnificent! One of the most favorite experiences of my career. She has an incredible ability to listen, to hear what's going on in each moment, to boldly pursue those elements. When we worked on adapting the book into a play, we literally went sentence by sentence. What was exciting was trying to find out what to leave in, and what to leave out of the book. When we mapped it out, ultimately, we found out the strongest story to tell and what events and characters served that story."

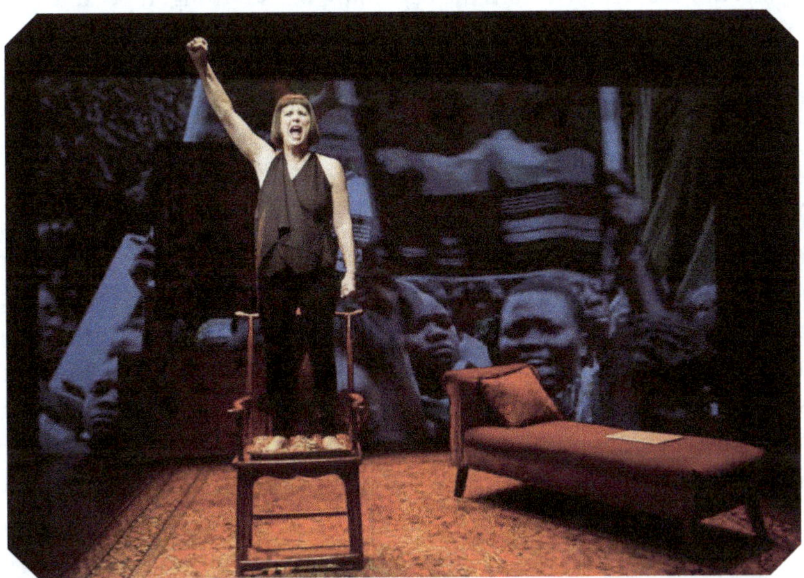

V (formerly Eve Ensler) in *The Body of the World*. (Courtesy Joan Marcus.)

- **How did you feel the first time you performed *In the Body of the World*?**

"I was really nervous because it's so personal, so visceral, so raw. That first night I thought I'd pass out before I got out on stage. But to see how marvelous the audience was, how generous in their emotional responses, and how willing they were to play, laugh, cry, and even dance. So many of the audience would come up every night to tell me afterward what inspired them about the show, to talk about their cancer or family member's cancer or their love of trees. And I loved that the final set-piece was such an astounding forest that the audience could visit and rest in, and where we held the talkbacks."

- **You conducted over two hundred interviews with women, which led to your writing the first draft of *The Vagina Monologues* in 1996, as you were writing the play. Did you see yourself performing it?**

"I think what happened was I did all these interviews, and out of them came a piece that was fictional—not the direct interviews. I would take a line or a theme or a paragraph from the transcripts, and I created the piece that way, and what became clear to me was what these women had entrusted me with their deepest secrets. When it came time for me to perform it, I knew because the material could easily be corrupted, and I wanted to protect it so that it would be transmitted in the most honoring way. The first performance was utterly terrifying, but the response from the beginning was so strong. It became the play that would determine so much of my life. It was really wonderful to pass it on to such extraordinary actors. I am beyond amazed and grateful to see the range of actors and women perform this play all over the world in these last twenty years."

- **What would it take for a greater respect for girls and women to occur on this planet?**

"I think it's always changing the 'ground story,' the cultural beliefs we live in, in a patriarchal society. I think the basic archetypal myths still have to shift. Art can work to make Transformation on those deeper levels. When I started, women couldn't say the word, 'vagina,' practically anywhere. Women have risked their lives to put on this show and perform in it. In the Philippines, they've been doing the show there for almost fifteen years, and it's helped change the laws on sexual violence against women. It was done in Pakistan where everyone thought it was impossible."

"In the Congo, after the ministers of the government saw the play, it caused a huge upheaval in discourse. I was present when I saw brilliant and brave women perform it in the Haitian Congress. It was performed by the female Members of Parliament at the European Parliament. To hear such powerful women moaning in those mighty halls was quite something. I've seen things I never dreamed would be possible. I think women have to constantly tell their stories and put out their truths. Women have to come back into their bodies.

"I think so much of ending violence has to do with men. I never understood why it became a women's issue. We actually don't rape ourselves. I think when men make this issue as important to themselves as it is to women, there will be real liberation. We move forward, we move back. Patriarchy is stubborn, and we know power is rarely given, particularly from the privileged and secure. I do believe that when men know in their beings, in their hearts, that their liberation is tied to the liberation of women, there will be a radical shift."

■ **And theater remains a place of creation for you—**

"I believe in the theater. It's of the body. It's where we're present together, in the moment. It's spontaneous, physical, political, psychological, spiritual. So much of this high-tech neo-liberal capitalist world takes us out of the present, isolates us, makes us lonely. Theater is a place of community, of revolution. We create it each night together. It's happening right now. It's of the body and of the moment. It's dangerous, and it's holy."

ELIZABETH VAN DYKE

Elizabeth Van Dyke is an award-winning actress, writer and director, and Artistic Director of New Federal Theatre in New York City. She received an Audelco Award and Ace Award as Lorraine Hansberry in *Love to All, Lorraine*, a solo play she adapted and co-directed with Woodie King, Jr. She made her Broadway debut in *Checkmates* and originated the roles of Fannie Mae Dove in Pearl Cleage's *Flyin' West*, Annie Talbot in *A Dance on Widow's Row* by Samm Art Williams. She played the leading role in *Zora Neale Hurston* at the Passage Theatre, *Antigone* at Lincoln Center Institute, and at the New Federal Theatre in *A Raisin in the Sun*, *Anna Lucasta* and *Daddy*. She has directed *Games, Sweet Mama Stringbean, Remembering WeSelves: The Black Renaissance, Zora* featuring Phylicia Rashad, and her own play, *Great Men of Gospel: Spirit into* Sound. Ms. Van Dyke is Producing Artistic Director of *Going to the River* and *The River Crosses River: A Festival of Short Plays by Women of Color* at EST. Ms. Van Dyke wrote the libretto, with music by Dr. A. Hailstork, for a Zora Legacy Concert, receiving its world premiere performed by the Orlando Philharmonic Orchestra in 2011.

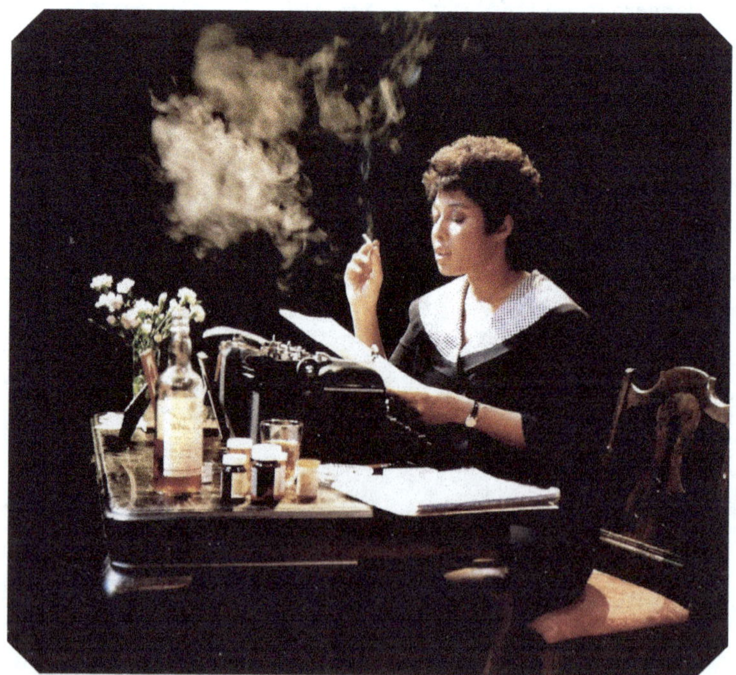

Elizabeth Van Dyke in *Love to All, Lorraine.* (Courtesy Elizabeth Van Dyke.)

▪ Why were you compelled to create *Love to All, Lorraine*?

"There were several reasons. Woodie King, Jr. had advised me that 'actors are for hire' and that it is best to 'activate work.' I had also directed *Young, Gifted & Black*, a play about Lorraine Hansberry, and was studying acting with Wynn Handman. I learned that as an actress, I was often 'in my head.' Lorraine was an intellectual, and there was something about her that intrigued me. A solo piece on Lorraine seemed the perfect project. Wynn allowed me to bring the piece into class, and I worked it out there."

▪ How did you go about exploring Lorraine Hansberry's life, as well as a host of many important individuals that played a role in her life, including Paul Robeson, W.E.B. Du Bois, and Langston Hughes?

"At some point, it became clear that one needed the rights to her life in order to do an 'authorized' version and be granted access to all of her work. After many conversations and negotiations with Robert Nemiroff, Hansberry's former husband and head of her estate—agreements were made—and I was given access to her private diaries and letters.

"In addition to many conversations with Robert and others who knew her—many trips to the Schomburg Library, books, magazines, articles, along with anything I could get my hands on about her—aided in my research—probing her short, yet impactful life."

▪ What challenged you the most performing in a solo play as Lorraine Hansberry?

"The dual-lens of playwright and actress was most challenging. Creating a historical or well-known character always requires some degree of exposition, which is rarely 'dramatic.' Leading to answering questions: Why are you on stage telling this story at this moment? What is the dramatic arc? The beginning, middle, and end. This is always the most basic, challenging aspect, and one that is ever-present."

▪ How necessary is it to keep a focus on the well-known inspiring figures who have forged a way forward for us?

"It may not be absolutely necessary to keep the focus on these great inspiring figures in terms of solo drama; however, the exploration of these lives who have a forged a way forward for us—is usually informative, uplifting, and encouraging.

"Most of these historical and well-known figures are human beings who overcame many obstacles in the effort to reach their goals. The knowledge and explorations of their journeys help us all—and can be affirmational and inspirational."

JEAN-CLAUDE VAN ITALLIE

One of America's most gifted playwrights, translator, painter, and teacher, his trilogy of one-act plays, *American Hurrah*, was hailed as the watershed Off-Broadway play of the 1960s. Mr. van Itallie was one of Ellen Stewart's original 'La Mama playwrights.' As principal playwright of Joseph Chaikin's Open Theater, he wrote *The Serpent*. His other plays include his often-produced versions of Chekhov's four major plays, *Tibetan Book of the Dead*, *Struck Dumb* written with/for Joseph Chaikin, *Bag Lady*, and *Light*. His translations include Jean Genet's *The Balcony* and Bulgakov's *Master and Margarita*. Mr. van Itallie had performed his one-person autobiographical shows: *Confessions and Conversation*, directed by Rosemary Quinn—and *War, Sex and Dreams* at La Mama in New York City, and at Highways in Santa Monica. He co-wrote the libretto with Lois Walden for the new opera, *Mila, Great Sorcerer*, with music by Andrea Clearfield. He taught workshops in Los Angeles, New York City, and at Shantigar Foundation. Mr. van Itallie's books include *The Playwright's Workbook* and *Tea with Demons, Games of Transformation*.

- **Why did you feel the need to create your two solo shows, *War, Sex and Dreams* and *Confessions and Conversation*?**

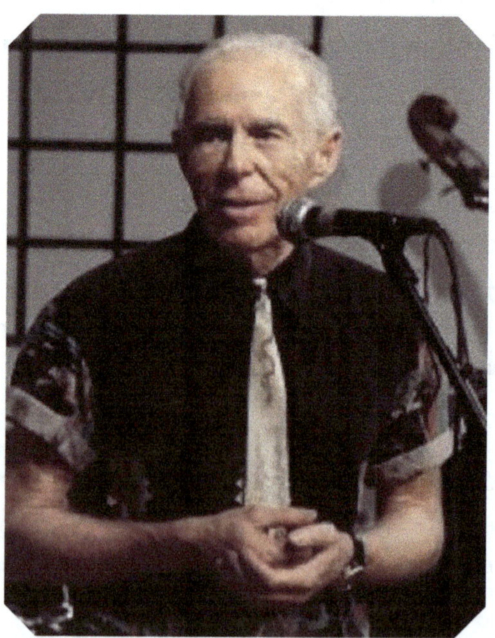

Jean-Claude van Itallie. (Courtesy of Jean-Claude van Itallie.)

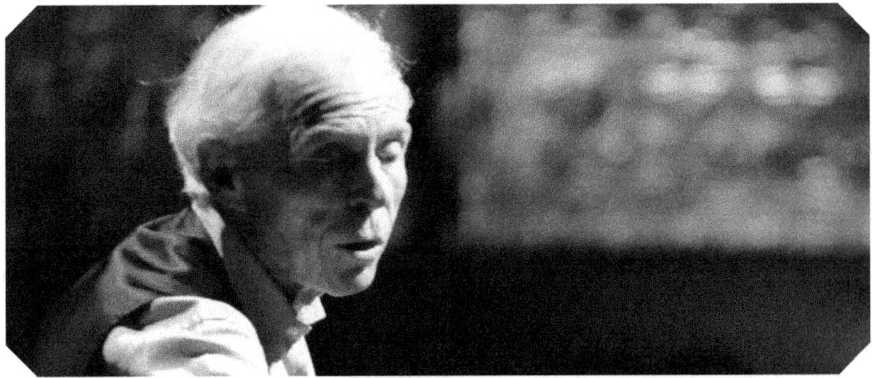

Jean-Claude van Itallie in *War, Sex and Dreams* at La MaMa. (Courtesy Josh Adler.)

"I felt as if the streams of my life were increasingly running into a single river. I wanted to demonstrate the currents of that river to friends, to physically show some of my dreams to an audience. I wanted to bodily release my secrets. Bottling demons inside is denying them. Writing them down wasn't enough for me anymore. I wanted to show them, exorcise them, embody them. I needed to expose my intimate selves, my rage, and fear. Would the audience recognize themselves in me? I didn't know. But I would, at least, be seen."

- **You teach a workshop entitled *The Healing Power of Theater*. Why did you choose that title?**

"Western theater began with the ancient Mysteries. The Mysteries were not a show you watched as a modern audience watches a play. You played your part in the Mysteries in order to become a more clear-sighted one in the community. You prepared by fasting, then eating a sacred hallucinatory substance. Priests and priestesses led you down into a dark cave. There they scared you out of your usual wits. After three days, you returned to earth's sunlight, bathed in the sea, and walked home with a strong sense of reality and what you needed to do in life.

"My meditative performance Workshop offers techniques for anyone, not just professional actors, to surprise themselves, to exorcise their demons, to dramatically tell a personal story. As movies, TV, and streaming monopolize entertainment, living theater can return to its sacred transformational origins. Disciplined performance practice is revelatory and revolutionary. A community of peers encourages a dedicated actor, amateur or not, to be present, true, and detailed—making space for inner change. This courageous, intimate work is what I call *The Healing Power of Theater*."

BEN VEREEN

A Tony and Drama Desk winner for his renowned performance in Bob Fosse's *Pippen*. Mr. Vereen's Broadway appearances include *Wicked*, *I'm Not Rappaport*, *Chicago*, *Hair*, *Fosse*, *Jelly's Last Jam*, *Jesus Christ Superstar*, and *A Christmas Carol*. Mr. Vereen appeared in the World Premiere of *Fetch Clay, Make Man*, directed by Des McAnuff at The McCarter Theater. Mr. Vereen continues to tour throughout the United States with his concert act, *Stepping Out with Ben Vereen*. His notable film appearances include *Rocky Horror Picture Show*, *Time Out of Mind* with Richard Gere, *Top Five*, *Idlewild*, *All That Jazz*, *Sweet Charity*, *Funny Lady* receiving a Golden Globe nomination, *Why Do Fools Fall in Love*, and *Once Upon a Forest*. His television appearances include the miniseries *Roots*, *Hot In Cleveland*, and *How I Met Your Mother*. Mr. Vereen has been inducted in The Theater Hall of Fame, The National Museum of Dance, and The Dance Hall of Fame.

- **As a humanitarian and arts advocate, you've spoken about "the breath of creativity . . . for the need of more arts in schools for children who can make a better difference in our world . . . to give them the tools that they need making a difference in other's lives." Was this something that was impressed upon you as a young person?**

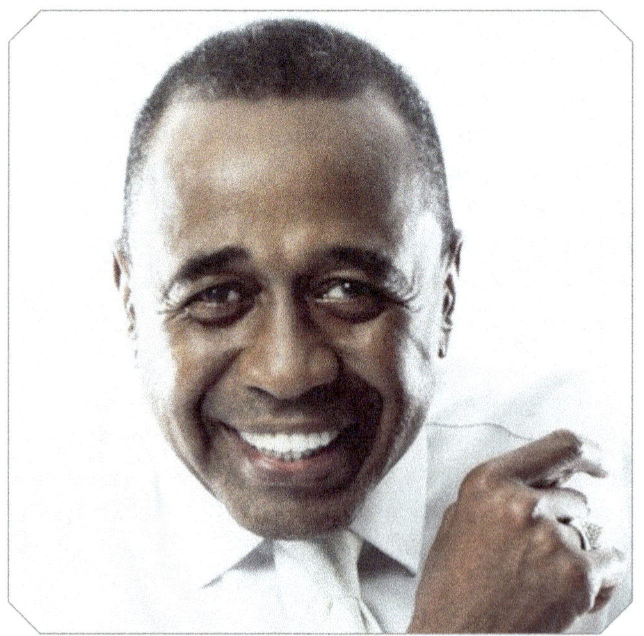

Ben Vereen. (Courtesy Isak Tiner.)

"Life is an art form—we have forgotten that. It's all in the Good Book as a spiritual understanding based on faith. A spiritual understanding, a secret to understand the power—call it Jesus, God, Buddha, Krishna, one power—and we're trying to understand that awesome power. In the beginning, a power was created, a creative power. I say: Why don't we use this creative power to come together instead of separating ourselves.

"What it is for me in the performing arts is that it's life itself. Any art form is life. It's a creative expression of who we are, and that creative spark is working towards the good in us. It allows you to express whatever avenue you want to go down in a positive way. If there's anger you're feeling, it's been created, but we can take it and entwine it in a way to learn how to live with one another. Each breath we take has been given to us, and we have to accept that out of that breath, all of us are given an opportunity to bring creativity into the world.

"When I was about twelve years old, I was living in Brooklyn. I grew up in the Pentecostal Church. I was a kid in a poor family, and I couldn't afford to go to the theater. It was also a time of great crisis; there were riots in Harlem. I remember I was traveling in a subway train returning to where I lived, and the riots had started in my neighborhood; it was all in flames. It was the time of Martin Luther King, Jr., Malcolm X, Huey Newton, Dick Gregory.

"I learned from them that we're here to make a difference in the world. I was part of that generation, so it was hard for me to sit still, and in the arts, I found a place where I could tell stories, to take the places I was feeling my anger in my heart, and to make something productive out of it. To offer something that could heal people, to be someone that could heal our nation, especially today when we need that more than ever. We need a 'coming togetherness.' Never mind what political party we're part of; we have to get it together. We need to love one another."

- **You studied under the world-renowned choreographers, Martha Graham and George Balanchine, Jerome Robbins—and you were directed by Bob Fosse, among many other extraordinary artists. What were some of the lessons that have stayed with you over the years?**

"Fosse gave me style. He wanted his work done well. He gave me a discipline from his experience. He'd say: 'You're free to do this,' and he'd bring things out of me, and then he'd shape them. Balanchine and Martha Graham were adjudicators at the High School of the Performing Arts. It's also where I saw the first modern dancer, Norman Walker. The way he danced just blew my mind.

"I had so much passion, and there were all these great teachers there that gave me a foundation. Working with Tom O'Horgan gave me freedom.

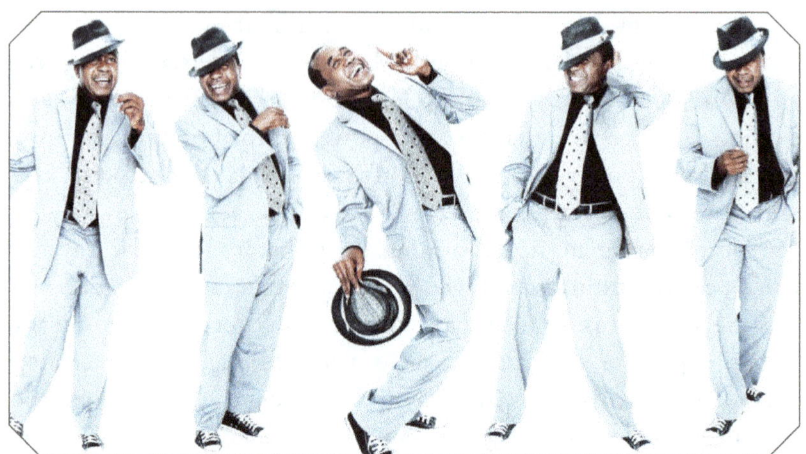

Ben Vereen. (Courtesy Isak Tiner.)

And before everyone, there was Ira Aldridge, an African-American actor who escaped slavery and changed the face of doing Shakespeare on this planet."

- **You toured the world with your one-man show *Stepping Out with Ben Vereen*, which I experienced and enjoyed in Detroit. Why did you originally want to create your own show?**

"The 'ham' in me. We sing, we act, we do it because we need to give away more love. My love was so big I had to get it out. When I did the shows I did, they were part of my life. I've been doing the show telling the spirit of my journey. All the songs in my show have a personal vibration inside me—from *Jesus Christ Superstar* working with Tom O'Horgan, singing "Corner of the Sky" from *Pippin, Sweet Charity*, singing the Sammy Davis songs, and *Wicked.* So I decided to put my act together right after *Pippen.* It's my gratitude show. I get to share with the audience where we've been together and to thank the audience for being here with me in this moment."

- **What continues to give you the greatest joy in life and on stage?**

"In my life, it's seeing my children blossom and grow. To see how young people grow through art. So many people come up to me and tell me: 'How wonderful it is to meet you. You changed my life.' or 'I saw you in *Pippen*, or you taught a master class, and it changed my life.' This is why we do what we do. We like to get paid, but the important thing is like the legacy you're laying down with your performances and your book *CREATE!* The real payback is beyond any monetary reward. It's the gratitude, the recognition that you touched somebody's life and made a difference."

TWELVE

Touching Lives Through Transformation: A Personal Memoir

A path lies before you just as it did for these performers who chose to fill a theater with their entire being to say what needed to come through them. They recognized a spark lay inside of them. A fuse that had to be lit in order to bring more light into the world. To me, each of them is a hero.

A hero is defined in many ways. Going forward with self-confidence in the face of great uncertainty. Determined. Courageous. Inspiring others with love, compassion, hope. Moving with the capacity to bring 'good' into the world through enormous skill and integrity. Willing to 'step into the shoes of another' selflessly. Bringing an empathy that needs to be felt by others. That kind of hero is inside of you when you become 'soul-driven.'

We all have, at times, been thrown out of alignment. What brings you back is 'that,' which is calling to you. It's where you'll find the strength you need. From your 'rock.' Think about the equation when the audience is 'one with one.' In that moment, all those who've come are joining forces with you to create an entirely new experience that has never occurred before in this singular moment. You have the power to bring great healing to the world through Transformation. There's no question we're living through a time of great stress and tension. It's important to be aware that by letting your 'goodness' shine through your creation on stage, it will help lead others towards the healing that needs to take place in the world right now. It's also just as important to deal effectively with your own fears, anxieties, tension, doubts, the different emotions you may have. Take the time to tap into the center of your peace. Allow yourself to be in contact with ways of grounding yourself and sharing all the goodness inside of you.

One summer, I had the delight to perform my solo play and teach my master Workshop at the Festival of Making Theater in Athens, Greece. I was struck by the exuberance of all the different teachers and students. Through our different techniques, we found ways to expand and connect with the students' consciousness in their exploration of creativity. Inside the robust intensity of each day, we'd experiment with sounds, space and time, movements, and language through our explorations into the mysteries of art and ritual. Whenever I perform my solo play, I always ask whoever knocks on my door to announce: "Places, Mr. Clurman." At this particular performance, the actress chosen for the task was surprised. She had never heard of anything like that before. Through the 'Art of Transformation, you cause a shift in the cosmic reality that's taken place—and everyone becomes a part of this Transformation.

At the end of the week, Evdokimos Tsolakidis, Artistic Director of the Theater of Changes in Athens, and the Festival Director arranged for the teachers to travel with him to one of the most beautiful sites in Greece—Epidaurus. Located on the fertile Argolid plain of east Peloponnese, we experienced the National Theater of Greece in their production of *The Persians*, the earliest Greek play to survive by Aeschylus.

As I sat on the ancient marble of this elegant outdoor theater designed by Polykleitos the Younger during the 4th century BC, I was surrounded by more than thirteen thousand spectators. Because of the extraordinary acoustics of the theater carved into the side of Mount Kynortio, without the performers' use of a microphone, I could hear every single word in Greek from the last row I was sitting in, hundreds of feet away from the stage. The rows of limestone seats formed an acoustics filter reflecting the voices of the actors on the stage. It was simply magical!

At Epidaurus, known as the birthplace of Apollo's son—Asklepios, the healer had treated patients at the nearby 'healing center.' Afterward, they were brought into the theater to watch the immortal Greek tragedies and comedies. It's a well-known remedy that by experiencing a 'catharsis,' you can be healed by liberating your emotions inside. The Ancient Greeks knew this was necessary to accept and understand the pain in their lives.

That evening, as the dramatic performance unfolded before me, I felt connected to the past ages and to all those around me. Above my head, a carpet of stars danced as a cool breeze played across my skin. We sat there together, much like the 'polis' that had joined together as an audience thousands of years before. We—a community of brothers and sisters—experiencing one of the oldest rituals on the planet—allowing us to breathe as one. Reminding us, this is what it means to be human.

With each day I spent in Greece, more and more of my connection to its earth, its sky, its land, and people passed through me. Here was Athens—where Socrates taught that 'love of wisdom' was connected to the 'art of love,' telling his students, "wisdom begins in wonder." When I walked to the Acropolis and ascended the pinkish-colored steps on its rocky hill, I stood before the Parthenon, the symbol of Ancient Greece. My eyes came to rest on its massive Pentalic marble pillars, holding up a temple built over twenty-five hundred years ago. I could feel the intense strength in each column, the rotundity of the earth in its stone, knowing it had weathered time and wars and cataclysms, and still, it stood.

When I turned, below me I caught in my gaze, two of the oldest theaters erected to celebrate fertility and rebirth—the Odeon of Herodes Atticus and the Theater of Dionysus. Images raced before my eyes. Here, during competitions, for the first time—plays by Aeschylus, Sophocles, Euripides, and Aristophanes were performed. The first actor stepped out from the chorus; some refer to him as Thespis. Aeschylus added a second actor, a third by Sophocles—and thus, modern drama was born.

When I left Athens, I traveled to Mykonos, known as the 'Island of the Winds.' I had been invited to stay at the house of a dear friend, a musician who played in one of the clubs on the island, on the top of a hill overlooking over the crystalline aquamarine Aegean Sea.

One afternoon, I descended the hill to the shimmering waters below. Walking barefoot down the beach, I stopped, turned, and looked back. There in the sand, I had left impressions. The earth had received them. But no sooner had I perceived this, that a large wave washed ashore. In a blink of an eye, my imprints were gone, lost forever. Still, the memory of that moment lingers inside of me. Reminding me of the cascading moments of time we all experience from the time we're born. Waves wash over us. Memories come and go. Some remain imprinted, residing deep within the contours of our soul. Whispers of past experiences. Lessons learned. Mistakes to be forgiven. We step forward. One day at a time. In gratitude.

During my stay, I ventured to the night scene to hear the deafening music in the nightclubs playing till all hours of the night. One, at which my friend was playing with her band. After a while, I wandered outside to observe the full moon smiling on the harbor filled with fishing boats lit up by its glow, slightly swaying in the moonlight. I was miles from the house I was staying at, but I decided to walk back. I somehow thought I could sense the route I had taken on a motorbike. So off I went.

Of course, at night, one hill starts to look like the rest. I was completely alone. Except for the sound of the waves crashing ashore. The steady evening wind blew across the fields. My breath came fast from my onward pace. Stars, endless above me, shining down brightly. Before me—the island stretched out—surrounding me on all four sides. I kept walking. Slowly it dawned on me. I was lost. I didn't have a clue where I was. Was I on the right road? When I came to a crossroads, each direction looked exactly the same. One was the way forward. But which one? I could sense a direction, but I wasn't sure.

Finally, I gave over to my inner guide—my 'inner compass.' It knew the way back, even if I didn't. So, I listened and went forward. Somehow in the darkness, with the wind whistling at my back, my path lit from the shining orb above, I could see my way. Slowly I began to recognize where I was.

Soon, before me, the hill I was seeking appeared. I had arrived back at her house, where I could rest and find comfort for the night. I took an extra breath. Saying a prayer of thanks, I began my ascent. When I finally laid down and closed my eyes, it was only a few hours before dawn. At the same time that I had become apprehensive, I wasn't worried. I knew somehow I'd find my way back.

We each carry a compass that guides us to a 'safe harbor in a storm.' You hold it within you. It will never let you down. You also hold a 'moral' compass—one of 'right and wrong.' That's why the 'Art of Transformation' rests upon these 'moral truths' you hold inside. They're connected to your heart and soul.

When I returned to America, I traveled to Massachusetts to perform in my solo play and teach my master workshop at Shantigar—the home and educational retreat of my dear friend, renowned playwright Jean-Claude van Itallie. Each time I had arrived, I always felt like I was returning to a 'safe shelter in the storm.' I had the good fortune of working with Jean-Claude for a couple of years as an editor on his memoirs.

With each visit, no matter the season, he would generously take me on a meditation walk through his cultivated and tranquil forest, adjoining his beautiful farmhouse near Rowe. Within the woods, he had divested the forest of all tree limbs on the ground and within reach—to allow the graceful features of the rocks and trees to emerge. Delicately, he had placed Chinese sculptures at various spots along the path. One continuous environment of peace and harmony.

As we moved slowly across the carpet of moss—with each step we took in silent mediation—it was as if time had stopped. It reminded me of the movements found in productions created by my dear friend, Robert Wilson. When I was a guest performer and teacher at his Watermill Center out on Long Island, at one of his sessions during the morning exercises with his students, they would move slowly across the studio at a snail's pace. In slow motion. Immediately allowing me—the viewer—to become aware of the human body in motion. I was invited to join in the slow-moving line of actors across the floor. I allowed my body to move effortlessly. To rise and fall in grace.

This kind of movement forces you to slow down. To be a witness to actually 'feel and see' in a much clearer way. I've used this movement exercise in my Workshop classes at acting schools and universities with students around the world.

Progressing further through the woods with Jean-Claude, it was as if the ground rose up to meet me with each step we took, adding to the buoyancy and movement. I felt I was met by lingering echoes from the many different natural pools of water we passed. When we stopped near a bog, no doubt millions of years old, we settled into stone seats in a sacred circle on the top of a small hill. Probably distant ancestors had once joined together here in sacred rituals. Around me, I felt an eternal connection between the nature surrounding me and the molecules in the air. In each tree. Stone. Flower. The sky above. Surrounding us. Intertwined with each breath we took.

As I sat there, I thought about how nature continually shapes and re-shapes us. Many times, unknowingly. By the tides of the moon. A sunset. The canopy of distant lights in the sky. We grow and change, and at the same time, this magical planet sustains us—as long as we respect what we've been given. A gift of life upon which we're able to share our art. To try and make this a better world—with the responsibility of taking care of it.

Everything you say and do every day becomes a reflection of who you are as an artist. Each environment you spend time in has a life of its own—its own shape and form. Many times, we take a lot for granted. We don't really see what's around us. Stop right now and look around. See something you haven't noticed before. It will heighten your awareness—bringing you a greater perspective and vision as an artist—as a human being.

With each performance, wherever I happen to be in the world, it's always a wonder how everything comes together, whether I'm in Kenya or Kuala Lumpur. Just a subtle shift of a chair or a different colored scarf on a table changes the entire tone and tenor of the space completely. Because everything speaks. Bear that in mind for the effect you're working to achieve through your storytelling. Nothing can be left to chance. And yet, everything is chance. Every moment has never occurred before. It all comes together in one beautiful arrangement. That's essentially your 'gift' to the audience. In this moment, you're saying: 'We exist together with one another right now.'

Sometimes, there won't be special lighting available, except the natural light of day. When I performed in my solo play in the centuries-old Dar al-Makhzen Palace in the Medina in Tangier, bright sunlight streamed down into the marble open courtyard. Accompanied by occasional shrieks and cries of swooping seagulls flying overhead, it led to a most unusual stage for Clurman's New York City apartment! Coupled with the sounds of crashing waves of the Mediterranean a few hundred yards away, it certainly had its own authenticity in the moment.

On my first journey abroad with my solo play, I had traveled to perform in Tbilisi, Georgia, in The GIFT Festival. My performance took place inside The Cave Theatre. Yes, it was a cave, and the stage that held Clurman's apartment was no more than six feet wide and four feet deep—with the roof of the cave only a few inches above Clurman's fedora. Nevertheless, with only one light illuminating the action—the audience, sitting a few feet in front of me—was transfixed by Clurman's passion. The intimacy lent itself to a feeling as if we were being 'woven together inside a womb' by the stories Clurman brought to life in this singular moment.

Later that evening over dinner, when I talked with the Russian director, Anatoly Vasiliev, I told him how different my performance was in a tightly enclosed cave, but no less intimate to the feeling I experienced from what he had achieved with his acting company in a Chekhov production at the Georgian National Opera Theater a few hours before. This is always the marvel of performing in so many different spaces, whether you're indoors or outdoors. It's part of the Transformation. The stories remain the same, as does the storyteller—yet, each time, it's an opportunity to renew the meaning of existence.

Several times I have crisscrossed India on different tours, performing and teaching at many different theaters, universities, colleges, acting schools—and even under the stars. Every time I have arrived in India, I feel like I've 'come home.' I can't describe it in any other way. India holds a magical place in my heart because of the vast beauty of its land and history, music, art, architecture, and extraordinary temples—and I always make new friends. Some of them include the filmmaker, Sachin Gupta; Artistic Director of the Auroville Theatre Group, Jill Navarre; the renowned conductor of the Indian National Symphony Orchestra in Bangalore, Dr. Ashley William Joseph; and two of my dearest friends was one of India's greatest playwrights, Vijay Tendulkar; and Alyque Padamsee, the patriarch of English theatre in India.

Alyque had been a world-renowned director who introduced *Evita* and *Jesus Christ Superstar* to India. Considered the brand father of Indian advertising, he was a fine actor and had played Muhammad Ali Jinnah in the film *Gandhi* opposite Sir Ben Kingsley.

When I first met Alyque, I was standing outside the National School of Drama in New Delhi, and we struck up a conversation. I mentioned that I was going to be staying in Mumbai with a young actor known as 'Q,' short for Quasar. He told me: "That's my son." You see, that's the magic of India! Full of amazing and life-changing coincidences! Instantly, we became good friends, seeing one another on my many different tours to India.

When I had been invited to perform and teach at the Cpracsis Conference for Asian Performance, I traveled to the south of India to the city of Thissur in Kerala. Walking through its colorful beehive of markets filled the streets of fresh fruits and vegetables, wares of every shape and size, above me loomed a large white Catholic cathedral overlooking the busy streets. While not too far away stood ancient and noble temples with majestic colorful towers.

In the evening, my performance came to life outdoors beneath the glittering stars. Tall cypress trees stood watch to the right and left of me; Clurman's apartment floor was on grass. I could feel the earth beneath my shoes—almost giving me the sensation that I was—indeed, one with the earth. At the same time, through my imagination, Clurman looked out the window of his apartment on West 57th Street.

On another trip, I was invited to represent the United States at the 2018 Theater Olympics. Connecting the past, present, and future, the Theatre Olympics celebrates the cultural diversity of different theater-makers from India and around the world. I was fortunate to give my first performance inside the Kamani Auditorium, considered the city's most prestigious Theatre Hall. Clurman met a large 'house' filled with a most enthusiastic audience, students filling most of the seats who gravitated immediately to Clurman's storytelling. The entire evening was one of a joyous sharing-together of laughter and passion. The next day, the National School of Drama invited me to teach my 'Art of Transformation' Workshop for their students. I read to them the words of Gandhi as we talked about Transformation, and how we're each responsible to help change the world for the better. It was gratifying to be in the middle of the Olympics, teaching at NSD, as it's referred to, where many of India's finest actors and actresses have learned their craft.

The following day before I flew to Kerala for my second performance, I visited Gandhi Smitri. It's known as the national memorial to the Father of the Nation—Mahatma Gandhi. I walked down Tees January Marg, a large boulevard lined with thick-leaved trees arriving for my second visit to the Birla

House, where Gandhi had lived for the last one hundred and forty-four days of his life, until his tragic death on January 30th, 1948.

Once inside, I stood alone at a simple doorway. In front of me, a sign read: 'Gandhi's Room.' Peering inside, on the floor, lay a mattress covered in bright white, on which he had slept. Nearby was a copy of the Bhagavad Gita. Before it, a small low wooden writing table where he had sat. Gandhi's Room has been kept as it had been on that fateful day. On a wall nearby, a large wooden frame holds Gandhi's last possessions labeled 'Worldly Remains.' I looked and found two spoons. Two forks and a knife. His reading glasses and a case. A pocket watch. A stone that he washed with instead of soap. A cutting knife, and his walking stick. On the wall above the stone fireplace, a second frame holds the inscription: 'My life is my message.' I stood in the room for the longest time. It was one of the quietest places I've ever been. I was entirely alone. It was as if I could reach out and touch the silence.

Silence plays a great role in the work we do on stage. Once you lower the 'noise' inside your head and you move into another sphere—you'll find a different kind of silence. Silence is always necessary to allow the organic process to occur. But it doesn't mean there's no sound. Slowing down gives you the opportunity to hear what you may not normally hear.

When I quietly stepped out of the room and closed the door behind me, I traveled along a garden path—next to another path which Gandhi had taken on his last walk –now holding impressions of his footprints. I arrived at an expansive lawn at the back of the grounds surrounded by fountains and Ashoka trees. Crows loudly cawing from their branches. Surprisingly again, I found myself completely alone in a country of a billion people. How this was possible, I haven't a clue. I stood silently at the spot where Gandhi had fallen. Nearby, close to the prayer ground, I read Albert Einstein's words: "Generations to come will scarce believe . . ." I closed my eyes and listened as the earth turned.

Wherever I teach my 'Art of Transformation' Workshop, I always hold up a copy of *A Gandhian Rosary*, which I had bought on my first visit at the Birla House years before, and I read aloud: "We must widen our circle of our love till it embraces the whole village; the village in its turn must take into its fold the district, the district the province, and so on till the scope of our love becomes coterminous with the world . . . The golden rule of conduct . . . is mutual toleration . . . Truth is like a vast tree, which yields more and more fruit, the more you nurture it. The deeper the search in the mine of Truth, the richer the discovery of the gems buried there, in the shape of an opening for an ever-greater variety of service."

"There should be truth in thought, Truth in speech, and Truth in action . . . I see and find Beauty in Truth or through Truth. All Truth, not merely true ideas, but truthful faces, truthful pictures, or songs, are highly beautiful. People generally fail to see Beauty in Truth, the ordinary man runs away from it and becomes blind to the Beauty in it. Whenever men (and women) begin to see Beauty in Truth, then true art will arise."

I tell my students: "You are 'Truth.' You are 'Love.' You are 'Peace.' Each of you carries a gift to the world to tell your stories. This is how we heal one another."

When I arrived in Kerala for my second performance during the Olympics at Thiruvananthapuram's famed Tagor Theatre, its entrance was graced by immense bamboo trees all lit up in bright lavender and pink, green and purple hues. On the stage, with every seat taken, I was delightfully grateful to find my hosts had placed an antique Asian elaborately-carved wooden ceremony chair at Clurman's desk, which lent a great deal of authenticity to the occasion and to Clurman's apartment.

On one of my tours when I had traveled to Mumbai, I had been invited by one of India's premier actors, Anupam Kher, to perform my play and teach his students at his prestigious Actor Prepares School. After my performance, I was delighted to see not only Anupam but Alyque had come as well. Over dinner later, Alyque told me: "What a great influence Clurman and his book *On Directing* have had on my life, from the beginning. Clurman and his book taught me everything was possible," he told me.

As I've gotten to know many different artists around the world, I find how much Clurman and his books have had a lasting impact on so many lives. When I performed at the National Theatre in the Cayman Islands, Henry Muttoo, the Artistic Director of the Cayman National Cultural Foundation told me, that: "Clurman's book changed my life when I read it during my days in college. It helped me to decide in which direction to go as a set designer and a director."

John Patrick Shanley, the well-known playwright, and screenwriter of the film, *Moonstruck*, told me when I interviewed him that when he was going to direct the film version of his play, *Doubt*, with Meryl Streep, he used Clurman's book as a guide.

During my own preparations, I also used *On Directing* when I was invited to direct a production of the hit comedy, *LUV*, in Bosnian, at the Chamber Theatre 55 in Sarajevo.

In Mumbai, each day when I traveled along the Indian Ocean inside a teetering three-wheel Tuk-Tuk to teach at the Actor Prepares School—I'd pass by a glistening large memorial statue sculpted by Deviprasad Roychowdhury—depicting eighty marchers with Gandhi leading them in the twenty-four-day salt march they had endured from Sabarmati to Dandi in 1930. What I enjoyed the most about the statue was the details of each person in line behind Gandhi. You could feel their determination, their persistence to realize their dream in how the sculptor shaped each figure.

One morning, soon after I had arrived, all the students and teachers stood up and began proudly singing India's National Anthem. It was the 60th anniversary of the founding of India. As I stood beside them, listening to their soaring voices, I couldn't help but be moved to think how young a country India is. Yet, how far they've come, with such an extraordinary history.

Before I departed Mumbai, Anupam Kher and I sat down to talk together. I asked him, "How did you begin as an actor?" He laughed. "I was a ham. I wanted to stand out in a crowd. I loved watching films, but I never entertained the thought of having a life as an actor." He had started out acting in plays in school and studied at Punjab University. "I understood the importance of training," he told me. "So, I went to NSD after that. I was lucky to have a very fine teacher to help me discover who I was as an actor, as a person. After my first play, Dolly Thakore's mother came to see me act. She wanted me to meet Alyque Padamsee. At that time, he was considered the 'God of the Theater.' Alyque didn't want to even take a look at me. He said: "I can't meet every Tom, Dick & Harry!"

"It took me three years of struggle. But I believe, if you want something, you go about it fruitfully and honestly, and you'll achieve it. Finally, when I had a meeting with the film director, Mahesh Bhatt, he said to me: "I hear you're good." I told him: "I'm not good. I'm brilliant!" I got the role of a 65-year-old man in his film, *Saaransh*. I found a way to express the great emotional pain of this man by drawing upon the immediate reality. I know there's more to life than acting. It's just as important to grow as a person. Teaching young people, interacting with them means so much to me. It goes back to the same journey I started with." From an early age, Kher knew what he was born and destined to become. I understand that.

When I was about five years old, I was already imitating everyone and everything in my path—I was like 'a child on fire.' Always moving, always climbing in every possible direction. I think the only way that my parents could deal with me was to get me out of the house—and into the house of an acting teacher, who had a stage in her dining room. As soon as I met my new teacher, Esther Brezo, I was 'in heaven.' There had to have been about ten or twelve other children and teenagers in the class, and we'd sit around a long table and read poems and Shakespeare out loud. When it was time, we'd get up on stage and act out scenes using words we'd randomly pick out from a large glass bowl. Like 'gold,' 'rich,' 'boat.' I'd unfold the paper and look at the words in my tiny fingers, along with two other children who also did the same. Then we'd rush around on the stage, putting the words into a story—making sure we used each of the words. You had to be quick. In improvisation, it's all about keeping everything going, like juggling five balls in the air at the same time—like performing in a solo play.

It so happened one afternoon—a moment came that changed my life forever. That's the only way I can describe it. I was in the middle of one of those improvisations, and everything seemed to be building to a climax. Someone had lost a valuable necklace. The princess had to have it back, or else the kingdom would be lost forever. No one knew where it was. It had disappeared. Until one of the children on stage loudly cried out: "He took it!" Pointing directly at me. I thought it was all fun and games up to that moment. I was in shock! I think if there was anywhere else I wanted to be—it certainly wasn't there. I wanted to crawl under a rock and disappear forever. I knew I hadn't taken it, but everyone was looking at me like I had. Like I was guilty already. I could see myself being taken away to a dungeon or even worse. Losing my head or being thrown into a burning pit with a thousand wriggling snakes.

I didn't know what to do. How was I going to convince them that I didn't have it? I started coming up with every reason in the world I could think of why I couldn't possibly have taken it. A whole dialogue of words poured out of my mouth. Where they came from, I had no idea. They just kept coming. I probably didn't know half of what I was saying. But I was standing up for myself! For justice! For truth! For everything that was right in the world! To prove to them that I hadn't taken the necklace. Everyone looked at me in shock when I was finished, as if they didn't believe me. I was shaking so much, I had to sit down, and I started crying. I thought no one in the world believes me.

Mrs. Brezo came over and held me. She explained that what I just did is called acting. And today, I had become an actor. At that moment, I knew what I was going to do for the rest of my life.

For me, South Africa has always been one of those countries far, far away. Like on the other side of the moon. When I was about seven or eight years old, I began collecting stamps. I knew a lot of famous people did the same thing. President Franklin Delano Roosevelt. Queen Elizabeth. Over the years, I had accumulated so many that my Father finally bought me a stamp album. I probably had stamps from every country in the world, in every shape, color, and size. You, no doubt, have your own hobbies. Things you collect that inspire you.

What fascinated me the most were the stories they told. Right on the face of the stamp is a country's history or a fascinating face of someone who has changed the world. America's stamps have our founding fathers. Famous and important moments in our country's history. Individuals that have made a positive difference. When I held up a stamp and looked at the Battle of Yorktown, I imagined I was there facing the British. Cannons roaring! It became real to me.

It so happened that on the back page of the album was an essay: 'I am a Postage Stamp,' that described where postage stamps could take you all over the world, to places I could only dream of going—Nepal and South Africa. India and Thailand. Places where I'd eventually tour with my play and teach others what I had learned. Little did I know what's carried on the wind.

One afternoon, my grandmother, who sometimes would come for a visit, sat down next to me and watched as I carefully placed stamps inside my album. I proudly showed the paragraph on the last page. While sitting next to me on the porch, she asked me to read it to her. I had never read it out loud. I couldn't pronounce half the words. For some reason, as I kept reading it, the words seem to take on a life of their own. As I spoke each word, I could see them dancing in the air in front of me. A minute ago, they were just words on a page. Now they were places all over the world coming alive. I could feel them inside of me.

When I finished, my grandmother said to me, "You're going to go to these places one day. You'll see. One day." I looked up at her, into her bright blue eyes. I didn't know why but I believed her. How could she possibly know something like that, I thought to myself.

On one of my tours, my play indeed brought me to South Africa. Just as my grandmother had told me I would that day when we were sitting together on the porch. I had been invited to perform and teach at the Festival of Fame held by the National School of the Arts in Johannesburg, South Africa. An exhilarating experience it certainly turned out to be! Following my performance, I held my acting master Workshop for more than seventy-five excited young students, placing into each of their hands a copy of Stanislavski's chart. I slowly explained who Stanislavski was and how he put his chart together as we sat in a large circle.

"He started out not knowing what it meant to be an actor. But he had a lot of dreams like you do. He had a great passion for what he loved, and he loved the theater." Several of the students had come from the nearby township of Soweto.

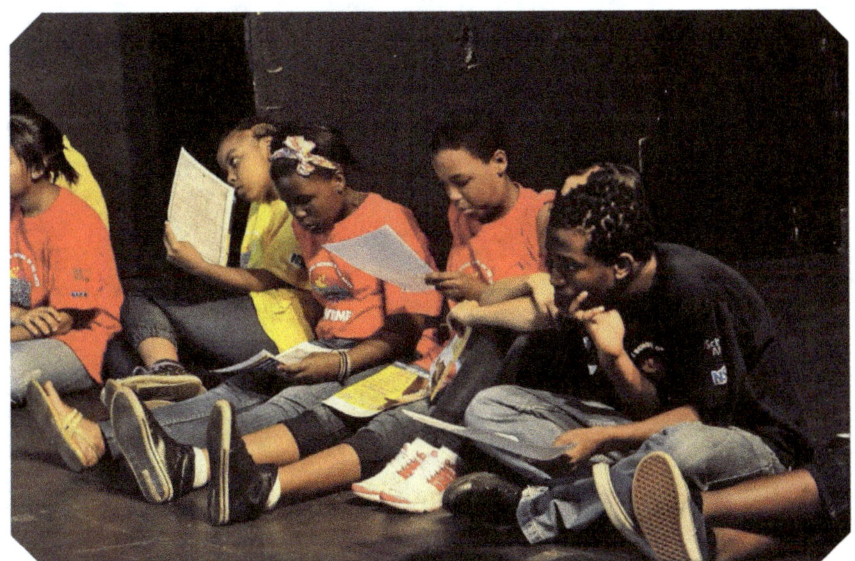

During Ronald Rand's Workshop during the Festival of Fame at the National School of the Arts, Johannesburg, South Africa. (Courtesy Ronald Rand.)

"Each of you can grow up like he did, just like Mandela, like Gandhi, and change the world for the better. Stanislavski did this through the theater. But he had to learn *how* to do it. Once he did, he wrote it all down, and these tools on this chart are a map that teaches us how to tell stories. A way to transform yourself into another person. Out there—(pointing out the open door)—are a lot of animals in the jungle. They also can tell us stories. They teach us how to live."

At that point, I asked some of the students to come into the circle and become any animal they wanted to be. I told them they had to relate to one another as their animals. It's a great lesson to see how Transformation occurs. I invited one of the students to tell a story as her 'animal' to everyone else. She began walking around in the circle, taking everyone on a joy-filled journey as if she was the animal telling her story. A perfect example of being free enough and letting the story be your guide. She also happened to add a lot of humor. Everyone joined in the 'fun,' and which happens naturally when we release all of our inhibitions and let the playfulness inside us soar.

One time in southern India during my acting Workshop, a young actor had dissolved himself to such a degree as a tiger that when he suddenly turned and growled, some of the other students jumped up in fright and ran away. It appeared as if he had allowed the spirit of the animal to come into him

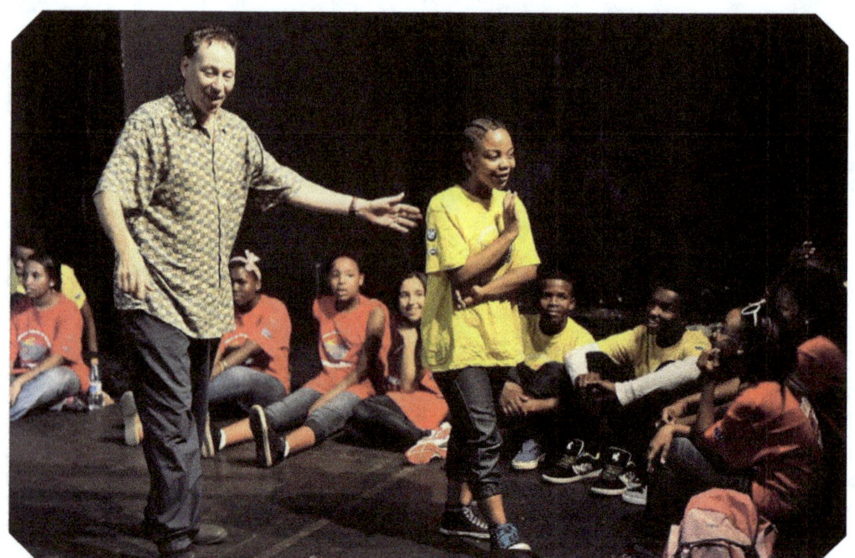

During Ronald Rand's Workshop during the Festival of Fame at the National School of the Arts, Johannesburg, South Africa. (Courtesy Ronald Rand.)

through his imagination and willed his body to change. When I looked into his eyes—as I had told everyone afterward—I saw a tiger looking out at me. It made the hair on my arms tingle. True organic life through Transformation can happen in an instant.

On a sun-showered afternoon, I walked up the steep Constitution Hill. Before me stood the massive walls of Johannesburg's Old Fort, a grim late 19th-century jail where tens of thousands of prisoners were once held, including two of South Africa's Nobel Peace Prize winners, Nelson Mandela and Albert Luthuli.

Entering its Number Four building, I had to bow my head to step inside the cell where Gandhi and Mandela had been held. Through its thick bars, I looked out at a patch of blue sky. Nearby, I could see the Women's Jail where Winnie Madikizela-Mandela, Albertina Sisulu, Ruth First, and Fatima Meer had also been held as prisoners. Both Gandhi and Mandela had 'grounded themselves' in isolation and pain, alone, unbowed, but with patience, they each retained their hope for freedom and peace.

In the museum, I gazed at a pair of sandals that Gandhi had made while he was a prisoner in his cell. After he was released, he sent the sandals back to his gatekeeper—as part of his philosophy—'satyagraha'—which means 'truth.' To him, that implied: 'love and firmness,' which served Gandhi during his life as a synonym for force. During that time, he reminded everyone that through the power of 'Transformation' the world can change. That we can become what we believe ourselves to be. It's truly one of the great lessons of life.

After I left, I visited a large modern building right next to the Old Fort. From more than 150,000 bricks taken from the former jail stairwells, a new Constitutional Court rose. Mandela stood there in 1995 at its opening and presented the new South African Court to his people. What a powerful and meaningful place for justice and human rights to be preserved. Taking a negative space of repression and incarceration and turning it into one of hope and positive energy. I entered and observed the Court in session. From out of their struggle for freedom, a social Transformation arose for a new future for the constitutional democracy of South Africa. It's both heartening and spiritually uplifting.

Before I departed Johannesburg, one of the parents of a student I had taught, who had participated in the uprising in 1976 as a young man, drove me for a visit to Soweto, which had been the largest black Township in the days of South Africa's apartheid—a symbol of resistance to the racist regime. Everywhere on many of its streets, I could see faces of courage and struggle painted on walls. Among them, Mandela's shining portrait. We visited the Hector Pieterson Memorial commemorating the role of students in the anti-apartheid movement. I learned that Pieterson was only twelve years old when he, along with more than a hundred and seventy protesting school children, were killed.

When we stopped at Mandela's original home, as I approached the door, I could see bullet holes that still remained in the walls from when he had lived there in 1946. He actually spent little time in the house before he was forced to go underground, living a life 'on the run' until his arrest and imprisonment. After his release from Robben Island in 1990, Mandela returned to this house, but just for a brief eleven days.

We stopped at the Regina Mundi Church, referred to as 'the people's church.' Mandela had described it as 'a literal battlefield,' where students had fled to escape the dogs, bullets and, tear gas canisters flying all around them. Bullet holes remain in the ceiling and in the altar where Mandela and Archbishop Desmond Tutu had once spoken. Standing before Mandela's image in a stained-glass window on one side of the church, in my ears reverberated his words: "We can change the world and make it a better place. It is in your hands to make a difference . . . It always seems impossible until it's done . . . What counts in life is not the mere fact that we have lived; it is what difference we have made to the lives of others that will determine the significance of the life we lead."

His words held a special significance and meaning for me when I flew to Zimbabwe. I had been invited as the first American to perform and teach at Harare's Buddyz 'Bafa' Festival of Arts. Arriving in October of 2010, the country was in the midst of a 'power-sharing' between President Robert Mugabe and Prime Minister Morgan Tsvangirai. When I took a walk from my hotel in downtown Harare to Africa Unity Square, drenched in sparkling sunlight, I had a chance to move among its people under the vivid purple blooms of the Jacarandas Trees.

Since my performance was going to take place the following day, I was taken to see some of the Festival. Dynamic dancers in dazzling red, green, and yellow costumes performed in tribal dances, filling the stage of a large white open-air bandshell theater. Thundering drumming, leg rattles, pounding musical gourds pulsated through the air. Dance is a cornerstone of Zimbabwe's heritage, a celebration of their culture.

I stepped inside a large wood-framed circular Shona Tribal Hut on the grounds of Harare Gardens to see the Ziya Theatre from Masvingo in a play about the discrimination of disabled people. I joined several others sitting on wooden bleacher-style rows stretching around in a circle, rows and rows, one on top of the other, reaching almost to the open roof in the center of the roof. It was a most engaged audience. So much, in fact, some were making it clear that they didn't like what was happening on the stage. They began talking loudly directly to the performers. Attending performances around the world is always an education in how different audiences react. The actor onstage 'broke the fourth wall' and started talking directly to the audience member, denying that he was doing anything wrong. Several in the audience booed him. That didn't stop him. Back and forth they went until an actress on the stage 'shushed' everyone, so the play could continue.

Theater has always had an element of confrontation, all the way back to the Greeks. Now, more than ever—it's back, front, and center—as a powerful catalyst for change.

In the Tribal hut, when the audience saw how the disabled person in the play overcame the antagonist despite his limitations, immediately there was a rousing enthusiastic response from the audience. Shouting gleefully in the air, they danced with each other in the bleachers. I wondered what would happen the following evening when they met Harold Clurman.

After the performance, I talked with the young performers, presenting them with copies of my newspaper, "The Soul of the American Actor," which I had brought from America, as a way of saying 'thank you' for their performance.

That evening as I prepared in my 'Creation Room' inside a small hut on the grounds, I could hear drumming in the distance. When Clurman entered 'his apartment' inside the large Tribal hut, over two hundred Zimbabweans filled the bleachers to the roof. There wasn't a single space to be had. Some even sat at both of Clurman's elbows on chairs. When Clurman sat down at his desk, the tribal hut was packed. After a few moments, several in the audience began to murmur and register their delight, loudly talking to one another about Clurman's cape and fedora, as if they were in a café loudly discussing an event they had seen the night before. Some called out in agreement to what Clurman said when he gave his 'Talk' to the actors, which Clurman took as a natural response, acknowledging everything they said—responding and plowing forward. He felt 'right at home,' totally enjoying the tight intimacy and great enthusiasm from the audience.

At the end of my solo play, Clurman always says: "And if it's a bad situation in the theatre, what's the answer? The answer is to go out and do your darndest to do the things that are proper to do them any way you know how to do them! Truth is like castor oil. It's bitter to swallow. People don't want it. So, you make them laugh! And when their mouths are open, you pour it in! But to do the things that are necessary to do, and to fight for those things! And to be yourself with people! Because only people like you can create a new world! Someone who's articulate enough to fill their mind full of thoughts! And your heart full of passion!"

There was complete silence. Clurman had spoken the 'unspeakable,' especially in Zimbabwe. Such words could easily get one thrown into jail. Before the performance, I wondered: 'Would I be able to leave when it came time for me to board the plane?'

After every performance, when Clurman disappears, and I return for the 'Question and Answer,' of course, I begin speaking in my own voice. I always say a few sentences of personal thanks in every language of each country I perform in. This time I gave a short speech in Shona to thank the organizers of the Festival. Talking about how art and theater plays a great role in bringing us together to share our humanity.

Suddenly, several young men in the audience stood up and started shouting, jumping up and down, pointing and gesturing at me. Others in the audience tried to calm them down. I soon found out from another member of the audience who explained: "They thought you were Harold Clurman. Now you have become possessed by someone else with a different voice. A 'spirit' has appeared and taken you over."

For over a thousand years ago, the Shona had built great cities in Africa. In the Shona Spirit World, it's a common belief that spirits and spirit possession exist in this world and in another world, interchangeably. That a 'n'anga,' a medium, can become possessed by one of these spirits during a trance and also have the power to heal through being possessed. That a person can also be entered by a 'svikiro,' an ancestral spirit, and receive advice that way.

I tried to assure them, explaining I go through a Transformation that allows Clurman to come, that it's part of my acting process. They were transfixed and wanted to know more about it. I told them, "Come to my Workshop tomorrow. It will all be explained." Some of the perplexed young men kept staring at me, keeping their distance warily. Wondering if I had indeed become possessed by another spirit who was still inside of me and where did Harold Clurman go.

At my Workshop the next day, inside a different tribal hut on the grounds, I talked about my organic process of the 'Art of Transformation.' I could see several of the young men lingering in the back still had reservations about who was really inside of me. I answered all of their questions as we examined Stanislavski's chart together. They wanted to understand the connection between what Stanislavski meant about creation and how I became someone else during my performance. Their eyes lit up when they began to see how I had made the leap through Stanislavski's System. That it was there, right in front of them, as they looked at the chart. That was how I 'became' Clurman. At the end of the Workshop, the group of young men came over and shook my hand. "We understand now," they told me. But then they asked: "Where did Harold Clurman go?"

I encountered a similar political dilemma when I traveled to Minsk in Belarus to perform as the first American to perform in a Solo play in over twenty-five years on the stage of the Palace of Culture of the Trade Unions Theatre. At the end of the performance, which has been translated into Russian on a large screen on stage next to me, audience members came up, and under their breath, asked me how I could get away with saying such things since saying them out loud was forbidden in the last surviving dictatorship in Europe. I replied, "But it's not me saying them. It's Harold Clurman. I can't stop him from saying what he has to say." It's never my intention to provoke a political discussion in one way or another or to turn my play into a kind of a polemic or make a statement. Clurman has to say what he has to say. As we know, every play *is* 'political' in nature because it's about issues that confront us every day of our lives. They need to be spoken, heard, and discussed.

The following day, I held a Workshop on the stage of the large auditorium at the Belarusian State University. I must have handed out over a hundred copies of Stanislavski's chart between those on the stage participating and those in the audience observing. I could feel their excitement to actually hold Stanislavski's chart in front of them. Nothing we do in the theater exists in a vacuum. Together, we explored and fervently discussed and worked together on exercises.

I told them: "The actor's constantly challenged to bring to the stage the richest characterization possible. But we have to keep our minds open because there's a world of difference between who you are and who you're bringing to life on the stage. We all come from our own lives. But when you go inside a play. Ah . . . now—you're inside a totally different world. The world of this 'other' person—and everything they have to deal with. The 'Art of Transformation' allows this to come through me when I'm preparing from a deep place in my soul—from a deep understanding of who I am and who other this person is—and why it's necessary that I'm bringing them to life. So when I put all of this into action—that's what is coming through me in every gesture, in everything I say—my body expresses what must be shared. In this way, the art of storytelling becomes an organic process happening in the moment."

When I was invited to Colombia to perform at the 'International Theatre Festival of Peace under the 'Big Top' in Barrancabermeja, I traveled to the north of their country, on the shore of the Magdalena River. During Colombia's forty-year civil war, Barrancabermeja was the most dangerous city in the entire country. With over a million people and the nation's largest oil refinery, with gold and nickel lying buried in the nearby San Lucas mountains, surrounding on all sides, there's also thousands and thousands of acres of coca fields. During that period, delegations of women, all in black, called for protests to stop the armed conflict's violence that ended up claiming more than 30,000 lives. Now the city was quiet, although the guerillas were still in the hills and mountains not too far away.

Arriving in Barrancabermeja, I boarded the 'festival' bus, and even though we all came from different places around the world, and for the most part, everyone aboard spoke Spanish, we all laughed and joked together, as if we were old friends, happy to be together at a theater festival for peace. When we stepped off the bus, before us stood one of the largest circus tents in South America, over sixty feet tall. Bright, colorful flags waved in the breeze at the top, and inside stood a large stage. We were told that some of the trapeze artists from Cirque du Soleil come and use it during their off-season.

In the evening, we were taken to a local restaurant that had been created by a courageous woman who stood her ground during the 'hard times.' She had delivered food she had grown to the poor across the river and led peace marches through the city in the face of death threats. Somehow, the guerillas never touched her. All the different foods we were served that evening had been her personal recipes. Naturally grown, plain, and delicious—maiz, Arroz con Pollo, Arepas, traditional dishes referred to as comida de la gente—food of the people.

Several of the Festival performances took place beneath the 'Big Top,' and I'd sit delighted watching exuberantly colorfully dressed South American dance companies and experimental plays mostly all in Spanish performed with enormous puppets and masks. On one of the evenings, we swatted away thick bands of mosquitos sitting outside watching an 'environmental' performance play under only a couple of colored lights. Of course, it was hot. No, it was extremely hot! But we were there for the love of theater, in support of peace. And the audience would always show up with a great outflowing of support—even when the power went out, and the large fans stopped turning.

When it came time for my performance, I was told it would be inside a large theater space in the college next door. I took a look. The back wall was so far away from the audience, it would be impossible to project the script translated into Spanish from that distance and for it to be visible. What to do? The only solution, I was told, was to have a person on stage translate every word. Would I do it? Of course. The real question was: would Clurman go along?

I had to quickly involve a young translator into the performance to make sure she understood what Clurman meant by everything he said in the play. So we went over the script together, so she could translate his words immediately into Spanish.

That evening during my preparation, I told Clurman: "There will be a student in your apartment who will be speaking Spanish. She will be translating everything you say. You'll need to stop after a sentence or two, so it can be translated. I had no idea what would happen or what he would do. We were both sailing into uncharted territory.

It turned out to be one of the most engrossing stage experiences I've ever had. Clurman did exactly what he needed to do. He spoke one sentence or two at a time. Then he'd stop, but he didn't wait. He'd busy himself with what he had on his desk. He'd work on his essay or examine a letter someone had sent him. It was a lesson of 'living in the moment.' How he occupied himself while his words were translated into Spanish.

When the performance was over, I thanked everyone in Spanish, including my translator, and almost by rote, she began translating my words 'into Spanish,' which made everyone laugh. I always make sure in my remarks to the audience that I speak the words as correctly as possible, having written them down phonetically. Afterward, I come down into the audience and shake hands with every person. At this performance, many in the audience didn't want to leave. They came up on stage, standing around Clurman's desk examining every book, every piece of paper, telling me how much it meant to them to have heard Clurman's words. One woman said to me: "It was exactly what I needed to hear. It was 'medicine' for my soul."

A day later, I was invited by the former mayor of a small town, San Vicente de Chucuri, nestled in the San Lucas mountains, to come and do a special performance for their town. They had never had an American perform at their theater. "Of course," I said, without realizing where I would be going. San Vicente de Chucuri was a dangerous town in the region during the armed conflict in the 1980s. Now it is one of the largest cacao producers in northern Colombia.

When the next morning arrived, there he stood, waiting patiently next to his shiny, sturdy pickup truck. Climbing aboard with two other dancers, I loaded my wheeling bag and Clurman's clothing for the performance, and off we went. Up we climbed, leaving Barrancabermeja behind, winding our way across the San Lucas mountains through its plush tropical forests, with the jungle soon enveloping us—and the pavement of the road soon changed.

Did I say 'road?' The flat asphalt soon became a completely broken jagged lane filled with pieces of stones and small boulders which made us rock from side-to-side, making it feel like we were floundering on a ship in the North Sea, and that any second I'd be thrown 'off the bronco' out the window and down the side of the rugged mountains. On we plodded until there wasn't even a road any longer. At one point, we literally slid forward on the wet mud. Obviously, our host had made this journey quite a few times before. He knew exactly how to maneuver, especially when we came within, at least it felt like, a couple of inches to the drop-off and the valley below, he'd immediately swing the wheel, and on we'd climb. At one point, to the right and left of us, stretching for miles as far as the eye could see, were bright green cacao plants. Were there guerillas in the fields and in the mountains around us? Of course. The historic peace agreement that ended fifty-two years of fighting wouldn't be signed for four more years.

When we turned a bend, there in the valley below us lay San Vicente de Chucuri, surrounded by a gorgeous vista of sky-reaching mountains.

I soon found out again that no one would understand a word of the performance without a translator on the stage repeating everything Clurman said. Luckily, they found a student of the English language, but he had never been on stage before. I had my work cut out for me. Luckily, it all worked out beautifully.

During my preparation, I told Clurman there would be a student again in his apartment who would be translating everything he said into Spanish and that he'd need to stop so that it could be translated. During the performance, Clurman did exactly what he needed to do.

Try it sometime as an exercise when you're working on your solo performance, by taking breaks between the dialogue and living in the space—moment to moment.

In my 'Creation Room,' looking out through the window in front of me, I could see the beautiful tall mountains ascending above the rich green canopy of the dark Columbian jungle. Loud native birds and monkey chatter floated over the sounds of the rushing stream below as the molecules took off and began to fly.

After the performance, I looked out onto the theater filled with the townspeople—families with small children, many students—who all graciously thanked me for coming afterward. When I read my prepared words in Spanish, I told them that it was an honor to perform for them in their beautiful theater. During the 'Question and Answer' with the audience, question after question

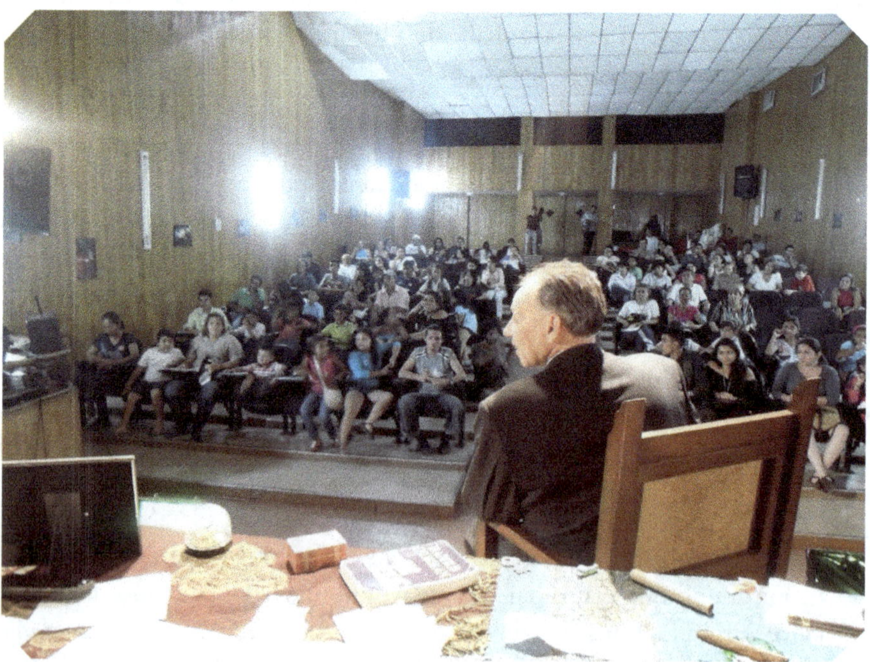

Ronald Rand with the audience after his performance in San Vicente de Chucuri, Colombia. (Courtesy Ronald Rand.)

kept flying in my direction: "What did I think about being in Columbia?" "What's America like and New York City?" "Do all the people live in cities?" "What kind of food do you eat?" "What kind of movies do you watch?" And so on. Certainly going on almost as long as the performance. No one wanted it to end. I have to believe Clurman's 'down-to-earth' common sense and humor had touched their hearts, and through theater, we became 'a family,' even though we didn't speak the same language and came from completely different cultures. We spoke the 'language of the heart.'

If history has taught us anything, it takes a willingness to build trust by coming together in person. Through the power of storytelling, a dialogue can take place, transforming into an entirely new dynamic of understanding, of empathy—sharing what is basic in all of humanity.

As I write these words, my heart is heavy learning the news of the loss of an individual who stepped forward in the service of others when the stakes couldn't have been higher. Showing us how necessary it is to live a life filled with dignity in pursuit of justice, freedom, and common decency. John Lewis, the son of sharecroppers, rose in stature and position to become a U.S. Congressman and led the fight for the Voting Rights Act of 1965. He was an original Freedom Rider, arrested more than forty times. He marched over the Alabama River and was beaten at the bridge that leads from Selma to Montgomery on 'Bloody Sunday,' attempting to commemorate the death of Jimmie Lee Jackson. Bloodied, he still rose up, following Martin Luther King, Jr.'s inspiring dream. He continued to stand up for the future of all people. His words remind us how much courage it takes—in the midst of overwhelming circumstances, to stand shoulder-to-shoulder against injustice, as his words reflect: "It is the power in the way of peace, the way of love. We must never, ever hate. The way of love is a better way."

Inspiring figures throughout history have led us forward. You can continually draw strength from their example of human decency, courage, and faith as you work on your solo play. Maya Angelou, Mary McLeod Bethune, Anne Frank, Delores Huerta, Helen Keller, Martin Luther King, Jr., Abraham Lincoln, Rosa Parks, Eleanor Roosevelt, Sacagawea, Harriet Tubman, Mother Teresa are just a few who have shown what the human spirit is capable of—transforming darkness into light. Powerlessness into strength. Pain into humor. Through their actions, they influenced others—encouraging us to take a harder look at the values that bind us all together.

In 1943, the future of democracy and freedom of the world hung in the balance. Four U.S. Army chaplains: Army Lt. George L. Fox, a Methodist;

Lt. Alexander D. Goode, who was Jewish; Lt. John P. Washington, a Catholic; and Lt. Clark V. Poling, a Dutch Reformed minister, were aboard a converted U.S. Army Transport troop ship crossing the submarine-infested icy waters of the North Atlantic off the coast of Greenland. In the middle of the night, the USAT Dorchester, with over nine hundred sailors aboard, was struck by a torpedo. Shattering its hull, the darkened ship exploded. Fire engulfed every deck and passageway. While the ship filled with water, many men were trapped below deck. Sailors fought their way out as the ship began listing to one side. In the midst of it all, these four chaplains never stopped helping soldiers get off the ship into lifeboats. Lt. Goode even handed his gloves off to one of the sailors. When the supply of life jackets ran out, they took theirs off and tied them on to other sailors. In the frigid waters, the two hundred and thirty in lifeboats could hear above the waves, the four chaplains ministering to the many wounded men still on board, leading them in prayer with comforting hymns—as the ship went down.

What does the life of John Lewis and reading about these four chaplains mean to you? What would you have done in their place? Selfless acts of courage by individuals throughout history, especially by those on the front lines today faced with an almost unstoppable Pandemic, teaches us a grace 'under fire.' Nelson Mandela said: "I learned that courage was not the absence of fear. But the triumph over it. The brave person is not someone who does not feel afraid, but the person who conquers that fear."

Think of the times you have may have felt fear in your life and how you overcame it. Out of the strength inside your heart comes your courage. Alfred Lord Tennyson reminded us: "My strength has the power of ten because my heart is pure." The compassion and empathy you feel for others, no matter the situation, is a reminder you may not always know why you're being asked to do what you're being asked to do. But when you are, give more.

History has shown us time and again that a person's character may 'change' from good to bad in an instant. We have seen it happen in those created by writers in literature, writers writing for the stage, film and on television—and what you need to try to understand is how 'human nature' does that. Why an individual brings 'light' into the world—or is tempted to the 'dark' side?' Psychiatrist Carl Jung referred to it as a 'dark shadow' of the psyche. Those qualities we don't want to acknowledge, and we may repress. During your career, you may be called to an audition or bring to life a human being who acts from a strong moral character, or on the other hand, someone who operates from their 'dark side'—allowing their ego, low self-esteem, or personal inferiority to overwhelm their judgment. There are many factors that affect a person's behavior in how they think and feel, what they do, and whether they respect others or not.

Everything you do every day, the projects you work on, the shows you perform in, and when you perform your solo play—will affect the world we live in. Some refer to it as the 'ripple effect.' It's part of the mystery of life. Mother Teresa told us: "I alone cannot change the world, but I can cast a stone across the waters to create many *ripples.*" We are all connected to one another on this planet. How willing you are to live with a genuine acceptance of your responsibility will bring you a 'clarity' that will guide you—so you'll be able to make the right decisions as you go forward, touching lives in a positive and compassionate way.

It's why I continue performing in my solo play, as 'a bridge for greater understanding between peoples.' When my destiny was shown to me, I made a conscious decision. I was no longer willing to go to the 'dark side'—to act as an 'evil' person, or work on any project that has violence in it, on stage, in film, or on television—even though I had made a good living acting in hundreds of plays, films, and TV shows. Someone said to me: "Well, you can't bury your head in the sand. Ignore the real world. You're talking about giving up playing some of the great 'characters' like Iago, Richard III, and others." It's a choice we all have to make. I choose to contribute my thoughts and actions as much as I can towards the betterment of the world. You decide what 'mirror' you're willing to share with others.

In 2013, an opportunity came to me to make a space for hearts and minds to meet through theater, to allow meaningful intercultural dialogue to take place. The U.S. State Department chose me as the first Fulbright Specialist to teach and perform in Sarajevo. I had always read about Bosnia & Herzegovina since events that occurred in Sarajevo led to the beginning of World War I. And I certainly watched the exciting 1984 Sarajevo Winter Olympic Games.

My first visit to this city of 'hope and reconciliation' was to perform in the Sarajevo Winter Festival. When I arrived, heavy snow had blanketed the city, and even though Bosnia's National Museum had closed its doors after more than a hundred years due to a lack of funding, the Festival went on. Everyone I met embraced me like a friend. On the sides of buildings, pavements, everywhere you turned, you could see the scars of the longest siege of a capital city in modern history.

When I returned in 2013, it felt as if I could hear chimes in the air. Molecules were leading me forward to new vistas, new friends, new experiences. The Chamber Theatre 55 and the University of Sarajevo's Academy of Dramatic Arts invited me to come to share my performance as Clurman, to teach the 'Art of Transformation,' and to direct an American play translated into Bosnian.

As my plane approached Sarajevo in the bright sunlight of the day, I could see on the tops of all the hills surrounding the city thousands of white tombstones. Back in 1980, Bosnia was a multi-cultural country with Bosniak Muslims, Serbs, and Croats living peacefully within its borders. When Bosnia declared its independence from Belgrade, after the death of President Tito—at the same time, so did Slovenia and Croatia. However, Serbs living in Bosnia wanted to stay with Serbia. The Croats with Croatia. In 1992, the Siege of Sarajevo began. Bosnian Serbs formed an army calling themselves Republika Srpska and, supported by Serbia, began shelling mortars down on more than half a million people living in the city. Across the country, many Muslims fled from their homes. The Siege lasted five years until 1996. Nearly fourteen thousand people perished. Today, many years later, when Serbs, Croats, and Muslims work together, they help heal the scars of the war through tolerance and reconciliation.

Walking through the streets, I was surrounded by a bustling city filled with mosques, orthodox churches, cathedrals, and in the center of the square, townspeople playing chess, moving large black and white chess pieces across a painted board on the pavement.

For several weeks, with the talented students of the Academy of Dramatic Arts, off we set on a journey into what Transformation is all about. Empowering their imagination to take off and fly, we pored over Stanislavski's chart, talking about the great 'leap of faith' that's required in the art of acting. "During your life, others will depend upon you," I told them. "This art is a collaborative art demanding a generous heart. Putting other's needs above your own." Quoting C.S. Lewis: "A willingness to do the right thing even when no one is looking."

"Each day, you'll discover it's a constant transformative journey of the Self. Only by taking a good look at yourself—acknowledging your strengths—your weaknesses—your common sense—your intuition—you'll begin to get a sense of what Socrates was talking about when he said: 'Know thyself.' But nobody can do it for you. How well do you handle the 'voice' inside your head when things go wrong? When you hear negative comments about you. Criticisms. LET THEM GO! Put your focus on your 'path.' Let me ask you: What does it mean to have a 'third eye'? It's your 'sixth sense.' It's where the center of your intuition resides. Giving you the ability to let go of all fears and doubt."

"Who's heard of the 'Law of Attraction'?" I asked. "It's probably the most powerful law in the universe. Lots of books have been written about it. Folks have reminded us of the truth inside it. I think a lot about what Buddha said: "You are what you think about all day long." When Esther Hicks says: "Tell yourself: everything is always working out for me." They're not just words. It's believing you have the power over your life and can manifest what comes to you. The strength you carry within is what you share through your art."

"As powerful as the 'Golden Rule' is," I continued, "the 'Law of Attraction' can help make your dreams come true. Simply put, if you think negative thoughts, negative energy will surround you. But by sending out positive energy, focusing on what you want to happen in your life in a positive way, energy vibrations respond. Molecules take off and resonate. Every conscious thought you think, including the ones in your subconscious, is picked up by the universe. So, it's not only thinking about what you'd like to happen in your life—you have to actually see yourself already doing it and to act as if it is already happening to you. I know, that's a tall order. But that's the way it works. The universe picks up on every single one of your vibrations."

"So think big! Dream big! Little did I know when I saw myself traveling to my first country to share my play and Workshop, that all these years later, I would have performed in all the countries that I have! It's more than I ever thought was possible. That's the power of opening yourself up. Believing in infinite possibilities. It's a part of the 'Art of Transformation.' Knowing there's nothing in your way except the limitations *you* put there. Release all self-doubt. Bring to the world everything you are. Sometimes fate will step in and show you a direction that you can be in service in ways you never imagined. That's why I'm here in Sarajevo with you! The wonder of life is doing what you love and loving what you do."

Now I took them 'flying'—one of the exercises I use when I teach. "We all have the ability to 'fly.' And when I say that, it's a process of 'giving yourself permission' to allow your imagination to take off in flight as if you're a bird." It's always inspiring to see how each student defies gravity as I walk them through the exercise. Afterward, they tell me that they actually experienced the sensation and saw themselves flying like a bird. "The body, the mind—all that you are becomes an instrument for the imagination. By not getting in your way, it will take you wherever you want it to go. It will completely believe whatever you tell it."

Another Transformation exercise I use is called: 'Stepping Back in Time.' All the students immediately became part of a tribe twenty thousand years ago. Each student chooses a task for their village. Some fish, others hunt. A group makes baskets, while some cook and prepare meals. One becomes the shaman, another the chief.

"You carry within you the ability to transcend reality," I told them. "To 'time travel.' To dip into your unconscious. Now it's time to go through 'your' ritual. The ritual of your tribe. You already know what it is. It's the only way you can survive." Immediately the students gathered together, holding hands. Humming. Chanting. Moving in unison. They knew what their ritual was because it was inside of them. It's in our DNA. We're all a part of the tribe. Our ancestors gave it to us. This is how 'a leap of faith' takes place through the 'Art of Transformation.'

A few weeks later, the students I taught came to see me in my solo performance as Clurman at Chamber Theatre 55. I had been invited to perform and be a Festival Judge in the oldest theater festival in the Balkans, the M.E.S.S. International Theatre Festival. For over two decades after the war, the Festival has gone on—full of spirit and courage—raising the question about a person's 'right to happiness.'

Actually, the United Nations created an International Day of Happiness, declaring it as a 'universal human right.' So, let me ask you—when have you stopped and looked at what gives you your greatest happiness? Your greatest joy? Every single day comes along. Are you doing everything that's leading to your bliss? How else will you be able to share what's inside of you with others? To let your talent flourish. It certainly brought me a great 'feeling of joy' when, after my performance in the Festival, some of the students told me they kept wondering when I was going to show up. It finally dawned on them that I was the 79-year-old Harold Clurman in front of them.

During my time in Sarajevo, the Artistic Director of Chamber Theatre 55, Dragan Jovičić, and one of Bosnia's finest actors became a dear friend. He had invited me to come as a Fulbright Specialist, and during my time with him, he taught me many valuable lessons. Dragan was a unique artist with a great strength of character, humor, generosity, and a deep belief in truth and goodness. His talented wife, Mirjana, translated the play I directed at the theater. They became dear friends, and this is why you're blessed and learn so much from traveling to other countries to share your art and creativity. Learning not only about yourself but so much more!

Dragan invited me to become the second American in the history of the Chamber Theatre 55 to direct a production at their theater. The theater had been founded in 1955, and over the years, their audiences experienced a wide repertoire of avant-garde experimental theater and new plays. The street in front of the theater was known as Sniper Alley during the Siege. But that didn't stop people from coming. Somehow miraculously, twenty-eight plays, including *Hair*, were staged by the actors during the Siege.

Dragan told me, "I stayed in Sarajevo along with other actors, and even with the snipers in the hills, we'd move through the darkened streets and the rubble to get to the theater to perform for those who risked their lives to come. There was no electricity. No running water. Admission was a candle. Each audience member would light their candle in a circle for the actors to perform in. We all came because we couldn't survive any other way."

When the audience would leave that theater, in the middle of such a horrifying reality, they had been transformed. When you act, act because it's the only way you can survive. The only way you can live.

Today, at the corner, right outside the door of the theater, stands the Eternal Flame. Bullet holes remain in the wall above it as a reminder. Dedicated in 1946, it is a memorial to the military and civilian victims who perished during the Second World War.

Dragan and I talked about how important it would be to make people laugh—to bring humor into the lives of the audiences of Sarajevo. What about an American comedy? So I chose Murray Schisgal's hysterically funny award-winning play, *LUV*, which takes place on the Brooklyn Bridge. I had actually played one of the leading roles a few summers before at the Barnstormers Theater in New Hampshire.

You might ask: How do you go about directing a play in the Bosnian language that you don't speak and can't read? You rely upon 'the kindness of friends'—in this case, Dragan, the talented cast, my assistant director and dramaturg Vedran Fajkovic, and the entire staff and designers. While the words naturally hold meaning and express what each person in the play is saying, they come out of a deep-seated need. By the time I came to direct the play, I pretty much knew every line and the motivations of each individual, so I knew exactly what they were saying. Directing is always about letting discoveries happen 'in the moment,' when molecules are set loose and begin flying in the rehearsal room. You can try and plan 'happy' accidents in comedy, but they discover themselves through spontaneity and synchronicity. A lot of timing comes down to the actor's natural impulses—letting them discover the complete opposite of how one might react when you're confronted with an impossible situation.

At the first meeting sitting around the table as director with my cast and an incredible array of theater practitioners, designers, technicians, production designers, I knew, above all, we were going to have a lot of fun. That always requires hard work, preparation, and there's never enough time. The designer of the set and costumes, Vanja Popovic, had designed the costumes for the Opening Ceremonies for the Winter Olympics.

I was fortunate to have three of the most talented young actors in the country—Zana Marjanovic, Muhamed Hadsovic, and Moamer Kasumovic.

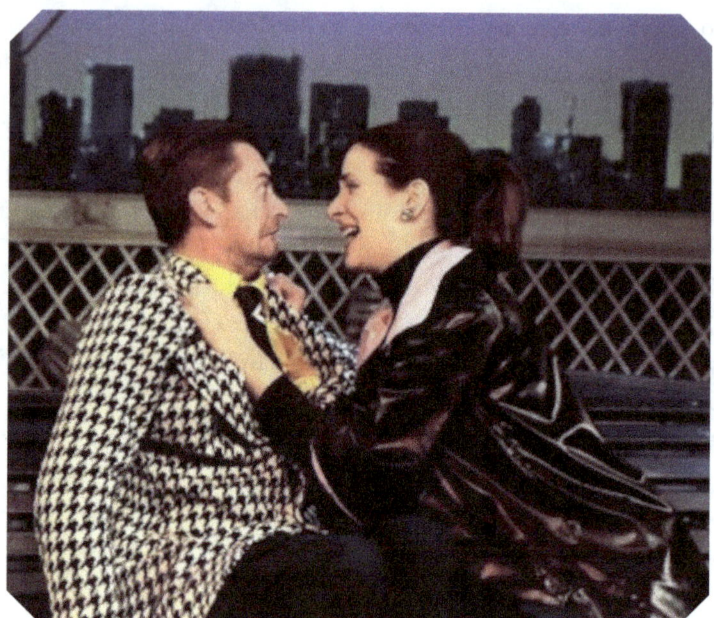

Moamer Kasumovic and Zana Marjanovic in *LUV*, directed by Ronald Rand, Chamber Theatre 55, Sarajevo, Bosnia & Herzegovina. (Courtesy Faud Foco.)

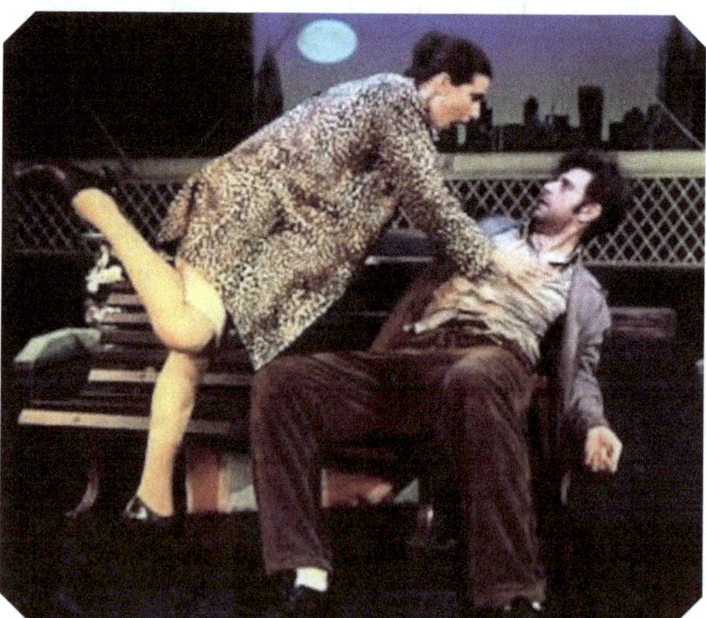

Zana Marjanovic and Muhamed Hadsovic in *LUV*, directed by Ronald Rand, Chamber Theatre 55, Sarajevo, Bosnia & Herzegovina. (Courtesy Faud Foco.)

With just a hint of a direction to Zana to go in—the reality of a 'sneezed-in' handkerchief to Muhamed—or a swagger or "become a musical instrument, Moamer"—immediately, they unleashed newfound truths revealing hysterically funny moments. One feeding into the next. Releasing what each of the three human beings in the play is feeling by immediately transforming everything they felt into physical behavior.

Of course, you never know what will happen until opening night. In this case, every seat was taken with an audience that included the Sarajevo Canton Minister of Culture, Ivica Saric; and the Director of Public Office Affairs at the U.S. Embassy, Elizabeta Delalic. Soon, it became a laugh fest from start to finish. *LUV* has been continuously performed for almost a decade since it opened, except for a few months during the Pandemic.

One day, Dragan and Mirjana took me for a drive, heading up above the city to Trebevic Mountain, the original site of the '84 Olympics. Each curve revealed buildings in decay, rusting metal, crumbling cement from all that remained when soaring athletes lifted themselves and soared above the city. We came upon the abandoned bobsleigh track, now completely covered in colorful graffiti art. It had taken on an entirely new existence.

Everything reminded me of when I saw the graffiti art under the M1 highway in Johannesburg. Up and down tall cement pillars—on walls beneath the roadway—were colorfully sprayed artworks of huge elephants, intricate science fiction scenes, portraits of Mandela and other leaders—some by South Africa's finest graffiti artists—stunning and luminous. Covering sides of buildings with stunning art is continuing to happen all over the world. It shows us creativity will always find a way.

Dragan wanted me to speak at the high school which he had graduated from—Druga Gimnazija Sarajevo High School, and where President Bill Clinton had spoken in front of the school when he visited Sarajevo in 1997. At that time, the school wasn't opened yet for students because during the Siege, it was on the frontline filled with sniper shelters and bunkers, and the school was completely destroyed.

Now I stood in the auditorium of the beautifully re-built school, greeted by over a hundred excited students, including the principal, with warm and welcoming smiles. They wanted me to talk about how I transform myself into another human being and how the art of creating on stage can bring healing to the world. It was amazing how we could all come together and share in the transformational power that peace can bring.

Right outside Sarajevo is an invisible border. I didn't realize it was that close until Dragan drove me through the mist across the Inter-Entity Boundary Line into SAO Raomanija of the Republika Srpska. On both sides of the road, there were signs in Serbian. On the buildings. Billboards. Barbed wire strung across roads, bringing home to me the reality of the separation that still exists so close by.

It also became clear when I was driven to the south of the country to teach the 'Art of Transformation' with young adults of the Mostar Youth Theatre.

Mostar remains a city of great division, so I wondered: How could I, through my teaching the Stanislavski chart and its tools reveal to them a dialogue about coping and cooperation? Truth and re-building? Living together within strife and friction?

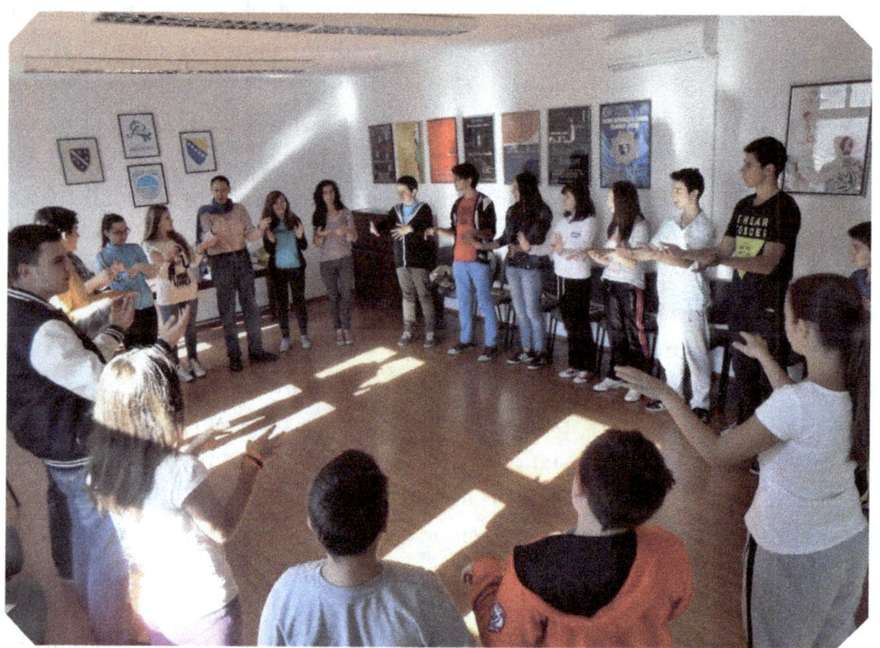

During Ronald Rand's workshop with students of Mostar Youth Theatre in Mostar, Bosnia and Herzegovina. (Courtesy Ronald Rand.)

I told them as they each held a copy of Stanislavski's chart: "Stanislavski showed us that truth carries within it a deep vibration that comes from the soul. That's why we're all connected to one another. If anything, art teaches us that we each carry the tools to transform not only our own lives but to share truths about how to live with those around us. You're already doing it through the shows you're putting on the stage." Many of the young students came from different ethnicities, different religions. They talked about the pressures that their families, their parents are faced with on a daily basis. We talked together about the effect that it has on them. How they've chosen to shape their frustrations into creative expressions of storytelling.

"Who is your heart beating for?" I asked them. "It certainly beats for your family, for your country. It also beats along with every other heart that beats in this city. We're all connected to one another. Even when there are differences, what brings us together? Transformation. We keep finding ways to teach each other a way forward, which we may not have recognized a moment ago. We can only find a way forward through peace, through love. The Transformation I go through to become Harold Clurman is a process built on truth. Once I discovered a 'deep well' inside—and let the stream of consciousness of what's true in every detail come—it takes me forward. You also carry within you this 'deep well' you can draw from every day that will guide you to let all doubts fade away. Through the power of your art, you can inspire others to come together to live in harmony."

As we did movement and singing exercises together, heart-warming light burst through the windows. We had become 'a family' in just a few moments, so it was hard to say goodbye. I sincerely hope one day to return.

When I walked across the famous Mostar arching bridge, I stood on its reconstructed cobblestones and looked out at the city. My thoughts were about its history. How members of one family had served in three different armies facing one another. The graceful span had stood for four hundred and twenty-seven years before it fell during the recent war. It was rebuilt, to perhaps say—to Mostar's Croats, Bosniaks, and Orthodox Serbs facing one another—the future is in your hands to live together in peace. It moved me to create a painting and to write this poem.

'As I Step out on Mostar Peace Bridge'

Ancient stones arching through space—tell me your story
Emperor Suleyman the Magnificent
ordered Mimar Hayruddin,
"Build me a bridge across the mighty Neretva,
but if it falls—you fall."
Mimar began building.
"Build, Mimar, build for your life," the people exclaimed.
So he built and up went the bridge. This in 1566.
And as he built, he dug his own grave.
The bridge reached and soared, but would it stand?
Would his life be sparred?
Four hundred and twenty-seven years
the stones held—blessing all who crossed.

Over time, battle upon battle were fought upon its pedestals.
Stand, mighty bridge, stand!
Connector of all people.
Muslim in the east, Christian in the west—Stand!
But lo, a new blast of war came.
Turn away, Mimar, turn away!
As stone upon stone fell into the mighty Neretva.
"Take us out!" submerged under the water, the stones cried out.
"Though we are mere stones, we carry your peace!"
So, the people listened.
Up went your bridge, Mimar, with your same stones.
"Walk again upon us." they said.
"But never forget,
Each step carries your courage, your love, your peace."

It takes a great deal of forgiveness to live in harmony with one another. It's a constant challenge. But through Transformation, we can face one another with a smile in our hearts.

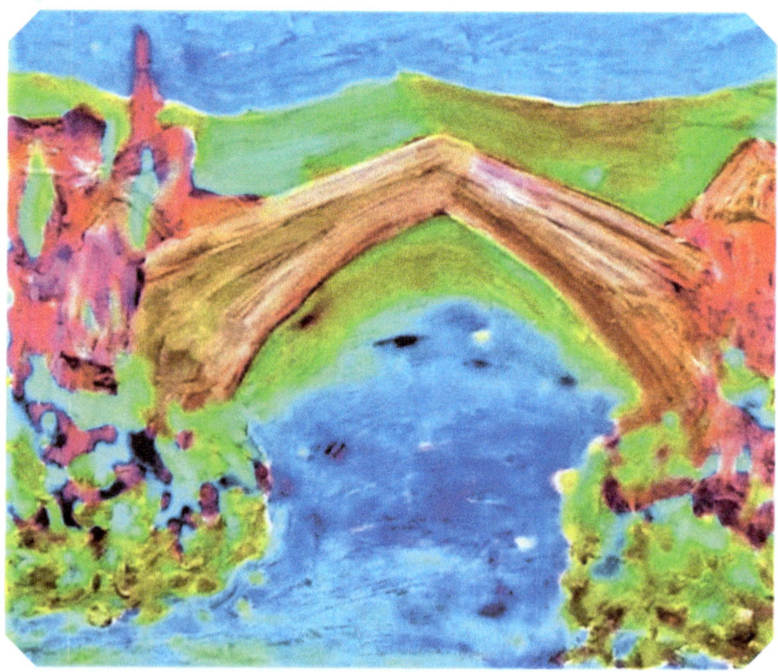

Painting: "Mostar Peace Bridge" by Ronjay, known as Ronald Rand. (Courtesy Ronald Rand.)

These words I write today on Thanksgiving are with a heavy heart, as I try and cope with the news I learned from Mirjana that Dragan, while acting in a performance at Chamber Theater 55, contacted the Covid-19 virus. She wrote me he fought, but he lost the battle. Dragan was a true warrior for art, a rich soul whose life-giving example as an artist of the stage showed us a way forward. It's almost indescribable the loss I feel. I think the best way is allow Dragan to say what came from his heart about his work.

"The universal language of theater speaks to the human spirit about common values that we all share, no matter where we come from. No matter how big or small each role I played, it had its demands and challenges. From each, I discovered something about the human soul and nature, and each of them required my absolute devotion and commitment."

"What I actually love the most working in the theater is the creative process—the birth of a performance—the weaving of the threads that each member of the team brings into a fine fabric of art. It is the focus and concentration that you need. Being a fisherman is very similar to being one with the fish/the role—clinging to it while diving into the deep waters."

He will surely be missed.

Little did I know a fortuitous meeting in the middle of the Pacific Ocean would lead me on an extraordinary journey bringing my solo play and master Workshops across Asia's 'melting pot of cultures' to Malaysia two years later. I happened to be giving my 'Art of Transformation' Workshop in Honolulu at the Hawaii International Conference on Arts and Humanities, and after everyone had finished 'flying' and it was over, a distinguished gentleman came up to me. As we talked together, I soon found out that Professor Zainal Abd Latiff was a renowned teacher in Malaysia and had created his own method of training actors using martial arts and Silat training. The more we talked together, the more we found out how much we had in common. Eventually, it led to an invitation for me to come as the first Fulbright Specialist to teach and perform at the Cultural Centre of the University of Malaya in Malaysia for six weeks.

Malaysia is known for its generosity of spirit and harmony. During my time at Malay University in Kuala Lumpur, which is known as 'KL,' I combined a study of the 'Art of Transformation' and the Art of Directing, along with inviting students to study different techniques of acting and directing, including Clurman's book, *On Directing*, and from my second book, *CREATE!* Within its pages are many interviews with actors and actresses, including Sabera Shaik, one of Malaysia's most versatile actresses. During my time in KL, I had experienced her emotionally powerful solo performance in *Puteri Saadong*, bringing alive Malaysia's legendary warrior princess, accompanied by musicians on traditional instruments. A perfect example where language was no barrier because of her richly textured storytelling.

After my performance for the students at the University of Malaya, I talked about how far Transformation can take you. The continual impact it can have on your life when you decide to create your own solo play. "I'm here because of my dreams. But how do you turn your dreams into a reality? Through the power of Transformation. Of course, I was inspired by my parents, teachers, and those I have read about, as I'm sure you have as well. But what led me forward was a deep belief in knowing that I had something to say to the world. When I discovered my destiny was to travel around the world sharing Clurman's passionate ideas through a solo play, it clearly showed me that there's an innate wisdom at work in the universe. That we're all here for an important purpose."

"The most important thing is finding out what it is that drives you forward—how you can give away to others, in a sense, why you were born—with all of your talents and your abilities. You see, you've been given this path, and it's up to you to let nothing stand in the way of it. It requires a singleness of purpose. Once you acquire a craft, you keep performing and performing again and again until you allow all that's inside of you a way to create through the 'Art of Transformation.' Always remember you're in service to others."

When I told the Cultural Centre of my great desire to reach out and touch the lives of more students across their country—it became a perfect example of the 'Law of Attraction.' All of a sudden, off we went 'on the road' across Malaysia, with the support of the JKKN National Department for Culture and Arts on an educational tour, bringing me to five of Malaysia's thirteen states with my solo performance and teaching master acting Workshops. It was the first time in their country's history that an American performer was invited to perform in a solo play at their State Theaters, and at universities, and that Malaysian actors and students would learn about Stanislavski's 'Method of Physical Actions' chart.

Heading north in a small van, aboard was Dr. Suboh, new friends to assist me with translating during my Workshops and assisting with the set, lighting, and sound at each theater. We first passed through the famous Cameron Highlands, known for its tea-covered hills. After a quick visit to the famous Perak Cave Temple and its forty-foot Buddha, our first stop was the capital city of Ipoh in the state of Perak, where I met the gracious Artistic Director, Mariam Sulaiman. She told me, "We're so glad you've come, but audiences don't usually stay to the end of the show. It probably will happen because they only speak Malay and Cantonese."

Well, after my performance, I gave a speech of thanks in Malay; we had a spirited 'Question and Answer,' I shook hands with everyone in the audience—and nobody left early. On top of that, almost everyone in the audience came up on stage to see Clurman's desk and everything it held. They didn't want to leave! Clurman's passion, his energetic life force had swept across the 'footlights. ' It would be the same everywhere we traveled.

The following day in my Master Workshop with over sixty young students and teachers, my words were translated into Malay and Cantonese. After we did several exercises together, and everyone held a copy of Stanislavski's chart in their hands, I explained: "Stanislavski went on a journey much like you're going on today—to uncover how to transform yourself to become another person, especially when you tell stories through a play. Everything you see around you right now is real—it has its own truth. But when you're on the stage and let's say in the play, you're in a jungle, there's nothing there on the stage except for the walls or a black curtain and some scenery, so how do you make it real for yourself? This chart is like a 'treasure map.' It will lead you step-by-step—through using these tools will help you to bring alive the person you're playing through your imagination—and will be built on truth."

Traveling north, we crossed into the state of Kedah, known as the 'Abode of Peace,' close to the border of Thailand. Kedah is also called the 'rice bowl of Malaysia.' As far as I could see, stretching out in every direction on both sides of the road, were paddy fields filled with rice, palm tree-fringed villages with Kampong-style houses. And rising up in front of us—'Gunung Keriang,' known as 'Elephant Mountain,' with its towering limestone cliffs jutting out from all sides. Inside, rare crystals lay buried among its bat caves. We arrived in the city of Alor Setar, right at the edge of the Malacca Strait, separating Malaysia from Indonesia.

Prof. Zainal had flown in from KL, and at my Workshop the following day after my performance, he did a demonstration of his technique using Silat. He said: "There's no hesitation when it comes to the dedication it takes to commit yourself to the craft. The follow-through of each thrust builds in its power, taking you to a greater focus." When I talked to the students, I told them, "See, it's the exact same thing in storytelling. Building and building to a climax. Taking the audience with you. With no hesitation. The need is that strong."

When we traveled south along the coast, we arrived at the eight-mile Penang Bridge leading to the beautiful Penang Island, called the 'pearl of the Orient.'

More than fifty students and teachers, including some young children, joined me in my Workshop as we sat together on an outdoor stage at the Temple of Fine Arts Academy surrounded by a lush garden. The Academy's motto is: 'Art, just for the Love of it.' During the 'animal' exercise, even the young children jumped up and joined in as butterflies, scurrying around the other actors who became fish and eels, frogs, and swallows.

I talked about the 'surrender' that it takes for Transformation to occur. "In that moment, when you've made the decision to become an animal, another reality arrives. It only happened because you allowed yourself to become a willing vessel. You allowed yourself to be open enough to whatever needed to happen. Animals aren't self-conscious. They have no self-doubt. Only acceptance. It's the same way in acting. When you 'take the time and allow this 'acceptance' to occur to become another person—a new reality comes into being. And this person you're becoming. They've come to live their life. Art becomes a healing force when you restore balance in each person who comes to see you. When they experience what you've brought alive, you've given them the nourishment they need to live." Afterward, we all had a vegetarian meal in their garden restaurant, attached to their Academy. The director of the Academy told me as we ate together: "What you shared in your Workshop—for us is 'soul food.' As much as what we're eating right now."

The following day, off we flew across the country to the eastern side of Malaysia, landing in Kuala Terengganu, facing the South China Sea. Again they were concerned that the audience coming would leave, as they told me, because "they probably won't understand what you're saying. Not only is Malay spoken, but Kelantanese, Hokkien, Teochew, Mandarin, Tamil, Punjabi—and a little English." "No worries," I told them. "Let's see what happens once they meet Clurman." For the most part, the audience understood the stories he told—and again, when I walked off the stage and shook everyone's hands—no one had left early.

In the morning, when I stood on the beach facing the South China Sea, I greeted the dawn as it rose above the horizon. Nearby a fisherwoman stood silently—several thick nets wrapped around her, covering both of her shoulders. She peered intently out at sea, scanning the horizon. I could see fishing boats dotting the horizon miles away. She stood immovable. I could sense her anticipation in her gaze, in her posture. It was one of hope. Perhaps that one of these boats would return so she could climb aboard to catch food for her family.

When we returned to KL, more opportunities arose to perform and teach at the Universiti Teknologi Mara in Selangor and at the Islamic International

State University. When I was invited to perform at Aswara, the National Arts, Culture & Heritage Academy, in a just few moments, with over a hundred students and teachers on mats and cushions surrounding Clurman on three sides, laughter broke out, and an incredible give-and-take of exuberance swept over the audience. At the end of the performance, when I met the Director of Aswara, renowned playwright Hatta Azad Khan, he extended a generous invitation for me to return when I was able to and teach at Aswara.

The next morning when I held my Workshop with a large group of students and teachers, we talked about the meaningful choices we make in life. "Nothing stands in your way. Einstein told us: "Life will only change when you become committed to your dreams more than you are to your comfort zone." Go down the path that belongs entirely to you, and a new world will appear. It'll say: 'I can see further.' Because the path has chosen you."

I asked them: "How often do you listen to your gut? It's one of the most essential parts of who you are. Literally running your body. One of the miracles and mysteries going on inside of you. Your 'gut' brain is like a barometer, making your body function and react. Do we know anything about it? Practically nothing. But you have to trust your gut because it tells you how you feel. Directly connected to your emotions, lining the human gut, over a hundred million nerve cells send signals right to the brain when you feel elation, anxiety, sadness, anger, and joy. I'm sure you've heard the expression: 'You are what you eat. Well, everything you put in your body affects how you feel, and your 'gut' brain reacts to it all. It's directly connected to your body's ability not to get sick or depressed. All connected to having the energy you need to create 'life' on stage! That's your responsibility!"

The climax of my visit to Malaysia was an all-day Stanislavski International Forum sponsored by The University of Malaya to celebrate the work I had brought across the country. Guest panelists came and talked about the importance of my having introduced Harold Clurman through my performances and Stanislavski's 'Method of Physical Actions' chart to students for the first time across their country.

"This was an opportunity that had never occurred before," Dr. Zainal told the audience. "Your Transformation into Harold Clurman gave us a deeper understanding of how this process works. You opened the eyes of everyone who experienced your play about the American Theatre. At the same time, your Talks about Stanislavski gave us an entirely new understanding of his work here in Malaysia."

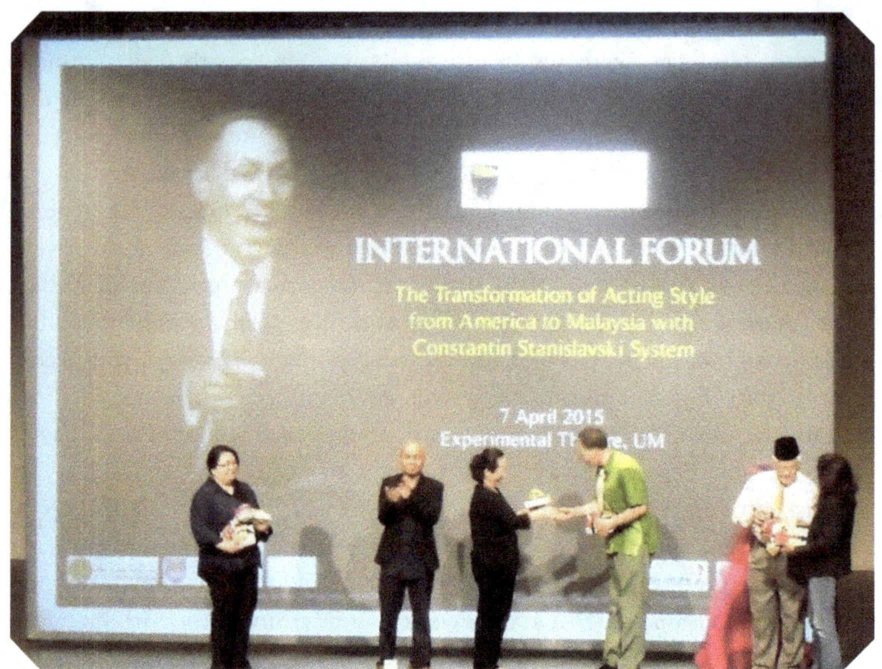

Stanislavski International Forum at the Experimental Theatre, 2015, University of Malaya, Kuala Lumpur, Malaysia. (Courtesy Ronald Rand.)

Before I left, I encountered a most unusual experience. At the base of a mountain in Gombak near KL, inside its jagged limestone, is a holy monument of complex grottos. The Batu Caves is one of the country's most revered sites, formed over four hundred million years ago, where once the Bersisi-Temuan tribe of indigenous people lived. Before I ascended the two hundred and seventy-two stairs to reach the caverns, I stared up, shielding my eyes from the sun's glare at a hundred and a forty-foot gold-painted statue of Lord Murugan, the third tallest statue of a Hindu deity in the world.

When I started up the stairs, I was immediately confronted. Mischievous monkeys had planted themselves right in front of me. Too late to go around. But I was prepared, dropping food and water for them. They scurried quickly, laying claim to their newfound bounty. One gulped down the water bottle, another with its baby clinging for dear life on its stomach, clutched a roll in its claws, and hurried away up a railing.

Stepping aside, I was glad I could 'be in service.' Entering the Batu Caves, uprose before me a vast cavern, giant stalactites, and stalagmites on all sides. Ornate Hindu shrines stood serenely nearby with their crags and crevices overflowing with every type of offering and prayers inscribed on papers left by a million pilgrims.

After I left the Batu Caves, I was faced with the choice of whether to ascend into the unknown or pass it by. Wanting to experience more than I know, I stepped inside the 'Dark Cave.' A tour guide handed me a safety helmet and a flashlight, adding, "It must always be pointed down." Where would the Dark Cave take me, I wondered? What was I getting myself into?

Joining a group of about nine people, we headed down a pathway, and immediately we were plunged into darkness. The only light came from our flashlights pointed down at the path as we headed deeper and deeper into the cave. Besides the sound of our footsteps on the thin cement walkway, there emanated extremely loud squealing sounds coming from directly overhead. The guide calmly assured us, "There's probably over two hundred thousand bats directly above you on the roof of the cave, and if you shine your light above you, you'll get an unwelcome gift." I definitely thought it would be good to keep my flashlight headed in the direction we were going.

Immediately my senses kicked in—an 'alert' instinct. I began to listen with my entire 'natural antenna.' Each of us has it. But it's not something we usually use until a moment like this arrives. Any kind of apprehension or doubt had to be jettisoned because we were going deeper and deeper into the cave. Into the darkness.

At one point, we stopped. "Turn off your flashlights." Hesitantly, we followed our guide's directions, and instantly, we were thrown into complete and utter darkness. It covered me like a wet blanket. Absolutely no light. Nothing. There were no bats above us now. I stood there. So this is what complete silence sounds like, I thought. Complete and utter darkness. I had disappeared. Most of us live our lives in a world of constant sound, light, noise. Never a moment without light. Now there was nothing except the sound of my own heartbeat. I 'saw' no form whatsoever. There was nothing except thoughts that kept coming—one after the next. My ears became my greatest extension. Faintly, I could hear a slight dripping sound. A scrap of someone's foot near mine. I felt like the 'I of me' had disappeared down a hole. It made me aware of the 'aura of light' that I began to see, which we all carry with us. Molecules surround our being. We sometimes see it portrayed in movies. But it's real. I somehow began to sense my form and others. When have you sensed that in your life? Many monks have retreated into caves to meditate. Now I understood why. In this kind of darkness, all you're left with is this 'voice' inside your head. Until finally, you have to let it go—to find another kind of peace.

For your entire life, there are two of you. That's right. Or at least, it appears that way. Day in and day out, there's you talking to you—and you listening to you. A *you* talking to you. So images come. Of course—feelings. Sensations like the chill in the air or the softness of sand between your toes. There's something else—like a dream. A thought comes until it's translated into words. It's how the mind speaks. You have an inner monologue, and as quick as a jackrabbit, molecules fly around inside of you, creating more thoughts. But how does all this happen? How does the mind do this? It's a complete mystery. It's part of your make-up. Everyone's mind doesn't necessarily work in the same way. Keep this in mind when you're creating another human being. Their mind doesn't think the same way yours does. They certainly don't look at the world the same way you do.

I always ask my students: "Are you in charge of your brain, or does it run you? Are your thoughts you?" It's amazing how many believe their brain's in charge of them. But you are not your thoughts. That doesn't mean you can't learn to see yourself from them. Try getting closer to your authentic Self. Some people say they hear voices. I certainly have heard words, as do all playwrights. People appear. They talk to us. If you're going to become someone who thinks that way, you have to understand what that means. Most people react from their unconscious desires, and it turns into a behavior.

We can't study our stream of consciousness. Because the second we do, it changes. We can't keep more than one thought in our head at any one time. Ultimately you have to come to peace with this 'voice' inside your head. To listen, whether it's a 'positive' voice or a 'negative' one. Behind all of this is your awareness of this 'voice.' That's what leads you closer to discovering another person and how they think. You're responsible to bring this entirely, completely different human being to life—their 'voice'—their soul—onto the stage.

When we turned our flashlights back on, we continued walking. Up ahead, light appeared. We came to another part of the cave. There was an opening at a rim above our heads. It was probably four or five hundred feet above us at the top of the cave. Bats flew in and out. Ah . . . so that's how they connect with the outside world. Some people on this planet spend their entire life studying the 'outside world' and other galaxies. It's incredibly vast, and when you look at the photographs beamed back from the Hubble telescope, you're immediately aware it's almost inconceivable how many worlds exist out there. All of that is also a part of you. That's part of the wonder and mystery of being alive.

Once we turned around, I realized we had to return the way we came. Each step we took led us past stalactite formations on the ceilings and the walls that had been forming for millions of years. Some of the water dripping down from above had already hardened into long shapes and was making a new formation on the floor of the cave. It would take many more millennia for them to meet. We may live a span of life for a hundred years or less or more. These stalactite formations have been dripping for millions and millions of years. It makes you stop and wonder. Being inside a dark ancient cave, I could have been overwhelmed, but I decided to merge with it. To accept it—as we accept light as natural.

In the depths of the sea, almost seven miles down, lies the Mariana Trench. In complete darkness. Yet fish live there. Somehow they've learned to adapt and to see. We've heard the expression: 'Seeing is believing.' Well, actually, 'not-seeing' is believing—because we believe in things we can't see. Molecules flying around us every day. The oxygen you breathe, you can't see it. Until it's a cold day, and then you see your breath. What about gravity that keeps you from floating off into outer space? Plus, your thoughts are invisible. So are your emotions until you look at another person's reactions and observe what their expression's telling you. Each day the mystery widens. The miracle grows. Let all the miracles happen to you that are meant to happen.

You can never underestimate how important it is leave yourself open to every new experience that comes your way. Embrace each without reservation, without doubt. Keep enlarging your vision because you have the capacity to show the world more than we ever thought was possible.

Again, the stars aligned two years later, and I was called upon to travel once more on behalf of the U.S. State Department as the first Fulbright Specialist in Paysandú, Uruguay. On my first visit to South America, I had performed and taught in Buenos Aires at the Kafka Theatre, sponsored by the Espacio Blanco Leis Acting School. As it turned out, I was also invited to be a Panelist at an International Stanislavski Theatre Conference, talking about Stanislavski's 'Method of Physical Actions' chart.

On that visit, I found out after I had arrived, by accident, I had left my cane at home. Clurman always arrives with a cane when he enters his apartment in my play. As fate would have it, Sebastian Blanco Leis gifted me with a cane for my performance. But this was no ordinary cane. It partly came from a Palo santo tree that had been uprooted in a storm. Palo santo means 'Holy wood.' For centuries, Latin American indigenous communities have used this sacred tree for rituals because of its enormous spiritual energy. It's sweet aroma of mint, pine, and lemon is known for clearing away negative energy and restoring tranquility. I felt aligned with the forces of nature as I placed this cane into Clurman's hand for the performance.

My first visit to Paysandú had actually occurred nine years earlier. Raul Rodriguez, a passionate theater practitioner and creator of the Paysandu Workshop Theatre, was also the Festival Director of the International Mercosur 'Atahualpa del Cioppo' Theater Festival—and had invited me to come and perform in my solo play. The Festival had been named after del Cioppo, one of the most inspiring figures across South America and one of the founders of the El Galpon Theatre. His actors had performed in plays by Gorky, Chekhov, Ibsen, Miller, Weiss, Hochwalder, and Brecht, and over the years, some of them had been persecuted, even jailed.

Del Cioppo believed: "that the writer, the artist, the theater doesn't solve the problems of society. That the most important thing is to contribute to the development of the audience's conscience and humanity. That only through justice can we affirm freedom. That a 'lucid conscience' can save us all from becoming beasts in these difficult times. We have to carry love in one hand and justice in the other."

During the Festival in Paysandú, I performed in the Teatro Florencio Sánchez, built in 1876, named after the most famous playwright of Uruguay. Its beautiful carved interior and thousand red velvet seats have greeted many of Uruguay's most important artists who have performed on its stage, including del Cioppo. The evening that I performed in the theater, proceeding me onstage, was an enormously loud Candombe colorfully-dressed band of dancers and musicians in bright orange and gold, pounding large drums and playing extremely loud trumpets in an Afro-Uruguayan rhythm.

My 'Creation Room' felt like I was inside one of those pounding drums. As I prepared, I overheard Clurman remark: "Must be a very loud concert in Central Park tonight!" For the most part, the audience only spoke Spanish, but many told me afterward, they could 'feel' everything Clurman said from his overwhelming passion. Later, I found out, during the performance, several in the audience translated what Clurman was saying to others.

When I returned for my second visit to Paysandu, Raul greeted me like I was 'a member of his family.' During the next five weeks, I was part of a solo play festival, along with solo performers from Mexico and Peru. And when I performed as Harold Clurman on the stage of the Paysandú Theatre Workshop, a translation in Spanish moved down the wall behind me, so the audience, which included several children, understood everything Clurman said.

When it came time to teach my Workshop, I went at it for seven hours, four days a week. The actors and students wanted to know as much as they could about Stanislavski and his chart. I was delightfully assisted by a talented actress and healer, Ilse Olivera. Full of energy, she translated every word I said.

I also learned she had a special diet—she only drank bird seeds in water for her three meals a day. Many people around the world actually use birdseed as a drink. It helps reduce weight and metabolism. I tried it and thoroughly enjoyed it, giving me a boost of energy. Keep leaving yourself open to discover new ways to infuse your health.

Raul also asked me to direct the actors of the Paysandú Workshop Theatre in an American play. I chose to create an adaptation, which Ilse translated into Spanish, from Thornton Wilder's Pulitzer Prize-winning play, *Our Town*. I was gifted with a talented cast that included Raul's daughter, Dulcinea, who played Rebecca. Ilse translated every direction as we rehearsed, and she also played Mrs. Gibbs, as we 'galloped' into Grovers Corners, New Hampshire, in 1901. None of the actors had ever been to America before, so I strove to bring to them the essence of what life would have been like if they had been living in New England at that time. They threw themselves wholeheartedly into the story of these two families.

Many of those in the audience who came to the Aras Theatre—the first time Wilder's words had been heard and performed in Paysandú—instantly recognized themselves in the townspeople of New Hampshire. The actors almost unconsciously applied what they had learned through our acting sessions together to make the story clear for the audience.

What touched me most during rehearsals was one of the cast members, Patricia Fernandez, who played Mrs. Webb, was at the same time battling

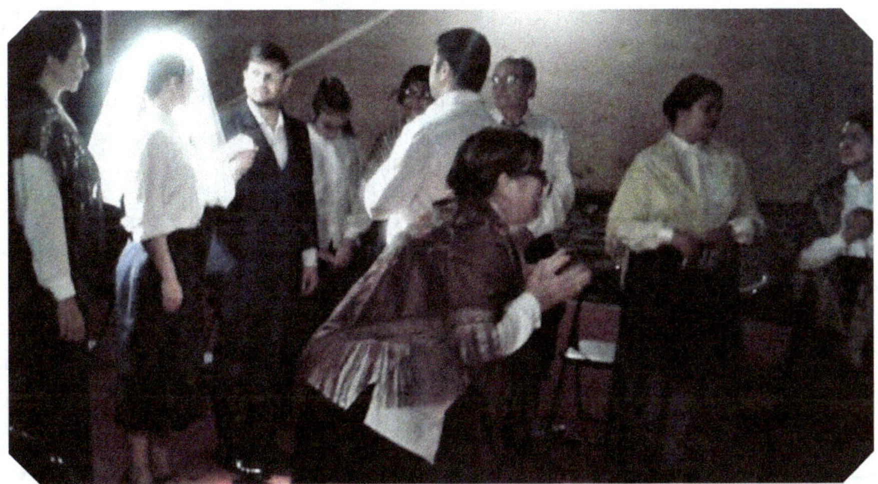

Thornton Wilder's *Our Town*, Workshop production, directed by Ronald Rand in Paysandú at the Aras Theatre, Paysandú, Uruguay, 2018. (Courtesy Ronald Rand.)

cancer. But she wasn't going to let that stop her. She'd come to the rehearsals completely committed to her role. Still, I could see the enormous effort and toll it took on her. I was moved by how much she transformed herself into a New England mother who cared deeply about her daughter's future.

At a cast party after the performance, we all laughed and danced together. Patricia told me she had chosen to use only natural therapies and meditation for her illness. She didn't want anything to get in the way of immersing herself in the reality of her role. You can see her standing at the far left next to Emily, about to be married to George. Alas, just a few months later . . . she joined the angels in heaven. Patricia continues to hold a special place in my heart. I can still see her huge broad smile at the end of the performance, having accomplished what she had set out for herself to achieve.

We're each given a certain amount of time on this planet. It's up to you to make the most of it every single day. To work towards improving the lives of those around you through the gifts you've been given. Mortality is a fact of life. Certainly, one of the greatest mysteries of our existence is where we're going next. Many poems and plays deal with what Hamlet refers to, as the 'undiscovered country . . .' How you deal with this inescapable part of life is a personal choice. We're both matter and spirit. But also know what drives you forward each day is your essence—your 'soul'—bringing new opportunities to live your greatest joy. To tell the story of your heart. To forgive others. To be a beacon of hope. You can hear it in the words of Anne Frank: "How wonderful it is that nobody need wait a single moment before starting to improve the world." You can feel it in the courage of those who have stood up against persecution in the face of overwhelming odds.

When it came time for me to depart, it was hard to say goodbye to all my new friends. As the bus took me south towards Montevideo, I gazed out at the Uruguayan countryside. Its seemingly endless pastures. Here and there, gauchos riding among the cattle. We're all part of a tiny planet that sometimes it seems quite vast. Yet, in a single moment, it reminds us how connected we are to one another.

The world can also be a dangerous place. This was made real to me when I was invited to represent the United States in Sri Lanka at the Colombo International Theatre Festival with my solo play. All of a sudden, the country was viciously attacked on Easter Sunday. Many of its people lost their lives. Of course, the Festival had to be postponed. Everyone prayed for their families, for the entire nation. A few months later, because art is such an important healing force, the Festival Committee decided going forward would be the truest expression of our humanity—to help heal through art. A different kind of Transformation was necessary in the face of such horror.

So when I traveled to Sri Lanka, Clurman's words took on an entirely different meaning. They spoke of courage, of coming together to lift spirits, embracing one another. That we have it within ourselves to do all we can to help heal others through art.

While I was there, I gave two performances, one at the regal Elphinstone Theatre, the second oldest theatre in Colombo as part of the Colombo International Theatre Festival, and a second performance at the University of Visual and Performing Arts for many of their students. They had never heard of Clurman but were fascinated by the stories he told. When I taught two master Workshops for over a hundred and fifty students, as we went over Stanislavski's chart, everything I said was translated into Sinhala and Tamil. Three different languages floated through the air.

"In the moment you allow Transformation to take place," I told them, "it takes on a life of its own. What's occurring is a shift in consciousness requiring that you make your way, step by step, finding out, first, who this other person is. How different they are from you. And once you discover that, you can begin the process of allowing them to come and merge with you. How does that happen? Begin with your breath. With each breath I take in the 'Creation Room,' I invite a new life force to enter me. By being a willing and open vessel, a new world appears I can step into. I'm no longer in my own. I've entered a new reality—their life. This is how the audience meets them. Through you."

After one of my Workshops, when we held hands standing together in a large circle, I could feel the energy flowing through the molecules uniting us. I heard my voice say: "What we have shared today has shown us a way forward. To see how expansive we can become. To look at one another with love, and know that we can, through our art, through our common bond, feel the grace of healing—to know we're all connected. The peace you seek is at the core of your being. Let the peace come and surround you with bliss. Be at peace, for only you know what you must do. Be the peace you seek. Accept the moment and fill yourself with light. Know you are never alone because we are all one. A community of artists connected by our love of humanity."

When I was driven downtown to visit St. Anthony's Church, which had been bombed on Easter Sunday, I stood silently inside the repaired and re-painted sanctuary with a prayer of peace on my lips. Around me, others prayed. I could see reminders from that fateful day—and new memorials. The restored interior said our greatest strength is that we will continue. Just as we did when we were faced with the aftermath of 9/11. In every country I visit, I always take time to step inside places of worship of different faiths. We're all brothers and sisters, and the work that you and I do is built on knowing that our goodness can transform darkness into light.

I'm reminded by Luise Rainer's words in my book *CREATE!*, when she says: "We all have to walk erect to see the sky, to know how little we are and how great. To look outside and not always within; that should be our goal and our health. Pain is a natural. It must be carried."

EPILOGUE

You can change the world for the better because of the power inside of you as a storyteller. Through your strength of Transformation—you'll bring an ever-changing, embracing life-giving force into the world. How often do you take the time to speak out loud in gratitude? To thank the universe? To thank God? To thank your guardian angels? To thank the powers that surround you and all who love you? Not only will it help bring you a greater peace inside and to those around you—the practice of gratitude offers an unlimited way to build upon your greatest resource—your transformative goodness.

As a solo performer, you're a part of the expansion that takes place when we all come together to grow as human beings—and it keeps growing when it's coupled with your deepest appreciation.

One of the questions I'm usually asked is—and this is on a more practical note: "How have you been able to get to all the places you go to and raise the money you need?" More than anything –where 'there's a will, there's a way.' It takes immense determination—perseverance—spending a great deal of time and effort on research and knowledge-building. On visualization. Trusting that the answers you seek will come. If reaching out to others for support doesn't come easy for you—fortunately, there are many avenues to go down today to fund your solo play, including fund-raising websites. By having the New York Foundation of the Arts as my fiscal sponsor has allowed me to accept financial support, but more than that, they've been there for me in innumerable ways. The most important thing is to seek out and open yourself up to all the opportunities that are available that will enable you to share all of who you are as a solo performer.

Be ready to be surprised. More than you could have ever wished for will come your way. So you have to be prepared. This is how you'll be able to continue performing in your solo play for many years to come—making your dreams come true.

Above all else, what remains the most important reason is *why* you needed to create your solo play in the first place—that your singular lifeforce must come through you in this way—and be shared! You have it within you to be a 'light' that will allow us to see further than we ever thought possible.

This journey that we've gone on together tells me: You want to reach out! You want to share all of who you are! Let nothing stand in your way!

Through Transformation—through an organic process in your preparation and on stage—you can allow yourself to show us a way forward. We can't survive without your storytelling. We need to hear what you have to say. Tell us!

QUOTES

VINIE BURROWS: "We're just human. Theatre can help us understand humanity. We're all the same. The body remembers, the muscles remember. The first time I knew of Rose McClendon was from seeing a photo of her. She was one of the great actresses of the past. I wanted to bring her out of oblivion with my solo show, *Rose McClendon, Harlem's Gift to Broadway.* I ended up performing over 6,000 performances with my ten different solo shows. We are not exempt from using our skills, our passion, our energies to make things right that are wrong in our world and our society. Within all of us, there is a kernel of understanding that recognizes that we are indivisible, that we must preserve, not only ourselves but our world."

LEN CARIOU: "The biggest thing is you're out there by yourself. When I did *Hemingway* and played William O. Douglas, I had to keep myself aware of the rhythm, the music of the piece, and moving it along. The audience gets ahead of you. Ernest Hemingway was pretty removed from the time I performed him in, and Douglas was one of the most important people in our society, but nobody knew him as a person, just as a Supreme Court Justice. We're creatures of habit. Our discipline is to know exactly what we're doing every step of the way. But I've had those wonderfully exhilarating moments after a performance when you say, "Oh my God!" And you sit down and say to yourself, "I went someplace I've never been before. Now how will I do that again!" But once you start questioning yourself, asking 'How?' you trip over yourself. The onus is on me to keep returning to the 'well' for what I need. That's my job."

OSSIE DAVIS: "We need again to see larger-than-life human beings clashing over big ideas, a sense of wonder in the work, of magnificence. That the life we're touching is human. That what we're writing about or portraying is throbbing, pleading life. We need to find our way back to the beginning of human life. Ruby Dee and I devoted our lives to telling human stories, and that's our function—yours and mine—to create humanity and to make it human. We've got to do it. We have no other choice."

RUBY DEE: "We're wrestling with so many things today we've never considered before. One of the functions of the artist is to put our times into perspective, into context. The artist puts a divine spin on things, carrying us beyond where the five senses take us. I see there's all this unfinished business following us through the spiritual growth of man. All these things are part of the long arc of history. Here we are on the same planet. Let us share. Let's not take what's not ours. If you wrong someone, make it right. We have to be patient with each other. There's always been a cost to sacrifice for freedom. We have to stand back and look at ourselves. History has chosen us at this time and place. When I was performing my solo show, *My One Good Nerve,* it was a privilege to share the words and ideas as they paint the time, like an artist with a brush, with the words as fluid as oil paint on a canvas. It comes from the knowledge of having absorbed everything, from my parents, my teachers, from history. I felt every sentence I said, and this stream fed me. You're never just saying words; it's what you're doing with them. It's a thrilling vocation—being a solo artist—through which doors fly open. And you let the subtleties, the music flow through you. If your instrument needs rest, if it's creaky, then you're not able to open yourself and let everyone into all the possibilities. You become the master of the ship by filling these words with the realities and the spirit they require. It's more than you that speaks. These ideas speak through you to live for others."

CHARLES S. DUTTON: "We change the world. We really do. But we only do it if we leave an ounce of our internal essence on the stage floor every night. If we don't do that, then we don't. When we do, someone who walks into the theatre at 7:45 in the evening, even if they already know it's a play, we suspend their disbelief. And even if they're thinking one way about life in the world, if we can get to them, when they leave, they're thinking an entirely different way—then we've done our job. Because the residue of that experience will remain within them throughout their entire lives as long as they're walking on this planet. And it will discover and re-discover their humanity."

TOVAH FELDSHUH: "The role as Golda Meir really chose me in the middle of my life. When you're willing to commit, to paraphrase what Goethe said: the universe conspires to support you. I learned from the Zen princes: You find beauty in everything. I get such pleasure from life, doing all the things I do every day, with the fullest commitment and with love. It's the little things that are a part of what you're trying to impart. It's a question of visualization. All that matters is having love and what you're trying to impart. And I believe that if you can maintain your relationships, you can have a career. I used to believe if you were excellent, all else would follow. It's not totally true. It's making sure you're good at your work and having loving relationships. And to live every day to the fullest. There are those who create their lives. It's up to you to live. That's what William Saroyan said: 'In the time of your life—*live*!'"

JULIE HARRIS: "Believe in yourself. Break all the rules. Do what *you* think is right. Don't lose faith in yourself. Don't be afraid of failure. As long as you have a taste for acting, the love of it, the courage to stick with it under the worst circumstances, no matter what, continue to go at your work with love, with honesty, and with courage. The rest will take care of itself."

HAL HOLBROOK: "Why did I do it? Why, because it kept me alive. It made my blood run. It made my heart beat faster every time I did it. Doing a show like *Mark Twain Tonight* keeps you young and interested and curious and passionate. It was hard sometimes. I did all my own research; I changed the material a lot. Sometimes, I never knew where it exactly would go. Twain did the same thing, you know. That's what he became—Mark Twain on the road, on tours—talking about America, God, politics, greed, the big business guys. He speaks to all of us. Because he does what other people don't do. He tells the truth, and the truth is always funny, because you hardly ever hear it. So people laughed, but they also listened."

JUDITH IVEY: "We have a tremendous acting tradition in America now, yet many young actors seem to feel separate from it or don't know enough of their roots and tradition. I literally go back to the caveman days. Somebody there said: "Tell a story," in whatever they spoke, and they did, and soon they started getting better and better at it. You can take it through all the centuries. It's part of our human culture; it's who we are. It's an honor to be an actress. I always say: I feel like a public servant. Because if I'm doing my job well, someone is being served in a special way. When I performed in *The Women of Lockerbie*, you could really feel you changed someone's life, that you had a profound effect, that they looked at themselves in a totally different way. I feel it's important that we respect ourselves and who we are. I honor that and don't want it dismissed. Others have misinterpreted the American experience. It's important that we honor and respect the culture we have."

SARAH JONES: "I think all performances are about getting inside the experience of someone who may be nothing like you. But the hope is that you find these points of connectivity . . . I have these characters in my repertoire from years of growing up in diverse communities that sound like music and what America is made of . . . And I want people to have those conversations with people that they might not normally rub shoulders with in their lives."

JOHN LEGUIZAMO: "I always find something troubling in my life and then create a show around it. That's the art that I do. Art is my therapy. With my newest show, *Latin History for Morons*, I had to juggle the history with the personal stuff. The genesis of the show was my son being bullied at school. So I created the show for him. I wanted to find the words to fight the bullies and beat them with information. So I did all this research, and I learned we helped build America. I mined the history along with the comedy. I tried to find that sweet balance through humor. By my three hundredth performance, I think I found the right ingredients, the right ratio. I always put music in my show because music and dance is such a huge part of Latin culture. The comedy, the writing, the performing, it's all needs to speak to people. The whole message of the play is: We are our own heroes. That's the uplifting message I want to put across."

LAURA LINNEY: "There's something terrifying about including an audience in your work. I'm glad I've been forced to deal with that because I think that fear for me now is permanently gone. That's what the experience of *My Name is Lucy Barton* has given me . . . There's nerves, and then there's fear, and there's a difference. Learning the role took a long time. There's no way around it. You can't fake your way through that. You just have to learn it word by word, and it's thirty-seven pages of single-spaced writing. It took me a while. I'm still just sort of stunned. I came offstage like, "What just happened?"

PRISCILLA LOPEZ: "I went to the High School of the Performing Arts. Playing Diane in the original production of *A Chorus Line* is my true story. I felt I had an incredible amount of freedom to explore during rehearsals, but Michael Bennett was very much in charge. He told us what it would be. We had the luxury of playing with what we did and creating inside it for over a year. The stories were all real stories, all based on truth. When I did the one-woman show, *Class Mothers '68*, it was the hardest I have ever worked. It took such stamina. I had to make each of the women complete within themselves. It was totally exhausting, but it was very rewarding. After I did the show, I felt I could do anything. That I had nothing to fear."

IAN McKELLAN: "Well, I think I like doing Shakespeare because it's difficult and it's complicated, and the actor's job is to absorb those complications into himself so that then they can be clearly expressed to an audience, who can then deal with the information they're being given. The real thing about acting in the theater is the presence of the audience, of course. And so, it's a shared experience. If there's no audience, there's no play. I want my breath that starts down here to pass across the very intimate parts of one's body out along through the airways, measurable, on to the eardrum of the audience. And there's a direct communication. That is life. That's people meeting each other."

MEREDITH MONK: "I have always felt that performance is a place of Transformation. Where else can you express one's self except through Transformation; it calls upon a special kind of energy. Performance is a place of cleansing. We're so attuned to habitual patterns of thought, but by letting there be these gaps, you can feel yourself. When we're unable to channel these energies, we lose time to have magic in our lives. The original idea of performance was literally negotiating and worshipping to nature, pleading, and a primal harnessing to alter nature. What do we have today that comes close to that? How do artists fit into people's lives? People get frightened, intimidated, it's a hard struggle, and a lot of the things are not done out of love. I'm so lucky to do what I'm doing. At a certain level, I'm almost willing to die for the experience of performing, to offer a new experience of human perception. It makes you aware of your responsibility—of not taking anything for granted."

DALE ORLANDERSMITH: "I want to look at how one person can embody a kind of humanity, aspects of humanity. And as the play goes on, I want other people to do it. I think that's interesting because it starts with one person asking. How does one person take in the world? We always see the collective, but the collective starts with the individual. Individuals form a collective, right? So how does one individual take in the world?"

RUBEN SANTIAGO-HUDSON: "What I try to do is understand the character. I read about the playwright. I read about everything I can get my hands on. Then I read the play over and over again, picking up all kinds of hints, listening to all the rhythms. I come in respecting the director's personality and style, and hopefully, I get the same back. I bring a lot to the table. I want to make mistakes exploring. When I was in college, one of my professors kept telling me how talented I was. He wouldn't let me forget it, so I began to believe more and more in myself and my abilities. That's what I tell young actors today. If you've got to be an actor—put your heart and soul into it. Not just in class but every day. That's the real learning process. Look at the stage as an opportunity to get up and act! It's like a rookie facing a batting machine. The pitch comes in with the same speed every time, but once you face a real pitcher—the whole speed—the pace and delivery changes. That's the only way you learn. Put your dreams into motion!"

ANNA DEAVERE SMITH: "Discussions are important because my goal is to bring people to the theater who normally wouldn't be in the same room together. It's using theater to create a kind of community. You see, my work, at least at this moment, isn't about unifying. A unifying idea is not enough. It's why I don't really put my own point of view into the piece, because once you put forward a powerful voice, be it truth or not, it makes the other voices seem smaller. My work is about giving 'voice to the unheard' and reiterating the 'voice of the heard' in such a way that you question, or re-examine, what is the truth. And we have to be able to tolerate more than one voice."

LILY TOMLIN: "It's only worth keeping a character going if you have something relevant to use them for. The central idea of a character has to be so strong that it keeps regenerating itself."

LUCY WANG: "It's crucial to do whatever it takes. To give each story the time it deserves and needs. To be kind to yourself in the process and not beat yourself up. Great work takes time and revision. And . . . who knows? You might be handsomely rewarded for your work ethic and natural talent. Sharing our stories about activism can transform and save lives. We all have our struggles, and these struggles can isolate and defeat us, but when we hear about others standing up for what is right, it can give us courage, community, and purpose. I think of writers as fighters."

ANDRÉ DE SHIELDS: "The harmony of humanity. We've forgotten it, but we can re-learn it. There are only four sources of humanity. One is air. One is water. One is earth. And one is fire. In these four elements is harmony, and harmony is vibrational. Each of these elements moves. Each of these elements has a rhythm. Each of these elements has a voice. Each of these elements has music as part of its essence, and that is where we discover everything we invent."

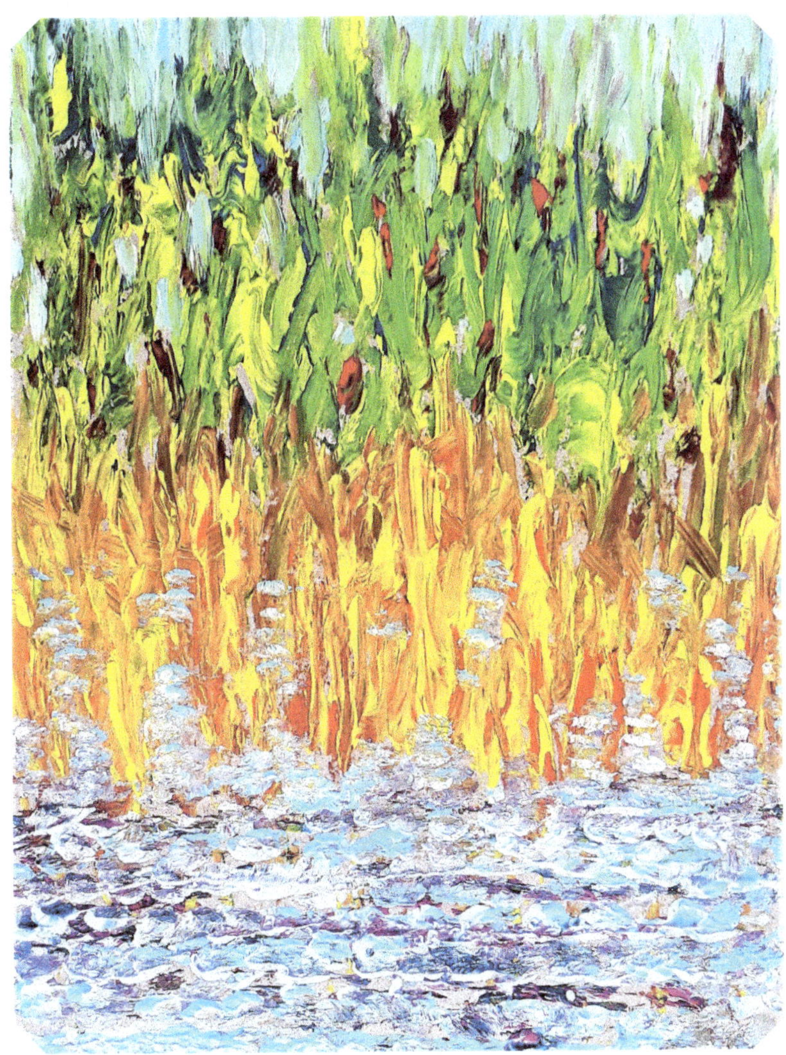

Painting: “The Harmony of Humanity” by Ronjay, known as Ronald Rand. (Courtesy Ronald Rand.)

RECOMMENDED READING

Adler, Stella. *The Art of Acting*. Edited by Howard Kissel. New York: Applause Theater and Cinema Book Publishers, 2000.

Adler, Stella. *The Technique of Acting*. With a Foreword by Marlon Brando. New York: Bantam Books, 1988.

Adler, Stella and Barry Paris. *Stella Adler on Ibsen, Strindberg, and Chekhov*. New York: Vintage Books, 2000.

Benedetti, Robert. *The Actor at Work*. Englewood Cliffs, New Jersey: Prentice Hall, 1976.

Boal, Augusto. *Games for Actors and Non-Actors*. London: Routledge, 1992.

Bogart, Anne. *A Director Prepares: Seven essays on Art and Theatre*. London Routledge, 2001.

Bogart, Anne. *The Art of Resonance*. London: Bloomsbury Press, 2021.

Bonney, Jo, ed. *Extreme Exposure: An Anthology of Solo Performance Texts from the Twentieth Century*. Theater Communications Group, 2000.

Brook, Peter. *The Empty Space*. New York: Touchstone, 1968.

Brook, Peter. *The Open Door*. New York: Random House, 2005.

Cameron, Julia. *The Artist's Way*. New York: Most Tarcher/Putnam Books, 1992.

Chekhov, Michael. *To the Actor on the Technique of Acting*. With a Foreword by Yul Brynner. New York: Harper and Row, 1953.

Cole, Toby and Helen Krich Chinoy, eds. *Actors on Acting*. New York: Crown, 1947.

Cole, Toby and Helen Krich Chinoy, eds. *Directors on Directing*. New York: Crown, 2013.

Clurman, Harold. *On Directing*. New York: Macmillian, 1972.

Clurman, Harold. *The Collected Works of Harold Clurman*. New York: Applause Theatre & Cinema Book Publishers, 1994.

Clurman, Harold. *The Fervent Years*. New York: Knopf, 1945.

Donnellan, Declan. *The Actor and the Target*. New York: Theater Communications Group, 2002.

Grotowski, Jerzy. *Towards a Poor Theatre*. Edited by Eugenio Barba. London: Methuen, 1976.

Hagen, Uta. *A Challenge to the Actor*. New York: Charles Scribner's Sons, 1991.

Le Gallienne, Eva. *The Mystic in the Theatre: Eleanora Duse*. Arcturus Books, 1966.

Lewis, Robert. *Method or Madness*. New York: Samuel French, 1950.

Linklater, Kristin. *Freeing the Natural Voice*. New York: Drama Publishers, 2006.

Moss, Larry. *The Intent to Live*. New York: Bantam Books, 2005.

Rand, Ronald. *Acting Teachers of America*. With a Foreword by J. Michael Miller. New York: Allworth Press, 2007.

Rand, Ronald. *CREATE! How Extraordinary People Live to Create and Create to Live*. Deadwood, OR.: Wyatt-MacKenzie Publishing, 2017.

Rodenberg, Patsy. *The Actor Speaks*. New York: Palgrave Macmillian, 2000.

Spolin Viola. *Improvisation for the Theater*. Evanston, IL.: Northwestern University Press, 1963.

Stanislavski, Constantin. *An Actor Prepares*. London: Routledge, 1989.

Stanislavski, Constantin. *Building a Character*. Translated by Elizabeth Reynolds Hapgood. New York: Theater Arts Books, 1961.

Stanislavski, Constantin. *Creating a Role*. Translated by Elizabeth Reynolds Hapgood. New York: Theater Arts Books, 1949.

Strasberg, John. *Accidentally on Purpose: Reflections on Life, Acting and the Nine Natural Laws of Creativity*. New York: Applause Theatre & Cinema Book Publishers, 1996.

Suzuki, Tadashi. *The Way of Acting*. New York: Theatre Communications Group, 1986.

Svich, Caridad, and Maria Teresa Marrero, Ed.. *Out of the Fringe: Contemporary Latina/Latino Theatre and Performance*. New York: Theatre Communications Group, 2000.

Yakim, Moni and Muriel Broadman. *Creating a Character*. New York: Applause Theater and Cinema Book Publishers, 1990.

Young, Jordan. *Spalding Gray and Solo Performance*. Past Times Publishing Company, 2012.

Zinn, Howard. *A People's History of the United States*, 2015.

CREDITS (for QUOTES on pages 210-215)

Len Cariou, Ossie Davis, Ruby Dee, Charles S. Dutton, Tovah Feldshuh, Judith Ivey, Priscilla Lopez, Meredith Monk, Ruben Santiago-Hudson: Interviews by Ronald Rand, 1998–2018.

Vinie Burrows: Interview by Gloria Messer, January 21, 2015.

André De Shields: Interview by Christian John Wikane, October 23, 2020.

Julie Harris: *Julie Harris Talks to Young Actors* by Julie Harris with Barry Tarsis—Lothrop, Lee & Shepard.

Hal Holbrook: Interview by Gary Tischler, Georgetowner.com, March 26, 2014.

Sarah Jones: Interview by Monica Bushman, Marialexa Kavanaugh, LAist.com, October 1, 2018.

John Leguizamo: Interview by Steve Velasquez, Curator, National Museum of American History, December 12, 2018.

Laura Linney: Interview by Joe Utichi, Deadline.com, June 19, 2018.

Ian McKellan: Interview by Christiane Amanpour, CNN, July 27, 2018.

Dale Orlandersmith: Interview by Sarah Brandt, The Repertory Theatre of St. Louis, November 16, 2020.

Anna Deavere Smith: Interview by Steve Profitt, Los Angeles Times, July 11, 1993.

Lily Tomlin: Interview by Amy Longsdorf, 'The Morning Call,' McCall.com, November 19, 1989.

Lucy Wang: Interview by Janis Butler Holm, July 26, 2020.

INDEX

ABOUT THE AUTHOR

RONALD RAND U.S. Goodwill Cultural Ambassador—Internationally acclaimed Solo Performer, he has received standing ovations in over 25 countries and twenty states bringing to life Harold Clurman, the "elder Statesman of the American Theatre," in his internationally-acclaimed solo play, *LET IT BE ART!*—in three critically-acclaimed productions Off-Broadway in New York City, representing the U.S. at the World Theatre Olympics in India, and for over twenty years galvanizing audiences around the globe on five continents, including in London, Paris, Frankfurt, Buenos Aires, Kathmandu, Kuala Lumpur, Colombo, Minsk, Sarajevo, Vologda, Johannesburg, Tbilisi, Harare, Bangkok, Paysandú, Eskişehir, Zagreb, Belgrade, Barrancabermeja, five tours across India, at Kenya's National Theatre, Cayman Islands' National Theatre Center, Tangier's Dar al-Makhzen Palace and at over a hundred theaters, universities, colleges, schools, and across twenty U.S. states. Rand created two other Solo plays as Charles Dickens reading a new adaptation by Rand of *A Christmas Carol*, and as Helen Keller's father, Captain Arthur Keller. He has appeared in several plays Off-Broadway & regional theater, including *Ma Rainey's Black Bottom*, *LUV*, *King Lear*, *Perfect Crime*, and in more than a hundred films and TV shows including *Homeless* with Yoko Ono, *The Family Tannenbaum*, *The Jerky Boys*, *Vanilla Sky*, *In & Out*, *Family Business* with Sean Connery, *Quiz Show* directed by Robert Redford, *Saturday Night Live*, and *A Marriage—O'Keefe and Steiglitz* opposite Christopher Plummer and Jane Alexander. An internationally celebrated Director, his production of *LUV* played for nearly ten years to sold-out audiences at Sarajevo's Chamber Theatre 55 with Zana Marjanovic. He is the Librettist of *IBSEN*, the first opera about Henrik Ibsen. Founder and Publisher of *The Soul of the American Actor* newspaper, online and in print for over twenty years, and best-selling author of *Acting Teachers of America*, *CREATE!* and *Solo Transformation on Stage*.

RonaldRand.com

LetItBeArt.com – SoulAmericanActor.com – IBSENopera.com – CreatetheBook.com

www.ingramcontent.com/pod-product-compliance
Lightning Source LLC
LaVergne TN
LVHW020509100826
845148LV00003B/730
9781620065716